To Anthonia
With much app:
and fervent love for
all your support during
our lengthy friendship.

In Christian love

Nellita Martin-Ogunsola

26 June 2007

# The Eve/Hagar Paradigm in the Fiction of Quince Duncan

# The Eve/Hagar Paradigm

## in the

# Fiction

## of

# Quince Duncan

Dellita Martin-Ogunsola

UNIVERSITY OF MISSOURI PRESS
COLUMBIA AND LONDON

Library of Congress Cataloging-in-Publication Data

Martin-Ogunsola, Dellita, 1946–
The Eve/Hagar paradigm in the fiction of Quince Duncan /
Dellita Martin-Ogunsola.
p.   cm.
Includes bibliographical references and index.
ISBN 0-8262-1525-4 (alk. paper)
1. Duncan, Quince, 1940–   —Characters—Women.
2. Women in literature.   3. Blacks in literature.
4. Social status in literature.   I.   Title.
PQ7489.2.D8Z75    2004
863'.64—dc22              2004004301

♾™ This paper meets the requirements of the
American National Standard for Permanence of Paper
for Printed Library Materials, Z39.48, 1984.

Designer:  Stephanie Foley
Typesetter:  Phoenix Type, Inc.
Printer and Binder:  Thomson-Shore, Inc.
Typeface:  Sabon

The publication of this book has been assisted by a grant from
Dean Bert Brouwer and the School of Arts and Humanities at
the University of Alabama at Birmingham.

*To my maternal grandmother,*
*Celestine Washington Martin Richard*

*(Affectionately known as "Mama Teen")*

*January 21, 1903–August 26, 1998*

# CONTENTS

# PREFACE

"They were bone of her bone and flesh of her flesh, her son's blood-line," muses the character Miss Spence.[1] With these words she evokes the ancient processes of marriage, procreation, and family that date back to the Garden of Eden. The irony of the character's meditation is that she is a single grandmother who cares for seven grandchildren left by a son who rejects marriage but not the pleasures of sex. Miss Spence also recalls the plight of the Egyptian slave Hagar, who was expelled from the household of Abraham when family tensions threatened to explode. The Eve/Hagar paradigm makes for a fascinating metaphorical representation of the perfect state of mind and body *before* the Fall. In this sense the model is gender neutral because Adam and Eve were created in the spiritual image of God with bodies that were to be immortal. However, spirit and flesh became dichotomized after sin entered the world, and a fierce struggle for dominance ensued between these two aspects of being. One unfortunate result of this broken relationship was the predominance of the male over the female principle—in concrete terms, the submission of the woman to the man. The latter, in turn, led to the development of patriarchy, which occasioned all kinds of troubles for women. Thus, the mind/body model was often read as male/female, man/woman, or husband/wife, even though it originally represented a mutual, complementary, and interdependent relationship. Through the lens of a double-edged metaphor originating in the historical figures of Eve and Hagar, *The Eve/Hagar Paradigm in the Fiction of Quince Duncan* examines women characters in five major works by Quince Duncan published during the 1970s.[2]

1. Dellita Martin-Ogunsola, ed. and trans., *The Best Short Stories of Quince Duncan/Las mejores historias de Quince Duncan*, 115.
2. The works to be included in this study are the following: *Una canción en la madrugada* (Dawn song) (1970); *Los cuatro espejos* (The four mirrors) (1973); *La rebelión Pocomía y otros relatos* (The Pocomía rebellion and other stories) (1976); *La paz del pueblo* (For the sake of peace) (1978); and *Final de calle* (Dead-end street) (1979). All translated titles and excerpts in this study are mine and will be cited parenthetically from these editions.

Moreover, the literary renditions of these archetypes produce a contestatory voice vis-à-vis the canonical texts that exclude and silence them. In that sense Duncan's fiction creates a counterdiscourse through female figures who often assume a rebellious posture.

Like writers of African ancestry throughout the diaspora, African Hispanophone writers in Latin America challenge the negativity of blackness in the Eurocentric hegemonic discourse. Thus, as Dorothy Mosby observes in her seminal study of black writing in Costa Rica, Duncan's stories and novels from the 1970s explore the topics of place, language, and identity.[3] In addition, his narratives present a holistic treatment of black characters in Latin American fiction, especially females. Using Mosby's model as a point of departure, the Eve/Hagar paradigm will be read as an allegorical representation of Duncan's quest to find a tenable position in Costa Rican literature through rescuing the black female voice, to negotiate multivalent linguistic systems that symbolize distinct and sometimes contradictory visions of reality, and to establish uniqueness as a public figure in the Western canon. As a form of resistance to the denigration of black womanhood, I first borrowed the phrase "female calibans" from M. J. Fenwick, who uses it to refer to feminist poets of the Caribbean. However, as this project moved forward, it was necessary to rethink the use of Caliban, a literary figure that originated in Shakespearean England and is still associated with the degradation of black masculinity. A good compromise was to subsume the Caliban model under the Eve/Hagar paradigm by retaining the adjectival form *calibanesque* as a synonym for *rebellious*.[4]

The question of race in relation to gender and class is important,

3. Mosby, *Place, Language, and Identity in Afro–Costa Rican Literature*, 1–31. Mosby's main argument is that the West Indian culture of Limón Province went through a generational transformation when it moved into the Central Plateau of Costa Rica. The result is an Afro–Costa Rican identity that is still "in process," according to the postcolonial principles set out by Stuart Hall.

4. Fenwick, "Female Calibans: Contemporary Women Poets of the Caribbean," 1–8. See also James Coleman, *Black Male Fiction and the Legacy of Caliban*, 1–17. Caliban is useful to this study, for just as the relationship between Prospero and Caliban is hierarchical, so is the relationship between men and women in patriarchal societies, or the relationship between the dominant and subordinate groups in colonial and neocolonial societies. Roberto Fernández Retamar depicts Caliban as a symbol of New World revolt in his study of European and Latin American relationships (*Caliban and Other Essays*, 3–55). This is the meaning intended in this study, where the Eve/Hagar paradigm feminizes the Caliban principle and, thus, achieves a balance.

but it should always be posed within a context of intelligent, informed, and sensitive dialogue. As Dominick LaCapra observes, "[T]he critical study of 'race' is central to contemporary thought. The very concept of 'race'—always to be read in quotes—is a feeble mystification with formidable effects; it is the crux of one of the most powerful ideological formations in history. To understand that ideology, its effects, and its intricate relations with such issues as class and gender is among the most forceful challenges facing history and criticism."[5] Entering the twenty-first century has not changed that fact.

*The Eve/Hagar Paradigm in the Fiction of Quince Duncan* accepts the challenge to explore the complex relationship among race, gender, and class with biblical archetypes as referents for some memorable female characters in Duncan's fiction. Specifically, the Eve/Hagar principle will be employed to examine how the essential aspect of femaleness plays out in the social constructs of blackness and caste. I am aware of the critical phobia associated with "essentialism." Nevertheless, a consideration of femaleness as a basic aspect of the human condition merits our attention because it is one of the most problematic aspects of the characterization of African-descended people in Western literature. Claudette Williams traces the portrayal of black and mulatto females in Caribbean poetry. She affirms that the "popular perception of the status, role, and destiny of three of the racial categories of women in the ex-colonies of Latin America and the Caribbean is condensed in the well-known saying 'the white woman for marriage, the mulatto woman for a good time, and the black woman for work.'"[6] *The Eve/Hagar Paradigm* illustrates how a prominent Costa Rican writer deconstructs that schema and in the process finds his own voice.

---

5. LaCapra, introduction to *The Bounds of Race: Perspectives on Hegemony and Resistance*, 1. Manuel Zapata Olivella contextualizes the constructs of race, class, and culture in New World societies in *Las claves mágicas de América (Raza, clase y cultura)*.

6. Williams, *Charcoal and Cinnamon: The Politics of Color in Spanish Caribbean Literature*, 1. Williams declares that "charcoal and cinnamon are two of the racial metaphors used to refer to black and mulatto women in Cuba's classic nineteenth-century novel *Cecilia Valdés*, by Cirilo Villaverde" (xi).

# ACKNOWLEDGMENTS

Whenever a person engages in a demanding task like writing, he or she must become *ensimismado(a)*, which means in Spanish "to go inside or become completely absorbed in oneself." It is vital that the critic become totally wrapped up in her own reason for being—in this case, the production of an enjoyable, meaningful, and sensitive work of literary criticism. The Spanish feminine form *ensimismada* conveys more succinctly than the above English definition the critical and creative processes involved in writing this book. Nevertheless, it would have been impossible to produce a refined product without the help of others. I wish to express my deepest appreciation to the following persons: Dr. Marvin A. Lewis, who made available his unique collection of resources at the Afro–Latin American Research Institute, University of Missouri–Columbia; numerous colleagues who provided encouragement and moral support during the extended labor/birth process of this work; Wealthy T. Ferguson, a dedicated office associate and great source of strength during my previous life as a department chair; David O. Ogunsola, my beloved husband, who periodically subsidized for me "a room of my own" at local motels in spite of questions about our sanity; and last, but certainly not least, my beautiful, brilliant children and grandchildren, who have been so lovingly understanding of their (grand)mother's "absences." All errors and omissions are mine. To God be the glory.

# The Eve/Hagar Paradigm in the Fiction of Quince Duncan

# Introduction

## Of Origins and Destinies

Eve and Hagar are two historical figures who have captured the human imagination across time and place—Eve because she is the archetype of womanhood, and Hagar because she is the prototype of the survival and resilience of femaleness in a patriarchal society. Moreover, the actions of these women offer compelling and contradictory models of behavior, not only for real people but also for fictional characters and artistic representations. Eve is the first woman presented in an overview of the Creation:

> And God said, Let us make *man* in our image, after our likeness: and let *them* have dominion over the fish of the sea, and over the fowl of the air, and over the cattle, and over all the earth, and over every creeping thing that creepeth upon the earth.
>
> So God created *man* in his *own* image, in the image of God created he him; *male* and *female* created he them. (Gen. 1:26–27; emphasis added)

In the above passages the word *man* is synonymous with humanity, which is then developed into its gendered, interdependent components. Man as male is not named until chapter 2 of Genesis, but it is clear that gendering is a fundamental part of the human condition. Thus, in chapter 1 "man/human" is to "them" as "man/human" is to "male and female," distinct but equal aspects of the same being. According to Edith Deen, "the fact that God did not give man dominion until he had woman standing beside him is evidence enough of her exalted place in the Creation." Thus, the Edenic model of humankind illustrates a relationship of parity and shared authority. A secular explication of the Creation portrays Eve as a "deposed goddess," or "humanity's earliest attempts to articulate the nature of Woman, the Feminine as a religious concept, and the very origins of human consciousness of the sacred." Another viewpoint attempts to bridge the gap between scriptural declaration and secularized analysis by presenting "the biblical Eve [as] our mother in myth, now joined by 'mitochondrial Eve' as our mother in genes."[1] These latter interpretations challenge the truth of inspired scripture in an effort to offer comfortable alternatives to those who reject the authority of the Bible. Yet all viewpoints acknowledge Eve as the female progenitor of the human race—whether in spirit or in body—and there is a consensus that she occupies a place of admiration and respect in the original scheme of things.

The second and third chapters of Genesis provide concrete details about the relationship of humanity to the rest of creation (2:1–15), God's first law (2:16–17), marriage (2:22–25), and sin (3:1–24), but little is said explicitly about the character of Adam and Eve. However, one can identify qualities that both possess in various degrees—intelligence, curiosity, and assertiveness, but also persuasiveness, naïveté, and vulnerability. Two ironies emerge from their broken relationship with God: Eve bravely and honestly admits her errors, which eventually gives rise to a misogynistic tradition of literature that vilifies her, while Adam tries to shift the blame to his wife and to God but is ultimately held responsible.[2] Viewed from a gender-neutral perspective, Adam and Eve reaped what they sowed because they exercised judgment through free will, apart from the relationship of complementarity, interdependence, and mutuality established by divine authority. Human beings have been dealing with the consequences of their choices ever since.

After the Fall the status of woman deteriorated. Concerning this decline, Rosario Castellanos traces the history of feminine mythification, asserting that the female principle more often than not is portrayed as antagonistic or malefic. She observes that

> throughout the centuries, woman has been raised to the altar
> of the gods and has breathed the incense of the faithful. That

1. Carol L. Meyers, *Discovering Eve: Ancient Israelite Women in Context*, 81–85; Deen, *All the Women of the Bible*, 3–4; John A. Phillips, *Eve: The History of an Idea*, 3; Tikva Frymer-Kensky, *Reading the Women of the Bible*, xiii.

2. See Leland Ryken, James C. Wilhoit, and Tremper Longman III, *Dictionary of Biblical Imagery*, s.v. "Eve"; and Henry T. Sell, *Studies of Famous Bible Women*, 9. Although Sell's work is early twentieth century, his statement that "there is not a trace of the Oriental idea of the inferiority, the degradation and slave notion—the shame and disgrace of the world—which were forced upon her later on" contains a powerful grain of truth. However, he ignores the Western notion of woman's inferiority as well.

is, when she is not locked up in a gymnasium or a harem to share the yoke of slavery with her own kind; when she is not confined to the courtyards of the unclean; when she is not branded with the mark of the prostitute; crushed by the servant's burden; expelled from the religious congregation, the political arena, or the university classroom.[3]

This negative attitude toward women became a function of patriarchal cultures that developed from the beginning of time and intensified over the millennia. Thus, by the era of the pre-Hebraic progenitors Abraham, Isaac, and Jacob, a hierarchical relationship between the sexes had been firmly established. For that reason Tikva Frymer-Kensky contends that "biblical Israel did not invent patriarchy.... The male Lord did not create patriarchy. The truth is just the opposite: patriarchal thought required that one Lord of all be conceived as a male and portrayed in a masculine grammar."[4] The Jewish heritage developed according to a global pattern.

The story of Abram, Sarai, and Hagar must be understood within the context of ancient patriarchy.[5] Two females of unequal socioeconomic status end up as the wife and concubine of a devout, wealthy, and respected man, not because it is part of God's plan, but because human frailty and whimsy are allowed to overrule faith and patience. In desperation Sarai, Abram's barren wife, follows the social practice of her time by insisting that he have sexual relations with her slave, Hagar, so that the latter can bear Sarai's child. According to the laws of Hammurabi, a woman who was unable to give natural birth could designate her personal slave as a surrogate. Like Adam, Abram is persuaded to take part in an affair that will have

3. Castellanos, *Mujer que sabe latín*, 9. See also Rosario Castellanos, "Woman and Her Image," 237. The title of Castellanos's collection of essays comes from a popular aphorism in the Spanish oral tradition that plays on the mind/body antithesis: "Mujer que sabe latín / ni tiene marido / ni tiene buen fin" (A woman who knows Latin / neither has a husband / nor comes to a good end).

4. Frymer-Kensky, *Reading Women*, xiv. See also John Henrik Clarke, "New Introduction," i–xv. Clarke contends that matrilineal descent was common to many African cultures, but others within that sphere revealed a healthy balance between patriarchal and matriarchal patterns.

5. In Gen. 17:5 God changes the name of Abram ("Exalted Father") to Abraham ("Father of Nations"); in Gen. 17:15 he changes the name of Sarai (meaning not given) to Sarah ("Princess"). Frymer-Kensky provides the meaning for Hagar ("stranger" or "foreigner"), whom she sees as a "co-wife" of Sarah (*Reading Women*, 226).

sad consequences for the family: "He came into Hagar and she conceived. She saw that she had become pregnant, and her mistress was diminished in her eyes" (Gen. 16:4). However, an unexpected turn of affairs occurs: "Hagar, who was supposed to be a neutral body being passed from Sarai to Abram, reacts. This 'womb with legs' is a person with her own viewpoint, and her mistress is 'diminished in her eyes.' "[6] Conflict between the two women is inevitable, and Sarai treats Hagar harshly. The pregnant concubine runs away, but she is persuaded by an angel to return to the household, where Abraham's first son, Ishmael, is born. One point of view about the strife between Sarai and Hagar is that it is a case of an "uppity slave" showing ingratitude to a "generous mistress" who raised her from bondwoman to concubine.[7] Considering the second-class or lesser rank of a second wife or concubine, this perspective is untenable. On the other hand, a portrayal of Sarai and Hagar as oppressed cowives who "vie for status in the household" is also flawed, for a free woman and a bondwoman are not equal to begin with. Therefore, they cannot compete for status in the home, although they might try to win the master's attention. From Abram's response it is evident that Sarai is not oppressed because she is the one who engineers the whole affair. When she does not like the outcome, she blames Abram for "mistreating" her, but she easily regains control of Hagar. Abram defers to his wife by restoring Hagar to her possession, so the concubine is victimized because she loses her "exalted status" as a "cowife."

Three years after the birth of Isaac, the promised son of Abraham and Sarah, Hagar is expelled from the household because Sarah cannot live with the reminder of her own role in the affair. Moreover, she sees the first-born Ishmael as a threat to the inheritance of her baby boy. The reluctant Abraham must choose between his wife and his oldest son, for the concubine is expendable: "And Abraham rose up early in the morning, and took bread, and a bottle of water, and gave it unto Hagar, putting it on her shoulder, and

6. Ibid., 227–28. See also Savina J. Teubal, *Hagar the Egyptian: The Lost Tradition of the Matriarchs*, 49–62. By a strange twist of logic based on her linguistic manipulation of Hebrew, Teubal considers Hagar not a slave or concubine, but Sarah's "companion" instead. This theory flies in the face of the events that unfold in the story when Hagar is banished at Sarah's command. After all, who would drive away her best friend and confidante?

7. Deen, *All the Women*, 12. The author's remarks are pertinent, but her tone is condescending.

the child, and sent her away" (Gen. 21:14–15). Hagar and her man-child then head for the wilderness to meet their destiny. Consequently, she becomes "a single mother, ... both father and mother, completing her parental duties by arranging for his marriage. Abraham has no role in shaping the future of Hagar and her descendants. He has relinquished that right by emancipating them; God has given Hagar that right by treating her as the head of her own family and lineage."[8] By dint of circumstances, Hagar ascends to a position of authority and leadership, and she must develop the qualities of aggressiveness, courage, persistence, ingenuity, and resourcefulness in order to survive and overcome adversity.

Addressing the issue of Africanity through a biblical paradigm in Quince Duncan's fiction seems contradictory. However, such is true only if one accepts the limited and limiting view of Christianity as a Western religion. The Semitic-based Jewish culture that evolved from the original Israelite clan of seventy that went into Egypt gradually incorporated other "racial" and ethnic groups through intermarriage and proselytizing over four hundred years.[9] Thus, the assembly of people who gathered in Jerusalem to hear the first Gospel sermon on the day of Pentecost in AD 33 was a multilingual, multiethnic, and multiracial group with religious ties to Israel. In short, the first-century church represented people from all the known nations of the Old World, which were scattered across various locales in Africa, Asia, and Europe. Furthermore, after Christianity began spreading with evangelistic fervor throughout the Roman Empire, it was eventually endorsed by the emperor Constantine in AD 313. The gradual paganization/Romanization of Christian doctrine by Hellenistic intellectuals *radically transformed* the church's original makeup such that it became a European and Europeanizing insti-

---

8. Frymer-Kensky, *Reading Women*, 236.

9. In *Africa and Africans as Seen by Classical Thinkers*, William Leo Hansberry states the following: "The territory included by the Greeks under the designation Ethiopia varies somewhat from age to age. Writers of the earlier period, particularly those composing the epic cycle, applied Ethiopia and Ethiopians to lands and peoples in both Africa and Asia; the latter continent was included apparently with good cause, for more recent discoveries and research have established that in ancient times a blackskinned people, or Aethiops, constituted an important part of the populations of Arabia, Mesopotamia, Persia, and India. Homer alluded to the Ethiopians of the two continents, noting that one division was situated towards the sunrise and another towards the sunset; for the Ethiopians are, says the poet: 'A race divided, whom the sloping rays / The rising and the setting sun surveys'" (6).

tution.[10] It was this adulterated form of the first-century church of Christ that entered the New World as a function of empire with its concomitant discovery, conquest, enslavement, and colonization of non-European peoples. Thus, Hagar is a strong link between Old and New World cultures. For example, in the African American oral tradition Aunt Hagar, a former slave and matriarch, becomes a symbol of everyone's mother, grandmother, auntie, and the like—the great nurturer of the black community. Hagar and her progeny are the real and fictional descendants of the Egyptian prototype, but the American figure is highly regarded as "Ishmael's Mama," just like Jesus is revered as "Mary's Baby." In written literature, Hagar is a figure of richly textured dimensions in the works of African American writers such as Paul Lawrence Dunbar, Frances Ellen Watkins Harper, Richard Wright, Langston Hughes, Maya Angelou, and Toni Morrison, among others who pay tribute to her.[11]

Ironically, Hagar also appears as a character in the writing of nineteenth-century white female writers, who appropriate her as a symbol of the suffragette movement. This depiction occurred after an intense struggle to erase or whiten (or both) the African origin of the Egyptian and her son, Ishmael. Janet Gabler-Hover comments: "Both nineteenth-century African and Anglo Americans knew that the black ethnicity of Hagar and her son Ishmael in the Bible served as a major source for the proslavery imperative to exclude African Americans from America's white power base." J. Lee Greene further observes that the expulsion of Hagar and Ishmael from the house of Abraham feeds into the myth of an American Eden from which the black mother and illegitimate son should be banished. Thus, Hagar is "culturally read" as African, and the implication is that she is black, even though there is not any biblical reference to her color. This problem is complicated by Savina J. Teubal's ambivalent perception of Hagar as "Egyptian rather than Hebrew (black rather than white?)." Again there is no biblical support of a black/white dichotomy between Hagar and Sarah, or between Hagar and Eve, for that matter, and it is much more likely that all three were closer in somatic appearance than contemporary thought would suppose. The Afro-Asiatic cultural sphere was very extensive in its reach, but

10. John McManners, ed., *The Oxford Illustrated History of Christianity*, 55–73.
11. Delores Williams, *Sisters in the Wilderness: The Challenge of Womanist God Talk*, 2, 245n2.

within that general rubric, difference was invariably measured according to language, ethnicity, religious beliefs, customs, traditions, and values—never color. It is only with the ascendancy of European domination in modern times that color/race becomes a gauge of culture. Thus, the strife between Sarah and Hagar is not necessarily a racial one, although it can be read that way from the perspective of the "colonised imagination."[12]

Concerning the impact of Hagar on the American mind, Gabler-Hover states that as "surprising as it may seem in these Victorian times of strict sexual rules, Hagar, the outcast bondswoman banished into the wilderness with her illegitimate son, gains iconic status in popular culture as a sympathetic figure. Hagar's hold on nineteenth-century American popular culture is implied by the numerous domestic fictions, poems, and graphic art depictions of Hagar." This contradiction makes sense when one considers that the figure of Hagar is "a radically hybridized symbol for white women dreaming black: African American ethnicity, albeit coded, empowered the white heroines in nineteenth-century American texts to rebel against the patriarchal mores of their time." At the dawn of the twentieth century, African American writer Pauline Hopkins deconstructed the sexualized blackness that Hagar came to represent for white female writers. In the novel *Hagar's Daughter: A Story of Southern Caste Prejudice* (1902), Hopkins "demystifies the African woman as a superhero who, because of her supernatural powers, bears the blame if her own womanly strength does not allow her to transcend social stigma. Hopkins actively resists the racial stereotyping of a black Hagar as inappropriately sexualized. And, cannily, rather than reclaiming the archetype for black women alone, Hopkins brilliantly reinforces the hybridization of a black/white Hagar through textual strategies." In this manner Hopkins shapes a politicized vision of black femaleness that reclaims the ancestral prototype and exposes the hybridized status of the Hagar heroines in nineteenth-century fiction by white females, which then

12. Gabler-Hover, *Dreaming Black/Writing White: The Hagar Myth in American Cultural History*, 7; Greene, *Blacks in Eden: The African American Novel's First Century*, 84–85; Teubal, *Hagar the Egyptian*, 21. On the African origins of mankind and the intercontinental connections among cultures, see Hansberry, *Africa and Africans*, 5–63; Cheikh Anta Diop, *The Cultural Unity of Black Africa*, 5–7, 107, 116, 120–21; Diop, *The African Origins of Civilization: Myth or Reality?* 1–9; Ivan Van Sertima and Runoko Rashidi, eds., *The African Presence in Early Asia*, 7–12, 15–51; and Jean Franco, "The Colonised Imagination."

points to the need for "twinned sisterhood between black and white women in America."[13] This twinning propensity also has implications for Central and South American writing in terms of color, class, and female depiction.

Many of the women characters in Duncan's fiction are imaginary representations of Eve and Hagar by virtue of their subordinate roles in postcolonial societies that are still stratified along racial, gender, and class lines. Nevertheless, these types are not all black. It will be evident in *For the Sake of Peace* that white women who rebel against the dominant value system are also cast out of the "Big House" and recast in the same mold as Hagar's daughters. Because Eve is the original "fallen woman," there is a constant effort to redeem her, as each generation of artists seeks to rescue her image from exile in the literary imagination. Because Hagar is cast as the proverbial wanderer, she becomes a magnet who draws all orphans to her, and like the elder women of traditional African cultures, she is cherished by virtue of her age, experience, wisdom, and nurturing propensity. In spite of humble origins Hagar is a figure who commands respect and admiration, even though she also elicits responses like rejection and condemnation. Essentially, Eve and Hagar have become potent symbols in a web of human ambivalence spun by the lack of reconciliation between the male and female principles.

To reiterate, the Eve archetype and Hagar prototype are coupled to determine how the confluence of race, gender, and class operates in the social constructs in which women find themselves. Concerning the two halves of the paradigm, Eve represents the pre-Edenic model of humankind in which the mind and spirit informed the body. Thus, sin was the result of Eve's assertion of intelligence and independence, not the offering of her body. Hagar stands for the post-Edenic schism between mind and body in which the body assumes primary importance. This means that women often fall victim to the "body trap," because in patriarchal culture there is an emphasis on their physical rather than mental and spiritual qualities. Sandra Messinger Cypess elaborates on the body-trap concept with the womb/tongue metaphor, an example of a type of synecdoche called "anatomical particularizing," or the process in which

13. Gabler-Hover, *Dreaming Black/Writing White*, 7. Hopkins quoted in ibid., 7, 123.

a distinctive body part is used to suggest the essence of the whole. According to this perspective, females are perceived by society primarily as conduits of reproduction (open the womb), not agents of production (close the mouth). J. David Sapir dovetails on Messinger's notion, observing that the female body part may also suggest her place as an object in a social hierarchy. Hence, issues of race/color, gender/sex, and class/caste influence the manner in which the female figures seek to find a voice. Their struggle is concretized in the womb/tongue, mind/body, head/hand dialectic—all subtropes of the Eve/Hagar paradigm. Ideally, these aspects of the paradigm are interactive, complementary, and interdependent.[14]

To the extent that the female characters in Duncan's fiction militate against negative images of themselves in the hegemonic discourse, the Eve/Hagar trope signifies those who try to reconstitute themselves by restoring a pristine balance. Only in this sense are they "calibanesque," or rebellious. One problem with the portrayal  of black womanhood through a male writer is the possibility of typecasting, which Martha K. Cobb addresses in her observation that "symbols often become stereotyped." "As with the female presence as an image of mother, home, sweetheart, authority figure, or even as sole provider, however, symbols must be taken into account where fictional characterization often mirrors real life and becomes an essential element in the portrayal of black women in fiction."[15] *The Eve/Hagar Paradigm* will explore Duncan's efforts to speak to the exotic "othering" of black womanhood in Latin American fiction. Furthermore, the trope will also be a sign for the author's progression from the portraiture of West Indian culture in *Dawn Song* and *The Pocomía Rebellion* to a probing self-analysis of cultural syncretism in *The Four Mirrors* and *For the Sake of Peace,* and finally to an oblique insertion of a hispanized black consciousness into the canon in *Dead-End Street.*

14. Cypess, *"La Malinche" in Mexican Literature: From History to Myth,* 101–2; Sapir, "The Anatomy of Metaphor," 16. The womb/tongue component is associated with physical reproduction (of human beings) and production (of speech); the head/hand pairing is linked to mental production (of thoughts) and reproduction (of writing). Their divergence is often cast as the mind/body antithesis, but in the original (pre-Edenic) state, these functions were in equilibrium. Therefore, their complementary, interactive, and interdependent nature will be the measure of analyzing the Eve/Hagar paradigm in Duncan's women characters.

15. Cobb, "Images of Black Women in New World Literature: A Comparative Approach," 238.

The twinned figure Eve/Hagar paradigm is a vehicle for measuring the degree of wholeness and equilibrium the female personae seek as they endeavor to shatter the pigeonholed images imposed on them by a national discourse that embraces European values. In a discussion of the Costa Rican canon, Duncan calls on writers to play a major role in the reconstruction of national, continental, and global discourses.

## GISELLA AND BONIFACIA; OR, THE MASTER'S TROPE IN COSTA RICAN LITERATURE

Duncan is a literary critic who is an integral part of the discourse on racism and sexism in Costa Rican letters. "El modelo ideal de la mujer" (The ideal model of womanhood) begins with the declaration that "sexism...does not refer to the natural differences between male and female, neither to the specialization of the work process, but rather to the hierarchical social structuring between the sexes that has roots in such differences. This process of hierarchical structuring is elevated to the category of myth and from it are derived immutable laws." In contemporary literary criticism the idea of "natural differences," or essentialism, is generally frowned on, but some scholars contend that there are physiological and psychological distinctions between male and female human beings that cultural factors do not eradicate. Yet such dissimilarities do not automatically imply a relationship of superiority and inferiority. Based on that supposition, Duncan explains sexism as a function of myth, or the fabrication of a vision of reality that does not correspond to historical fact. Moreover, myth is based on "the ideological current that attributes to the sexes qualitative differences of an intellectual and moral nature, thus establishing between them a hierarchical relationship...to justify the structure of male domination over females and to rationalize natural propensities in mythic terms."[16] Because "The Ideal Model" was published in 1985, it will

16. Duncan, "El modelo ideal de la mujer: Un análisis ficciológico de estereotipos sexistas en la narrativa costarricense," 97. All translated quotations from this essay are my own. See also Stuart Hall, "Cultural Identity and Cinematic Representation," 69–70. Hall posits a modified essentialism that is part of an "identity in process."

be interesting to see the extent to which Duncan's theory of female portraiture coincides with his praxis in the 1970s works analyzed in this study.

To summarize, in Costa Rican (and Latin American) literature race, gender, and class have intersected to produce a model of the perfect woman who is portrayed as physically attractive, submissive to male authority, and, above all, a paragon of motherhood. It is interesting that this pattern has been dominant regardless of the writer's gender, although there are notable exceptions such as Yolanda Oreamuno and Fabián Dobles. Three naturalistic novels show examples of conventional portraiture. *Alma llanera* (Rustic soul), published in 1946 by Edelmira González; *Pedro Arnáez*, published in 1942 by José Marín Cañas; and the short-story collection *Cuentos de angustias y paisajes* (Stories of anguish and landscapes), published in 1947 by Carlos Salazar Herrera, depict sexist, racist, and class-based stereotypes.[17] *Rustic Soul* illustrates how race, gender, and class interweave in the positioning of the female protagonist and antagonist. The poor but proud Gisella Ivanovich, wife of the rich landowner Simeón Calderetti, is described as an "angel of light" born to be a queen, an image that is derived from her European origin. It is implied that Gisella is virtuous because she is beautiful, and she is beautiful because she is white. By contrast, Bonifacia, a "home girl" from the northern province of Guanacaste, is portrayed as a crude, irrational woman from the plains, a *chorotega*, or indigenous person, which has the connotation "ugly." Duncan comments:

> Gisella and Bonifacia, as antitheses, show the connections between sexism and racism. In this case, it is a question of the deliberate use of a classic racist argument in order to justify their differences and upstage a certain model of womanhood: the white woman, of "authentic" European beauty, incarnated in Gisella, who becomes, *ipso facto*, virtuous. Bonifacia, on the other hand, is indigenous, the "country bumpkin," the "centaur," or half man–half horse.[18]

17. Duncan, "Visión panorámica de la narrativa costarricense," 91. All translated quotations from this essay are my own.
18. Duncan, "Modelo ideal," 99.

Thus, the aesthetic model that is codified in the discourse is the white, blonde, blue-eyed female. Because of her beauty and virtue, Gisella can ascend the social ladder through marriage to Simeón, even though it is suggested that she has "been around" in the provinces. Bonifacia, however, can never surpass the limits set by their society no matter what virtues she has or heroic deeds she accomplishes.

In *Pedro Arnáez* the female character Cristina is a hardworking, self-denying woman whose sole purpose is to produce an heir for her husband, Pedro Arnáez. After fulfilling her destiny, Cristina dies—poor serving woman, working woman, docile woman, but virtuous woman. Submission to male authority and the cult of maternity are also the cornerstones of the very popular *Stories of Anguish and Landscapes,* which was still used during the 1980s as an official textbook in the public school systems of Costa Rica. Duncan observes that female behavior in this collection is judged strictly in terms of the binary "virtue-vice" paradigm because the production of "women mothers" is the desired end. According to Duncan, this value is stressed in Latin America to socialize women into accepting their reproductive function as the primary or only means of fulfillment. These seemingly innocuous stories and novels also serve to program other members of society to accept unquestioningly gender, racial, and class differences as justifiable reasons for discrimination instead of viewing them as functions of biology, environmental adaptation, and history. Duncan remarks that "these stereotypes construct an ideal woman, an archetype characterized by a Europeanized code of beauty, and 'virtues' of a patriarchal society. In order to justify this model people resort to the most diverse arguments, including religious symbology, racism, and the cult of maternity." A connection is then made between the reductive process of stereotyping and the destructive impact of the colonial/colonialist discourse vis-à-vis gender, race, and class differences in the pluralistic communities of Costa Rica. Duncan concludes: "This sexist vision without a doubt responds to the preexisting model in Costa Rican society. It reflects the ideology of the dominant social sectors, Eurocentric in their aesthetic values, patriarchal in their vision of the role of the sexes. Feudal values survive in Costa Rican society." In short, Duncan elucidates the fundamental nature of the Spanish/European heritage in Costa Rican literature that has given rise to the *leyenda blanca* (white legend), or the notion that their nation is unique because of its ethnic/racial homogeneity in a region saturated with indigenous, mestizo, black, and mulatto populations.[19]

There were efforts by some Hispanic writers to address black culture. For example, *El negro en la literatura costarricense* (Black people in Costa Rican literature), a 1975 anthology, includes works by self-identified white writers as well as some of Duncan's early texts. Earlier, Carlos Luis Fallas had published *Canal Zone* (1935), the first novel in Spanish to fictionalize West Indian life in Costa Rica. *Mamita Yunai*, Fallas's second work, came out in 1942. Its title plays on a linguistic corruption of "United" (as in States) as it portrays the racial and class strife exacerbated by the dominance of the United Fruit Company in Central America. Next, Fabián Dobles wrote several short stories featuring Antillean characters, among them "El jaspe" (The jasper), "El gato con botas" (The cat who wore boots), and "La mujer negra del Río" (The black woman of the river). Finally, Joaquín Gutiérrez produced a trilogy about black people: *Manglar* (Mangrove swamp) (1947), *Cocorí* (The jungle book) (1948), and the popular *Puerto Limón* (1950). Among these writers Abel Pacheco seems to have presented a more "internal" perspective than the others because he was immersed in West Indian culture as a result of growing up on the Atlantic Coast. Nevertheless, Pacheco is still not considered part of the "in group" of West Indian–descended writers.[20] Duncan is contemporary with the white/mestizo writers Alfonso Chase and Laureano Albán, who are attempting to influence the aesthetic and social direction of Costa Rica's literature.[21] A discussion of the black writing tradition will be deferred momentarily.

There is a need to reexamine gender, racial, and class issues in the national discourse, for the relationship between fiction and society is a double-edged sword: the writing reflects the culture, and the latter, in turn, perpetuates the myths codified in belles lettres. Therefore, it is the writer's task to intervene at two critical junctures of the literary process: the moment of creation and that of publication. At the moment of inspiration, unconscious factors resulting from socialization inform the creative process, so that even those authors who theoretically reject sexism (and racism and caste) might

19. Ibid., 100; Mosby, *Place, Language, and Identity,* 23–24.
20. Ian Isidore Smart, *Central American Writers of West Indian Origin: A New Hispanic Literature,* 121.
21. Mosby, *Place, Language, and Identity,* 120–21.

show evidence of it in their works. Duncan contends that a writer's greatest responsibility is exercised at the time of publication, or the moment when the artist as representative of given cultural phenomena speaks publicly through the inscribed word: "Essentially, self-criticism is fundamental. It is a self-criticism that implies the humility to accept the fact that all of us are exposed to a process of social programming. Therefore, to declare oneself against sexism does not automatically produce the freeing of one's consciousness from the albatross of sexism." The author-critic, then, is the model proffered by Duncan, whose fictional universe runs the gamut from collections of folklore to short stories and novels of penetrating insight. Furthermore, "the plurality of ideological options makes possible a self-imposed reprogramming and the creation of a new, alternative fiction freed from the sexist vision of the world and from all the other structures of domination, a fiction that is open and liberated. And in this sense the literary critic has an important contribution to make."[22] Nevertheless, the challenge of developing critical theory free from Eurocentric biases is what intellectuals continue to wrestle with in the present age.

## AFRO-REALISM; OR, THE THEORY OF LIVED EXPERIENCE

Josaphat B. Kubayanda asserts that historically, Latin American critics did not develop the proper tools for assessing the growing body of black literature because they were hampered by their indiscriminate acceptance of the prevailing anthropological and sociological theories of race and class—concepts like acculturation, assimilation, *mestizaje, mulatez,* and *transculturación.*[23] Moreover, by virtue of the neglect and silencing of "minority voices," Hispanic discourse has denied the importance of a distinct African Hispanophone body of literature, a fact that the perusal of current anthologies confirms. Despite canonical exclusion, black writers from the Spanish-speaking nations have contributed much to our understanding of Latin American culture. Thus, Afro-Hispanic texts have been validated by a distinguished group of scholars in the United States

---

22. Duncan, "Modelo ideal," 101.
23. Kubayanda, "African Hermeneutics and the Rhetoric of *Transculturación* in Black Latin American Literature," 226.

and Canada who have "centered" these works not only by calling
attention to them in literary criticism but also by sponsoring international conferences to which their eminent authors have been in-
vited.[24] Richard Jackson summarizes the importance of this literature by declaring that "the black text is not hermetically sealed from
reality; it has power and authority precisely because of the reality
it reflects and represents. As Black literature emerges, it will continue to offer a challenge for admission into the canon 'worthy' of
Hispanic texts." Jackson also classifies Afro-Hispanic literary criticism according to four tendencies: black criticism; negristic or so-
cionegristic criticism; socialist, Marxist, or nationalist criticism; and
universal criticism. He observes: "Black criticism recognizes the
role ethnicity plays in evaluation. Negristic or socio-negristic criticism is interested mainly in the folkloric and atavistic aspects of
black literature or in defending blacks. Marxist, socialist, and nationalist criticism, by emphasizing revolutionary solidarity or *mestizaje,* are aimed, like universal criticism, at 'whitening' black authors
by playing down their black ethnic identity." However, these categories are not so mutually exclusive or uncomplicated as presented,
and critics of Afro-Hispanic literature are often leery of the myriad
schools of contemporary theories that fall under the general rubric
of postcolonial, postmodern, and poststructural studies. A major
concern is that the Eurocentric "post" theories might have some
value as strategies for approaching Afro-Hispanic writing, but they
might also ultimately distort the lens through which the works are
properly read.[25]

Among current theories the postcolonial critical perspective is
somewhat helpful in assessing black Hispanic literature because it
focuses on certain historical processes that all conquered/colonized

24. Several conferences were organized by Marvin A. Lewis at the University
of Missouri–Columbia in 1991, 1993, and 1999, in which African and African
Hispanophone writers and their mainly North American critics met. In addition,
international meetings of artists and intellectuals sponsored by the Afro–Latin
American Research Association took place in 1996, 1998, 2000, and 2002, in
Brazil, Haiti, the Dominican Republic, and Panama, respectively.

25. Jackson, *Black Writers and the Hispanic Canon,* 104, 169; Yvonne Captain,
"Writing for the Future: Afro-Hispanism in a Global, Critical Context," 3–8. Contemporary literary criticism based on an exclusively Eurocentric worldview has
made the explication of literature an increasingly elusive, complex, and *non*-user-
friendly activity. The objective of illumination, more often than not, gives way to
"obfuscation," a term borrowed from Nancy Carol Joyner, "Postprandial Postmodernism." Obfuscation detracts from the pleasure of reading good literature.

groups have undergone. Such processes include "migration, slavery, suppression, resistance, representation, difference, race, gender, place, and responses to the influential master discourses of imperial Europe such as history, philosophy and linguistics, and the fundamental experiences of speaking and writing by which all these come into being."[26] However, postcolonial theory still privileges the aesthetic and theoretical codes of a mode of thought basically extrinsic to African diaspora cultures. For this reason, we might consider instead an alternative suggested by Duncan called *afro-realismo* (Afro-realism), which is expounded in the following manifesto: "Afro-realism has its roots in the African and Caribbean griot of oral tradition. Therefore, it is a sonorous cry. That is, it announces things with intense musicality. . . . But it does not announce just anything. Afro-realism is the lived word, which means that it is based on experience. It is a construction and reconstruction of reality, without ceasing to be fiction, without losing the fantasy that makes us take delight in reading." By calling attention to key words and expressions like "griot," "oral tradition," "intense musicality," and "lived word," as well as terms dealing with the creative process, such as "construction," "reconstruction," and "fantasy," Duncan grounds his aesthetics in the syncretistic cultures to which all New World black writers are heir. He continues:

> On the other hand, Afro-realism carries within itself the ancestral word, everything that happened long ago and that still affects us. Those things that have traveled from mouth to mouth and that form our tradition, that which gives us an identity, that which legitimizes our survival. Through those twice-told stories we know that we are part of a fragmented community. Our culture was broken up by 500 years of oppression. Afro-realism announces and proclaims the tidbits of reality that we are left with, the remains of first covenants. But it is not limited to showing that the African consciousness is broken; instead it is preoccupied with rebuilding it. Therefore, Afro-realism is the dream of the reconstructed word.[27]

26. Bill Ashcroft, Gareth Griffiths, and Helen Tiffin, eds., *The Post-colonial Studies Reader*, 2.

27. Duncan, *Un señor de chocolate: Treinta relatos de la vida de Quince*, 10. Martha K. Cobb articulates an earlier version of this theory, which she calls "concepts of blackness," in her seminal study, *Harlem, Haiti, and Havana: A Comparative Critical Study of Langston Hughes, Jacques Roumain, and Nicolás Guillén* (1979).

The preceding quotation suggests that the theory (and praxis) of Afro-realism should be intrinsic to the Afro–Costa Rican cultural matrix. Furthermore, it must develop critical structures commensurate with its double-edged (African/European) heritage, but with roots in the remnants of "first covenants" (African modes of being), with branches throughout the world (diaspora connections) from the healing vine of a "broken consciousness," and with seeds (fragments of American reality) of the "reconstructed word." These are "the forms of things unknown" that every generation of writers and intellectuals must rediscover. The genres of the Anancy the Spider tales and calypso are some prominent forms of Afro-realism that characterize the black oral tradition in Costa Rica. Furthermore, the specific trope of signifyin(g) in Duncan's stories and novels falls within that general rubric, and it will be elucidated through the Eve/Hagar paradigm in the appropriate chapters.[28]

A second approach to decoding the female voice is Filomina Chioma Steady's concept of African feminism, which looks at the racial, sexual, class, and cultural aspects of oppression in an effort to place women in a holistic context in which their humanity is emphasized over their sexuality. Ideally,

> an inclusive feminism can signal the end of all vestiges of oppression, including those glossed over by revolutions based pri-

28. This concept is parallel to Henry Louis Gates Jr.'s theory of the Signifying Monkey in African American literature. That trickster figure is peculiar to black oral tradition in the United States, but the fundamental concept of signifying is cross-cultural. Out of a corpus of mythological sacred and secular narratives came figures like B'rer Rabbit in the United States and Anancy the Spider in the Caribbean. See Gates, "The Blackness of Blackness: A Critique of the Sign and the Signifying Monkey," 286–87. In his full-length study *The Signifying Monkey: A Theory of Afro-American Literary Criticism,* Gates distinguishes between "signifying," as it is used in the Western literary canon, and "signifyin(g)," as utilized by blacks in the oral tradition. Gates comments: "'Signification,' in standard English, denotes the meaning that a term conveys, or is intended to convey. It is a fundamental term in the standard English semantic order. Since Saussure, at least, the three terms *signification, signifier, signified* have been fundamental to our thinking about general linguistics and, of late, about criticism specifically. These neologisms in the academic-critical community are homonyms of terms in the black vernacular tradition perhaps two centuries old. By supplanting the received term's associated concept, the black vernacular tradition created a homonymic pun of the profoundest sort, thereby marking its sense of difference from the rest of the English community of speakers. Their complex act of languages Signifies upon both formal language use and its conventions, conventions established, at least officially, by middle-class white people" (46–47; Gates's capitalization and emphases). Anancy will be the focus in several chapters of this study.

marily on class conflicts. It can be argued that this type of feminism has the potential of emphasizing the totality of human
experience, portraying the strength and resilience of the human
spirit and resounding with optimism for the total liberation of
humanity. African feminism is, in short, humanistic feminism.[29]

This critical framework intersects nicely with Afro-realism.

Not only does Steady examine the roots of African feminism in
precolonial cultures on the Continent, but she also studies their
adaptation in the diaspora over a period of time. Moreover, without
romanticizing the African past, she confirms that "parallel autonomy, communalism, and cooperation for the preservation of life
are more useful concepts in developing an appropriate framework
for examining African feminism than the framework of dichotomy,
individualism, competition, and opposition, which Western feminism fosters." Finally, there is an emphasis on the complementary
relationship between males and females that ensures the totality of
human existence within a balanced ecosystem.[30] In much of Duncan's fiction one perceives the attempt to establish an equilibrium
between the male and female principles. For that reason, the Eve/
Hagar paradigm is a valuable interpretative approach to this study.

Although the methods used by international scholars are of great
value in gauging the works of a writer like Duncan, one must also
employ an analytical framework that focuses on Caribbean history.
Many cultural studies have been done in that area, but one of the
most outstanding in terms of literary analysis is by Edward Kamau
Brathwaite, who articulates the cultural connections between Africa
and the Caribbean and its implications for the study of literature.
Brathwaite confirms that "African culture not only crossed the Atlantic, it crossed, survived, and creatively adapted itself to its new
environment; Caribbean culture was, therefore, not 'pure' African, but an adaptation carried out mainly in terms of African tradition."[31] Like the island-based authors of Cuba, the Dominican
Republic, and Puerto Rico, Duncan writes in Spanish, but unlike
them he is a part of English-speaking (British) and African-derived
(Ashanti) forms of culture from Jamaica. In fact, multicultural and
multilingual structures have played a significant role in the devel-

29. Steady, "African Feminism: A Worldwide Perspective," 4.
30. Ibid., 7, 18.
31. Brathwaite, "The African Presence in Caribbean Literature," 73.

opment of the Caribbean discourse that links North and South Americas. Thus understood, Duncan's Afro–Costa Rican fiction is a branch of Caribbean literature and, simultaneously, an integral part of Central and Latin American letters.


## AFRO–COSTA RICAN LITERATURE

The presence of African-descended people in large numbers in Central America is a function of British and "Yankee" economic and political interests in that region in the late nineteenth and early twentieth centuries. In order to profit from the cultivation of bananas and coffee, entrepreneurs with capital and technology sought cheap labor in the islands of the Antilles, or West Indies. To facilitate the transportation of those products to European and North American markets, West Indian workers were recruited to construct the Panama Canal. As a result, many Antilleans were resettled along the Atlantic Coast of the western Caribbean basin, which today includes the rimlands of Belize, Honduras, Nicaragua, Costa Rica, and Panama. Ian Smart refers to the process of relocation and dispersion as "scatteration," which came in the wake of several historical population waves that began with the conquest of Mexico, crested with the recruitment of black labor from the Antilles in the late nineteenth and early twentieth centuries, and leveled off in the 1950s. No matter what ethnic or racial term one uses to classify the peoples of the Gulf of Mexico basin, "the African cultural heritage constitutes one of the defining features of Caribbeanness even in the fullest geographical sense, for the African cultural note is the dominant one, or one of the most prominent, in the peculiar cultures of all of the islands and rimland regions considered to be Caribbean."[32] Consequently, the affirmation of West Indian culture in Costa Rica is a defining feature of Duncan's fiction.

Born in San José, Costa Rica, in 1940, this grandson of Jamaican and Barbadian immigrants is the most prominent black fiction writer in that country. Dorothy Mosby situates Duncan within a strong oral and an emerging written black tradition, which includes

32. Smart, *Central American Writers*, 10–11, 12. The term *scatteration* is not widely accepted among Afro-Hispanic scholars, but Smart's analysis of Caribbeanness merits our attention.

the Anancy tales and calypso, as well as early writers like the "tailor-poet" Alderman Johnson Roden (1893–?) and short-story writer Dolores Joseph Montout (1940–1991). Some of Roden's extant poems in English are "Forget It," "Forever Faithful—To My Wife," "Nostalgia," "White Justice—Reality," and "The Outlaw," which include such themes as love, frustration, and oppression of blacks throughout the African diaspora and their rebellion against it, but most of his works never saw the light of day. However, they situate Roden as an important literary precursor to contemporary black writers because he is the link between their West Indian origins in Jamaica and the transformation of West Indian culture in Costa Rica. Joseph also wrote profusely in English, and the majority of his pieces are unpublished. One exception is *Tres relatos del caribe costarricense* (Three short stories of the Costa Rican Caribbean), which came out with a Spanish title, but is a collection of stories in English that depicts the daily struggle of people in Limón Province during the 1970s. For this reason, Joseph has been referred to as the "cultural historiographer" of the West Indian experience in Costa Rica. Both Roden and Joseph are the links between the oral tradition and the living generations of writers. Second-generation poet Eulalia Bernard (1935–) is the author of *Ritmohéroe* (Rhythm hero, 1982), *My Black King* (1991), and *Ciénaga* (Swamp, 2001). Fourth-generation bard Shirley Campbell (1965–) and Panamanian-born Delia McDonald (1965–) round out the literary landscape. To date, Campbell has published *Naciendo* (On being born, 1988) and *Rotundamente negra* (Unequivocally black, 1995), while McDonald's poetic outlay includes *El séptimo círculo del obelisco* (The seventh circle of the obelisk, 1994), *Sangre de madera* (Wood blood, 1995), and *La lluvia es una piel* (The rain is a skin, 1999). Bernard writes and publishes in Spanish, English, and Limonese Creole, but Campbell and McDonald use Spanish exclusively. Nevertheless, they all contribute to an emerging discourse of African Hispanophone writing in Costa Rica. Through the lens of postcolonial theory, Mosby identifies the "literary and social issues of marginality, subjectivity, immigration, nation, language, and literary production of texts by Afro–Costa Rican writers"; within the specificity of their sociohistorical reality (Afro-realism), she analyzes "the experience of West Indian migration, thematic repetitions, code switching (English, Spanish, and Creole-patois), notions of 'Otherness,' and engagement with Afro-Caribbean and African folklore."[33] In short, the above writers are the foundation of a literary tradition that reflects an Afro–Costa Rican worldview and fosters racial, ethnic, and gender diversity within the national discourse.

Although the lyric voice in Costa Rican literature is strong in the works of the above poets, the absence of a black female writer of fiction is conspicuous. Concerning this issue, we are reminded that "limited access to education, prescribed domestic roles, and exclusion from the literary marketplace have deprived Spanish-American women, particularly black women, of a voice."[34] However, that challenge has been met in the foregrounding of a tradition of black female writing in Miriam DeCosta-Willis's edited anthology *Daughters of the Diaspora* (2003). Compelled by a passion for the subject, other academics are producing studies that redeem/recover invisible/ lost authors. For example, Henry Louis Gates Jr.'s *Loose Canons* succinctly articulates the global thrust behind the recovery of texts and the elucidation of literature in African diaspora studies:

> Ours is a late-twentieth-century world profoundly fissured by nationality, ethnicity, race, class, and gender, and the only way to transcend those divisions—to forge for once, a civic culture that respects both differences and commonalities—is through education that seeks to comprehend the diversity of human culture. Beyond the hype and the high-flown rhetoric is a pretty homely truth: There is no tolerance without respect—and no respect without knowledge. Any human being sufficiently curious and motivated can fully possess another culture, no matter how "alien" it may appear to be.[35]

It may not be possible to fully understand another culture, but one can learn to appreciate cultural differences. Instead of tolerating "foreign" literature, people can mutually respect each other's con-

33. Smart, "Quince Duncan"; Mosby, *Place, Language, and Identity,* 25. Mosby's source for the scant biographical information on Alderman Johnson Roden is Donald K. Gordon, "Alderman Johnson Roden: The Tailor-Poet." In addition, she provides data on the poets Bernard (76–79), Campbell (168–73), and McDonald (209–10) in her study.

34. Miriam DeCosta-Willis, "Afra-Hispanic Writers and Feminist Discourse," 248.

35. Gates, introduction to *Loose Canons: Notes on the Culture Wars,* xv. On Dolores Joseph, see Donald K. Gordon, "Expressions of the Costa Rican Black Experience: The Short Stories of Dolores Joseph and the Poetry of Shirley Campbell."

tributions—a dream Aretha Franklin articulated quite well in her song "Respect" (1966). To this end, *The Eve/Hagar Paradigm* proposes to take the reader on an enriching journey by exploring a distinct way of seeing the world through women characters in Duncan's fiction. It is hoped that at least one of the "black holes" of contemporary Spanish American fiction will be illuminated.

## CHAPTER ORGANIZATION

The rest of this study comprises five chapters and a conclusion. Chapter 1, "Intimations of Womanism in *Dawn Song*," focuses on women characters during the period of transformation for West Indian culture. In this collection is a female presence that captures the early years of migration and resettlement from Jamaica to Limón Province on the Atlantic Coast of Costa Rica. The chapter is called "Intimations of Womanism" because its literary personae are composite sketches of black womanhood that are blended into a communal identity painted by the writer. Six characters are featured in chapter 1: Myra ("Dawn Song"), Ruby ("A Gift for Grandma"), Sophisticated Lady ("Sophisticated Lady"), The Educator ("The Watchman's Light"), an anonymous figure who assumes the form of the *samamfo* ("Two Roads"), and Miss Spence ("A Letter").[36]

Chapter 2, "Womanist Footprints in *The Pocomía Rebellion*," also features six personages—Mama Bull ("The Pocomía Rebel-

36. The term *samamfo* means a number of related things: "ancestral spirit," "the place where the ancestors meet with the living," "the spirit and heritage of one's ancestors," or "black spirituality." This is documented in Ian Smart's interview, "The Literary World of Quince Duncan," and it is repeated in the entry "Quince Duncan" written by Smart for *Dictionary of Literary Biography*. Duncan states in that interview: "I found [the term *samamfo*] in some book on African culture. I had been searching for a word that would express this idea we have at home that the spirits of our ancestors are alive, present all the time there with you. I well remember hearing my grandparents talking about the older people just as if they were still there. They really were there, the only problem was that they were, you know, still in Jamaica.... [T]he ones that had died in Costa Rica would be considered to be around. I remember many times, for example, at night when we arrived home after a walk through the dark, an animal or something might go by and the comment would be: 'Your grandmother walks with you to protect you.' So the spirits of the ancestors are here constantly with you. I couldn't find any way of expressing this in either Spanish or English until I ran across that term *samamfo*, which said exactly what I wanted to say" (102).

lion"), Aracely ("Go-o-o-o-al!"), Ma' Drusilda ("Family Ties"), Guadalupe ("Little Boy Blue"), Joe Gordon's wife ("The Legend of Joe Gordon"), and the Doctor's wife ("Ancestral Myths"). In addition, chapters 1 and 2 represent Duncan's tentative efforts at positioning an authentic black literary voice in Costa Rican fiction.

Chapter 3, "A Tale of Two Wives in *The Four Mirrors*, " examines two females that embody the double consciousness of protagonist Charles McForbes, who attempts to reconcile two mutually exclusive ways of life represented by the Central Valley (San José) and the Atlantic Coast (Limón). Moreover, the analysis of McForbes's first and second spouses through the Eve/Hagar principle highlights the conflictive nature of Duncan's posture with respect to the canon.

Chapter 4, "The House of Moody in *For the Sake of Peace*," studies five women figures presented in ensemble fashion—Sitaira, Mariot, Elizabeth, Margaret, and Mammy—but Mariot is the only one who has a voice. The novel covers a century of colonial and neocolonial turmoil encapsulated in the antithetical positioning of Jamaica (1833) and Costa Rica (1930s). Utilizing the technique of the new Latin American narrative, Duncan seeks in *For the Sake of Peace* to reconcile the conflict presented in *The Four Mirrors* by centering West Indian culture in its sociohistorical context rather than viewing it from the margins. In doing so the author reconstitutes his Afro–Costa Rican literary identity in relation to the canon.

Chapter 5, "A Voice from Down Under in *Dead-End Street*," examines the period of national reconstruction in Costa Rica from the Civil War of 1948 to its aftermath twenty years later through the eyes of one of the lowly—a female rebel named Doña Carmen. This "nonracial" novel won the Aquileo Echeverría national prize, even as it inserted within the national discourse an invisible (black female) presence that challenged the notion of a modern society based on the myth of white supremacy. With this novel Duncan radically transforms the canon in unique ways that emerge from a close reading of the text. Thus, the Eve/Hagar principle will be used to trace the female subject from its first manifestations in the short stories to full-blown characterizations in the three novels, and parallel to this the novelist's engagement with the literary canon.

The conclusion to this study evaluates the significance of male-authored female characters in gender studies. Specifically, we shall address a series of issues: How successful is Duncan's portrayal of female characters in terms of his own theories? How does his blending of seemingly disparate cultures impact the aesthetics and praxis of his writing? Can author, critic, and the public discover a happy meeting ground where the production, elucidation, and reading of literature are enjoyable, meaningful activities? This last question perhaps touches on a concept of humanism outlined by Jackson and other scholars in their literary studies. Through the Eve/Hagar paradigm this monograph will focus on Duncan's works from the 1970s in order to examine some of the most compelling issues of contemporary Latin American literature.

## A NOTE ON TRANSLATION

The analysis of literature has engendered all kinds of "studies" that are, more often than not, comparative, cross-cultural, interdisciplinary, multilingual, or all of the above—witness the plethora of intellectual ferment in African American, Hispanophone, Afro-German, Caribbean, cultural, Francophone, gender, Latin American, Lusophone, and translation studies programs in institutions on a global level. *The Eve/Hagar Paradigm* encompasses at least half of these fields, but translation is an issue that must be addressed before proceeding. This process has developed during the course of history in response to the need for communication among peoples, cultures, and nations. For this reason, Albrecht Neubert and Gregory M. Shreve suggest the phrase "language mediation" as a "collective name for translation and interpreting," thus highlighting the important role translation plays in human affairs. It is a job for the bold at heart, and translators have always done so at the risk of being misunderstood, although the reasons are not always obvious. Shreve sheds light on the practice as he points out that

> a source text is embedded in a complex linguistic, textual, and cultural context. Its meaning, communicative intent, and interpretive effect draw upon its natural relationships in that environment. It is a daunting task to pull a text from its natural surroundings and recreate it in an alien linguistic and cultural setting. The text belongs to a dynamic cultural and linguistic

ecology. The translator uproots it in a valiant attempt to trans-
plant its fragile meaning.[37]

I became interested in translation as a function of my research
and teaching of Latin American literature, and within that field
Afro-Hispanic writing. After teaching classes in African American
literature and seminars in the University of Alabama at Birmingham
Honors Program, and coteaching a humanities (interdisciplinary)
class, it became apparent that a translation project was in order to
satisfy an English-speaking audience that was eager to study Afro–
Latin American writers but could not read their works in the original language. Therefore, I embarked on a path that took me "where
angels fear to tread," and my first efforts to produce a vehicle of
linguistic and cultural mediation resulted in the bilingual collection
*The Best Short Stories of Quince Duncan/Las mejores historias de
Quince Duncan*. Overall, this volume has had a favorable reception, but there has been some fallout involving the use of variant
forms of English from the United States. In fact, the red (or are
they black?) flags of "Ebonics," "Eubonics," and "Southern black
dialect" have been hoisted.

In the first place, the models of English used in the translations
are not dialectal but vernacular, which are very different. Dialect is
the attempt by a writer or translator to graphically reproduce the
sounds of a language that he or she does not usually speak in order
to approximate the speech patterns of groups of which he or she
may not be a part. In other words, the characters are beneath or
apart from the writer; therefore, he or she wishes to maintain some
distance from them. Often, this distancing carries ethnoracial or
class overtones or both because it emanates from an abstractly
stratified, rather than functional, model of language. On the other
hand, vernacular involves the use of alternate forms of speech by
writers, translators, and speakers who have historically learned another or a different or a new language from the point of view of
their original mother tongues. Africans, Amerindians, and Asians
who experienced slavery and colonialism were forced to learn European languages by using the patterns and structures of their original idioms. With respect to this point, John Edgar Wideman pres-

37. Neubert and Shreve, *Translation as Text*, 1.

ents a brilliant analysis of the effects of engaging a "foreign" tongue on people of African ancestry. He comments:

> Tension and resistance characterize the practices African-descended peoples have employed to keep their distance from imposed tongues, imposed disciplines. Generation after generation has been compelled to negotiate—for better or worse, and with self-determination and self-realization at stake—the quicksand of a foreign language that continues by its structure, vocabulary, its deployment in social interaction, its retention of racist assumptions, expressions and attitudes, its contamination by theories of racial hierarchy to recreate the scenario of master and slave.
>
> Uneasiness and a kind of disbelief of this incriminating language we've been forced to adopt never go away.[38]

In short, the speakers of vernacular might be unschooled or very highly educated, but they engage in a form of code switching that is tantamount to bilingualism or multilingualism.

Second, some locutors employ the vernacular as a rule because they have little or no formal education and they have not learned to negotiate the socially acceptable registers of the dominant language. However, among the "illiterate" are many intelligent, resourceful, and creative individuals who *prefer* to speak in the vernacular as a form of resistance to a racially charged hegemonic discourse that often demeans them. Likewise, many formally educated people make a conscious choice to utilize multiple levels or registers of a given language, and they also *choose* to speak in vernacular in certain situations. In every nation where a European language is dominant there are alternate forms of the "standard." In the United States, New Englanders and New Yorkers speak differently; northerners and southerners do; and so do midwesterners and people in the Pacific Northwest. In Costa Rica those who live in the Central Valley speak distinctly from those who live on the Atlantic or Pacific Coasts. Essentially, Africans on the continent who went through colonialism, as well as their descendants in the diaspora who endured slavery, forged their own tongues out of the linguistic matrices of the European languages of conquest/discovery/empire, no matter where the latter originated.

38. Wideman, "In Praise of Silence," 548.

Third, there is a myriad of theories about translation, for the discipline of translation studies has developed exponentially in the past decade. Although scholars differ in their approaches, the overwhelming consensus is that a translator must capture the ambience, sociolinguistic context, and historical reality of the language from which he or she is translating, and then transfer that meaning into the target language. For example, Carolyn R. Hodges informs us that

> despite the many different precepts evolving from the debate on the art of translation, those who embark upon the task have a common goal—to transfer meaning: they also have a common understanding—that the final product can only be an approximation of the original. The attempt to transfer meaning, that is, to find an equivalent between the original text, or source language, and the language into which it is to be translated, or target language, suggests the possibility of finding *sameness in meaning*.[39]

According to the context of the source and target languages, sameness in meaning is the objective, not a word-for-word transcription.

The Jamaicans who migrated to Costa Rica were fairly literate, having a basic level of education equivalent to grammar school (eighth grade). For example, James Duncan, Quince's grandfather, was a very articulate and well-read individual, and he exercised a tremendous influence on the novelist. Moreover, there were many people, including common laborers, who spoke the "King's English," albeit with a Jamaican or Caribbean rhythm.[40] Conversely, there were and are many people in the Afro-Caribbean community who alternate(d) between "proper English" and Creole, a vernacular that is very difficult for a North American translator to handle if it is not part of her daily verbal repertoire. Therefore, by recreating Duncan's stories through translation, the attempt was made to transfer meaning such that an English-speaking audience in the United States could take pleasure in reading them. This meant that in some stories, I had to select forms of black vernacular used by mostly rural farmers or urban working-class people in the 1930s

---

39. Hodges, "Introduction: Reflections on the Art of Literary Translation and the Legacy of Langston Hughes," vii; emphasis added.
40. Duncan, interview by author, Guanacaste, Costa Rica, September 22, 2002.

and '40s in order to convey a *sameness in meaning,* not a one-to-one correspondence of words. It is a language that is not necessarily limited to the South (although it originated there), since many blacks who migrated to the North carried these forms of speech with them and passed them on to later generations.[41]

Finally, Duncan himself has authorized my use of the vernacular to translate certain aspects of his fiction in eighteen years of interaction through letters, telephone conversations, interviews, conferences, and in our respective home spaces. The first occasion of direct communication between writer and literary critic was at a conference at Dillard University in New Orleans in 1985, where he and the audience reacted favorably to certain passages of "The Legend of Joe Gordon" that I had translated; an earlier version by another translator had convinced Duncan that he had failed to convey the humor intended. Duncan stated: "I realized that the translation made the difference." On a second occasion in 1991, Duncan publicly expressed appreciation to me, commenting that "it takes a writer to know a writer." This was a priceless statement of validation.

There is much truth in the criticism that "Quince Duncan has a very clear political and philosophical reason for writing in standard Spanish—and *not* English, which he knows because he is bilingual, *nor* in the creolized Spanish of West Indian descendants. I believe that he wants to make it very clear that a West Indian–descended Costa Rican can master the dominant tongue."[42] To reiterate, Duncan is indeed self-conscious of language as seen through the eyes of the hegemonic discourse, and in his early works he shows the world that he can master the dominant tongue. On the other hand, it is already evident in a story like "A Gift for Grandma" (in which *the*

---

41. In the story "Dawn Song," the character Myra refers to her children's grandmother as Abuela, which when capitalized is translated as "Big Mama." If one asks many African Americans about terms of endearment for their grandmothers, the responses run the gamut from "Big Mama," "Big Mom," and "Mama" to "Muh Deah," "Mama Ella," and "Nana." Of my maternal grandmother's twelve grandchildren, only one of them, my younger sister, Selitta, ever called her "Grandmother." The rest of us said "Mama Teen." This kind of naming is common to a number of black communities in the United States and throughout the African diaspora. At a funeral during August 2003, the practice was coincidentally confirmed when I opened the program and noticed that the captions under the picture of the deceased woman referred to "Big Mama's" activities during her lifetime. Duncan capitalizes the word in the story to *name* the individual referred to, and thus identify her as an important figure in the extended family.

42. Comments from an anonymous reader.

*author creates variant registers, including a black vernacular*) that Duncan wishes to avoid the pitfalls of positioning himself as a "minority writer" who gives a knee-jerk response to a "majority discourse." This means that he does not necessarily wish to sacrifice poetic license for mainstream correctness, just as any other author would do. In fact, I took my cue from that very narrative. A rereading of *The Best Short Stories* and its Spanish counterpart will reveal that African American vernacular forms are used very sparingly (in those passages indicating conversations between characters or interior monologues of the same) and that the majority of the translations are from "standard Spanish" to "standard English." Consequently, the choice of this linguistic mode to make the stories accessible to an English-speaking North American audience is not a "misreading" but a *re-creation* of Duncan's texts. Presently, the Costa Rican author is working on an English-based novel, perhaps with other languages included, which illustrates that he has moved beyond a preoccupation with proving himself. As a bilingual artist, he can create a fictional universe of endless aesthetic, thematic, stylistic, and linguistic possibilities. The analysis of the Eve/Hagar paradigm in female characters is simply one way of reading Duncan's literary achievement in Latin American fiction of the 1970s.

# 1

## INTIMATIONS OF WOMANISM IN
## *Dawn Song*

*Dawn Song* (1970) presents stories about life in the Atlantic region of Costa Rica during the early years of the twentieth century, a period when the Antillean immigrants experienced many difficulties in adjusting to a new environment. Moreover, the incidents occur in Limón Province before and up to the Civil War of 1948, a watershed in national history. During this early period of migration, black women played key roles in the preservation of West Indian lifestyles and values within the conflictive, and often chaotic, setting of the Costa Rican tropics. Thus, their lives replicated the Eve/Hagar pattern as they sought to adjust to another world. *Dawn Song* speaks to other texts in the postcolonial discourse of Latin America in that it verbalizes the experiences of migration, oppression, and resistance among the first wave of Antillean immigrants to Costa Rica. This is evident in the lives of the six female figures who are prominent in the stories "Dawn Song," "A Gift for Grandma," "Sophisticated Lady," "The Watchman's Light," "Two Roads," and "A Letter." For the most part, the narratives are developed in a linear manner that incorporates the techniques of an omniscient narrator, character/narrators, flashback, memory, and interior monologue. With respect to the Eve/Hagar paradigm, the female personae of *Dawn Song* constitute intimations of womanism, or that principle of black femaleness through which one exhibits "outrageous, audacious, courageous, or *willful* behavior."[1] Instead of full-blown characters, these women are indelible sketches on the broad canvas of West Indian life in Limón Province. Along with the male characters they form a vibrant portrait of the era.

1. Alice Walker, "In Search of Our Mothers' Gardens," xi.

According to historian Trevor W. Purcell, "as increasing numbers of Blacks were brought into the economy of Central America's Atlantic Coast during the early twentieth century, Hispanics came to deplore the Africanization of the region."[2] Throughout Central America West Indian blacks were considered a necessary inconvenience for developing the lowlands, but when competition for jobs became intense, the government started campaigns to deport them. By the third decade Antillean immigration had slowed to a trickle for several reasons. For one thing, the banana crops had been destroyed by various diseases during the 1920s and '30s, which forced the United Fruit Company to shut down its operations in the Atlantic region. Second, the Costa Rican Congress under the administration of León Cortés issued a prohibition against people of color who sought employment in the new company enclave on the Pacific Coast, alleging that the inhabitants who lived there needed the jobs more. Thus, unemployment, starvation, and despair forced many Antilleans to seek a more favorable climate in Panama or other countries in Central America. Third, many West Indians migrated from Puerto Limón to more sizable towns in the eastern lowlands of the country, which began a process of cultural adaptation that would intensify after the Civil War.[3] No matter where they settled, the Antilleans were engaged in the struggle for a better life, and this battle brought out the heroism of a proud people, among whom were many women. A glimpse into the lives of these heroines (and their heroes) through the Eve/Hagar paradigm elicits a celebratory note in *Dawn Song*, which represents the nascence of West Indian culture in the national consciousness.

Duncan treats the themes of poverty and the de facto segregation that discouraged internal migration from the Atlantic Coast to the Central Valley, as well as the problems that racial and ethnic differences entailed in the dominant society. One point of view asserts that "the lighthearted slice-of-life title story" belies an increasingly pessimistic tone in *Dawn Song*, and observes that "this dark social context ultimately translates itself into individual existential questions and doubts about personal value, identity, and purpose— themes central to Duncan's later work."[4] It is true that one story in

2. Purcell, *Banana Fallout: Class, Color, and Culture among West Indians in Costa Rica*, 3.
3. Kathleen Sawyers Royal and Franklin Perry, "Costa Rica," 218.
4. Smart, "Quince Duncan," 101. For a general treatment of characters and

particular, "When I Lay My Burden Down," ends with the strange death (possible suicide?) of the young protagonist Bryan, but this is the exception rather than the rule in the collection, and it will not be treated in this study. *Dawn Song* contains the seeds of West Indian cultural affirmation that would blossom in *The Pocomía Rebellion* and undergo transformation in Duncan's novels. Not only does the title *Dawn Song* suggest hope and faith, but the majority of the stories also depict women who maintain both in the face of overwhelming odds. This allows the collection to end on an optimistic note with "A Letter," which counteracts the existential angst of "When I Lay My Burden Down."

The story "Dawn Song" illustrates the theme of physical, psychological, and spiritual survival of a family of Jamaican immigrants in which gender roles are not necessarily stratified. John and Myra are a hardworking young couple whose lives are filled with unprofitable labor, and their story is a brushstroke in which Duncan presents them as a symbol of life in Siquirres. The town is "a black portrait that rocks, that throbs with love in John's and Myra's hearts."[5] One can situate "Dawn Song" in its historical context because Siquirres is a small town in Limón Province, the heart of the Costa Rican black belt before 1948. Moreover, there are references to black music rooted in the traditions of the Anglophone Caribbean and United States (the blues and calypso) rather than Hispanic culture (boleros and *guarachas*). In "Dawn Song" Duncan contrasts the searing innervating daytime, symbolized by the tropical heat, to the cool, refreshing night when John and Myra relax in bed, represented by the translucent aura of the sky. The author extends this symbolic chart of opposites to the natural world, for the banana tree, cocoa plants, machete, and swamp are associated with pain, lack of fulfillment, futility, and danger, while distant objects like the sky, stars, moonlight, and clouds suggest joys, hopes, and dreams.

The motif of suffering is not upstaged in "Dawn Song," even though John and Myra represent the first generation of Jamaicans in Costa Rica, who experienced the worst living and working conditions but saw themselves as temporary dwellers. At first the United

---

themes in Duncan's fiction from 1969 to 1989, see Donald K. Gordon, *Lo jamaicano y lo universal en la obra del costarricense Quince Duncan.*

5. Martin-Ogunsola, *Best Short Stories,* 39. All subsequent quotations will be cited parenthetically. The publication is set up such that the English translations appear on odd pages, the Spanish original on even pages.

Fruit Company recruited men exclusively, because elements like the torrential rain, scorching sun, insects, snakes, and other nightmares of the tropics were too harsh for women and children to endure. In time improvements were made on the banana plantations so that better housing and provisions for health care attracted single women and married couples; however, maintaining a stable family life was still difficult.[6] The marital love depicted in "Dawn Song" provides thematic relief from the motifs of poverty and hardship, and it humanizes what might otherwise be perceived as stereotyped victims. Nevertheless, it must be pointed out that John and Myra are happy with each other, not with their abject conditions. Thus, their tragicomic stance is particularly evident in their enthusiastic response to the blues, an African American form of music that simultaneously laments and celebrates the black experience in the New World.

John and Myra embody the capacity to hold on to one's inner self and keep it inviolate from destructive external forces. Moreover, Myra's role is significant because she is a confident, loving, and well-adjusted person who is proud to be a housewife. In this sense, she embodies the original principle of Eve as suitable mate, the female part of gendered humanity. Although their relationship is one of equals, Myra is playfully deferential to John as he prepares to go to work in the banana fields:

> "Myra . . . Where the tea?"
> "What?"
> "The tea, for goodness sake, the train leavin' me. Cairo far."
> "I lef' it on the stove, honey."
> "On the . . . The tea not on the stove."
> "Huh?"
> "Wake up, now, woman. The train gon' leave me, doggone it." (39, 41)

John's authoritative, demanding tone is counteracted by Myra's soothing response, which manifests her assertiveness as one aspect of the Hagar principle:

> "So much rushin' around . . . *Cho*.[7] And what make me so mad is you ain't even washed your face."

6. Purcell, *Banana Fallout*, 4–5.
7. In the original, an asterisk appeared after the word *Cho*, indicating that it is in the glossary to Martin-Ogunsola, *Best Short Stories* (289). According to

"Hey, girl, just gimme the tea, will ya? And stop all that yackin'."

"Look, shuggah. You got it right in yo' hand."

"Kiss the back o' my neck."

"You mean to tell me you made me get up outta bed . . ."

(41)

One of the most significant features of the above passages is Duncan's use of language as a marker of cultural identity, for the Spanish of John and Myra's conversation is charged with the inflection and flavor of West Indian English. Moreover, this type of usage connects to Stephen Henderson's *mascon* concept, "certain words and constructions [that] seem to carry an inordinate charge of emotional and psychological weight, so that whenever they are used they set all kinds of bells ringing, all kinds of synapses snapping, on all kinds of levels." For example, words like *cho,* an expression of disappointment, disgust, or frustration, and the accentuation of the last syllable in "hombré" to achieve the *agudo* (masculine/sharp) stress, in contrast to the standard Spanish "hombre" to create *llano* (feminine/mild) stress, enrich their idiom with non-Hispanic speech acts. The use of "nation language," or vernacular forms of English like Jamaican Creole, engages the womb/tongue principle in Myra, enabling her to maintain home and family in an alien environment without missing a step.[8] As a consequence, her garrulous nature is a concrete manifestation of Afro-realism in the story.

Myra's assertiveness and self-confidence are evident in a scene where she takes charge of instructing their two children:

"There yo' teacher, now, go on. And you already know: no disrespect to Big Mama, no spinnin' tops, no marbles, no cards, no tossin' coins, none o' that stuff, 'cause today Sunday, the Lord's day."

"Yes, Mama."

"Besides, be careful not to git yo' clothes all muddy; and behave yo'selves. Be good, now."

"Yes, Daddy."

"Yes, Mommy." (43, 45)

---

Benjamín Núñez, *Cho* (or *Cha*) is "an Afro-Caribbean exclamation expressing scorn or annoyance" (*Dictionary of Afro–Latin American Civilization,* 120).

8. Smart, "Quince Duncan," 106; Henderson, *Understanding the New Black Poetry,* 44; Mosby, *Place, Language, and Identity,* 43.

Although both parents instill attitudes, beliefs, and values in their youngsters, the female's influence is stronger. This is indicated in the choice of words with which Myra reinforces her instructions—for example, the allusion to "Abuela" ("Big Mama"), an affectionate name for black grandmothers in many African-derived cultures throughout the diaspora. If a child does not listen to "Mama," he or she will invariably obey "Big Mama." In effect, Myra personifies the positive aspects of the Eve/Hagar model—qualities like self-confidence, ingenuity, and industriousness. For this reason, she takes control of her own life and guides that of her family in spite of her lack of power in the larger society. Within an ambience of hardship and hostility, the spouses enjoy true companionship in that they talk things over, worship and swim together, and accompany each other to the local tavern on Sunday evenings. This would hardly be the case if their relationship were stratified, for Myra might otherwise have to drag John out of the tavern, or nag him until he comes home. In effect, the Eve/Hagar principle in Myra's character reveals her interdependent, mutual, and complementary relationship with John.

At the end of the story, one is reminded that the world of John and Myra is not idyllic since they must face "Blue Monday," a reference to John's daily routine of unprofitable labor. Nevertheless, their positive relationship shows the ability of various members of a marginalized group to transcend mere existence, for John and Myra create an inner life that contests their sociohistorical conditions. Poet Nikki Giovanni articulates this healthy response to oppression when the persona in her poem "Nikki Rosa" comments: "I really hope no white person ever has cause to write about me / because they never understand that *black love is black wealth.*"[9] In short, the mind-set John and Myra choose to face hardship—whether hope or despair—is a function of their religious and moral values. Furthermore, the Eve/Hagar construct is operative in strengthening the character of a woman like Myra, whom the society pities or scorns.

In "Dawn Song" Duncan creates a sketch with no physical descriptions of the female character, but instead allows her language, behavior, and attitudes to define her. This contrasts sharply to the portraits of Gisella and Bonifacia discussed in the introduction to this study. Although race, gender, and class are factors in Myra's

9. Giovanni, *The Selected Poems of Nikki Giovanni,* 42; emphasis added.

life, they do not determine her outlook. Concerning the Eve/Hagar principle, Myra is "colored" by the experience of living in a neo-colonial plantation enclave that replicates the colonial structures in effect before the abolition of slavery. She is assertive and talka-tive, but also tender and good-natured. Inherently, she functions as woman/wife and woman/mother, and both these roles feed into the womb/tongue metaphor. However, the tension of polar opposites (mind and body) is held in check, and a balance is established. Like others of their generation, the couple yearns to go back to Jamaica. Kathleen Sawyers Royal and Franklin Perry state that "the pri-mary concern of the migrant workers was to make some money and then return home to their home islands. But although their labour on the railway and plantations sustained much of the na-tional economy, their wages remained meager. Few, if any, earned enough to re-establish family ties, and the threat of unemployment and poverty was ever present. Return to the islands was little more than a dream." Carlos Meléndez Chaverri and Quince Duncan in-dicate that the mentality of *provisionalidad* (provisionality) or *tem-poralidad* (temporality) constituted a form of self-deception that became the source of much emotional pain for the descendants of the immigrants. "Dawn Song" sketches broad strokes of a female type who reconstructs with her mate a "home" in the tropics, thus temporizing her family's pivotal role in the modernization of a trop-ical wilderness. That is, Myra is part of that first immigrant group who saw its role as a "civilizing" or taming mission for a country that was considered incapable of bringing about necessary change. Nevertheless, the reconstitution of self (identity) in the face of op-positionality meant that the West Indians had to recodify their con-cept of belonging even as they attempted to maintain their ethno-linguistic uniqueness in Costa Rica.[10] The use of the mother tongue (West Indian English and Creole) is an instrument Myra uses to re-make her identity in the new country. This challenge would also be faced by her descendants.

"A Gift for Grandma" is a delightful trickster tale about a middle-aged couple who are members of the second generation of

---

10. Royal and Perry, "Costa Rica," 216–17; Meléndez Chaverri and Duncan, *El negro en Costa Rica,* 103; Rosemary Geisdorfer Feal, "Reflections on the Ob-sidian Mirror: The Poetics of Afro-Hispanic Identity and the Gendered Body," 26; Mosby, *Place, Language, and Identity,* 25.

West Indian immigrants, who called themselves "Nowhereans." Unfortunately, these people "saw themselves as neither British, Jamaican nor Costa Rican. Although born in the country, none of them were legally its citizens. The United Fruit Company, the railway company, the Costa Rican government, the British consulate in Limón and the Jamaican government appeared to have washed their hands of them."[11] In this story language—or the literary invention of registers—serves as a mask to create a virtual female character. The ensemble cast includes Cocobello; his wife, Ruby; and their joint creation, the *abuela* (grandma). Not only is the family engaged in mortal combat with the rebel army, which sees itself as the "savior" of the Antilleans, but they must also contend with the official government forces. Cocobello and Ruby consider the opposing armies to be their enemies because both try to recruit Antilleans, who are not even citizens of the country. Thus, the narrative has two dimensions: an external framework that portrays a civil war in the nation, and an inner story that depicts the West Indian resistance to forced inclusion in that society. The two layers of the narrative structure are linked by the author's deft manipulation of various linguistic levels and by the unfolding of the Eve/Hagar paradigm through the two-headed Ruby/Grandma figure.

Like Eve, Ruby is her husband's helpmate. Her specific purpose in this situation is to help him escape the dragnet of forced recruitment by the Costa Rican soldiers. The first example of register is shown in the conversation between Cocobello and Ruby as they prepare to receive/deceive the soldiers who have just arrived by train in Estrada:

> "Ruby," his voice shook, "get the cushions."
> "I'm comin'."
> "Hurry up."
> "I'm comin'...go on, take off your shirt."
> ..."How do I look?"
> "Very nice, Granny."
> "Don't shuck and jive with me, now."
> "For goodness sake," Ruby exclaimed, "some of them comin' right this way..."
> "Okay, woman, calm down, now, calm down."

11. Royal and Perry, "Costa Rica," 218.

> "Yeah, yeah, all right. I'll be calm. But don't talk to me in
> that idiotic granny voice. Get in bed easy, now." (59, 61)

The above passage represents the literary use of standard and vernacular forms of language, as is pointed out in the following analysis: "When they are themselves, Cocobelo [sic] and Ruby speak a vernacular language, spiced with a few earthy expressions ('Shuck and jive,' 'Get in bed easy,' etc.), which is close to the standard. However, when confronted by the soldiers, who speak a variant folk idiom tinged with authority, Ruby's speech borders on dialect in order to maintain the protective mask of submission and ignorance, thus covering for her husband."[12] An example of linguistic marronage, this one-way communication is advantageous to Ruby since she understands the commanding officer but he cannot comprehend her.[13] One of the reasons Anancy the Spider is so successful in eluding danger is his or her ability to speak a foreign tongue, that is, to utter a discourse that his or her enemy cannot understand. Like the North American B'rer Rabbit, Ruby/Anancy employs the same words as the soldiers, but with a radically different meaning.

The reader assumes that Cocobello and Ruby talk with each other in English, for during the early years of their sojourn in Costa Rica, many West Indians resisted learning Spanish. However, the written language is Spanish because of the audience to whom the stories are directed. It is through the technique of stereotyped linguistic markers that Ruby is upstaged in the dramatic struggle between oppressed and oppressors because the squadron sees and hears only what it wants—two defenseless black women. Armed with the knowledge of her opponents' blind spot, Ruby acts to confirm their expectations. That is, she speaks "a jingle in a broken tongue," and her words literally become flesh right before the soldiers' eyes as the reader is also witness to the spinning of a tale within a tale:

> Then they heard voices in the hallway: hey, black gal, yessuh,
> where your husband, what husban', *your* husband, I ain't got

12. Martin-Ogunsola, "Translation as a Poetic Experience/Experiment: The Short Fiction of Quince Duncan," 46.

13. The word *marronage* is a borrowing from the French *marron* and, by extension, from the Spanish *cimarrón*. Please note that both words have a double *r*. The English term *maroon* doubles the *o*. See Núñez, *Dictionary of Civilization*, 306.

none, jus' kids, how old, the oldes' one 35 an' goin' aroun'
mixed up in dis mess, on whose side, Ruby was lying, she was
lying and she hoped she could keep her lies straight, whose
side is he on, who, aw, how I'm go' know, I don't know nothin',
I wanna know whose side he's fightin' on, with the Government or the Revolution, I don' know nothin' 'bout dis mess,
okay, there any soldiers in town? And that question pierced
the wall, lacerating Cocobello's ears, opening up his wound,
tryin' to get Ruby to take part in a matter in which she had
none. Soldiers? Man, even the flickin' mayor left, he went run-
nin'. Where? How I'm gon' know? I ain't no spy or nothin'
like that, okay, Brown Sugar, don't get upset, we gonna help
you all, y'all been exploited, we gonna come back later, four
of my men . . . What! to set up camp here. You gotta big house.
Well, it just that I only got two beds an' Grandma sick, an' . . .
No problem. They can sleep on the floor. Aw, s—t, man! What
did you say? Nothin', nothin', suh, nothin'. (61, 63)

Duncan skillfully juxtaposes different linguistic levels to suggest
the interplay of perceived roles, and thus Ruby's racial, sexual, and
social positioning as a Hagar figure:

> Several or more linguistic levels intersect in this passage and
> throughout the story: the formal level used by the narrative
> voice; the vulgar forms uttered by the soldiers among them-
> selves and the clipped vernacular directed by the soldiers to
> Cocobello and Ruby, the syncopated modified standard used
> between the married partners (indicated by elisions, rhythmic
> placement of words, and softening of vowels); and the totally
> non-standard level (graphically represented by the use of double
> negatives, zero copulative, etc.) employed exclusively by Ruby
> with the soldiers.[14]

Cocobello's resentment of his predicament is expressed through interior monologue, but the silencing of the male voice allows the
trickster couple to bring "Grandma" to life. In other words, his
manhood is compromised because it must be channeled into a
character who does not exist except in the "Eye of the Other."[15]
Consequently, the husband is outraged that he cannot confront the

14. Martin-Ogunsola, "Translation as Experience/Experiment," 47.
15. Sylvia Wynter, "The Eye of the Other: Images of the Black in Spanish Literature," 9.

military head-on, but he knows that kind of bravado is foolhardy. It would expose not only him, but also his six "draft-dodging" sons and other males of the community, who live in a constant state of alert.

The mind portion of the Eve/Hagar paradigm must quickly act to protect the body, so the character Ruby resorts to the time-tested black tradition of signifyin(g). That is, she lies, avoids the commander's questions about her sons, talks around the subject of war, but never quite comes to the point. At the same time, Ruby and "Grandma" make fun of the soldiers and their predicament by their use of strategic imaging and trickery.[16] The farce is successful because Ruby addresses the soldiers in a lingo they feel is appropriate for a woman of her station and because she reinforces the stereotyped image of the single black (and fecund) female, which readers in the United States might associate with the character "Bebe and her Kids." Nevertheless, Ruby's mask of helpless ignorance is also the thing that makes her vulnerable to the implicit threat of rape, which is suggested by the officer's intent to camp out in her house and is underscored by his audacious use of the term *Brown Sugar* to address her. Nevertheless, the womb/tongue dialectic is delicately balanced in that Ruby's intimate relationship with her husband (through her womb) is the very force that drives her to save him (through her tongue) and, by extension, their sons.

Within such a context, Ruby is heroic because she acts even though she is afraid of detection and punishment. In fact, the character does not limit herself to saying what the soldiers want to hear, but adds a note of defiance by injecting an expletive or two, a linguistic act that has traditionally been associated with male behavior. Role reversal, then, becomes the mainstay of this trickster tale, for the wife is the protector of the hearth and the husband, the dependent one. Another characteristic associated with male conduct is that Ruby gets temporarily caught up in the euphoria of war when she marvels at the blazing weaponry. The individual sacrifices her own well-being for the sake of family, which is common in female portraiture. Ironically, the denouement of "A Gift for Grandma" unfolds with Ruby back on her knees scrubbing the floor, while Cocobello releases his outraged frustration at being emasculated

---

16. Roger D. Abrahams, *Deep Down in the Jungle,* 51–52. See also Gates, "Blackness of Blackness," 288.

through ironic humor and understatement: "Well, I'll be d\ \d, underpants and silk stockings," and he guffaws. Laughing to keep from crying, Cocobello thinks about his sons. "What a blast!" he exclaims and stops abruptly: "Life is just as fine as it was yesterday" (65).

In one respect, the wife is cast in a supportive (Eve) role, for she is there to dry the tears and clean up the mess—in short, to comfort her husband. From another perspective, she has successfully negotiated the masculine/feminine dichotomy for the benefit of all concerned, which makes her "androgynous" in a double bind, like Hagar. In this sense, Ruby is the head/hand as well as the womb/tongue because she is the agent that metaphorically inserts black (West Indian) history into the national text. Furthermore, she affirms the gender-neutral qualities of the Eve/Hagar model not only by asserting herself in the farcical contest with the army, but also by assuming a position of leadership within her family and community when the situation demands. Nevertheless, a balance obtains in that there is an invisible network of men and women who cooperate to resist oppression, which is implied when the omniscient narrator provides the reader with additional details: "The fact is that Cocobello has six sons who are safely tucked away at his in-law's house. He won't let them fight in a war that's not theirs" (61). Undoubtedly, the heroic actions of women like Ruby led to the preservation of West Indian culture up to the 1950s. "A Gift for Grandma" is an excellent example of a literary sketch that utilizes the trope of virtual reality before the rise of computer technology.

"Sophisticated Lady" is an exquisite vignette of a young woman whose beauty, poise, and dignity challenge the conventional representation of black femaleness in Latin American literature. In terms of physical attractiveness, the character models the literary figure of the *mulata* of the colonial period. We recall that "charcoal and cinnamon are two of the racial metaphors used to refer to black and mulatto women in Cuba's classic nineteenth-century novel *Cecilia Valdés,* by Cirilo Villaverde. . . . As cinnamon is more appealing than charcoal, so too was the mulatto woman's perceived aesthetic and sensual attraction more esteemed." This kind of female characterization was and is an integral part of the canon. Moreover, the Eurocentric discourse is both an inventor and a product of the complex sociohistorical and cultural factors that manipulated race/

color, gender/sex, and class/caste into an ideology that supported the hierarchical structure of Caribbean and Latin American societies.[17] Duncan undermines the conventional literary model by investing the anonymous persona of this story, who will be named "Sophisticated Lady" for ease of discussion, with characteristics of the Eve/Hagar paradigm that she employs to continue the tradition of rebellion and subterfuge of other women characters. Ironically, Sophisticated Lady avoids falling into the body trap by a skillful manipulation of mind and body.

Set against a midwinter backdrop (stormy weather, gray-black clouds, dark days), the protagonist of the story goes to the state or regional prison with clothes for a male member of her family, who is about to be released. Historically, African-descended people have not had pleasant encounters with the law, whether the police or the courts. Thus, women who visit their interned loved ones have often had to downplay gender and class (since they cannot camouflage their race) in order to avoid assault, humiliation, and rape, especially in rural or provincial settings. There are three reasons that Sophisticated Lady is able to find a loophole in the system to complete her mission. First, she is beautiful, refined, and well dressed, with cinnamon-colored skin and long, delicate (well-manicured) fingers. This does not go unnoticed by the timid sentry at the jailhouse door, who sees only one dark and lovely figure, and it serves to "take him off guard." In short, the awareness of her body as a weapon of defense and her perceptive use of body language facilitate a smooth entrance into the jailhouse for Sophisticated Lady. Like Eve and Hagar, the female character in this story is more than what she appears to be.

The second reason the protagonist is successful is due to her perspicacity. She is able to assess the situation in a few seconds by realizing that the youthful watchman is expendable and powerless to withstand her spellbinding presence. He is her exact opposite—shy, lacking in self-confidence, especially with females, and probably plain-looking. At least *he* thinks so. In addition, the guardian of the jailhouse door stutters, a handicap that cannot be fully appreciated if one is not aware of the strong macho custom in Spanish-speaking countries that almost always spurs men to compose *piropos,* or expressions that signify upon the female body. A more self-assured

17. C. Williams, *Charcoal and Cinnamon,* xi, 1–18.

male character might try to proposition Sophisticated Lady with a statement like, "Baby, you got the keys to the kingdom," or something to that effect, before allowing her to enter the prison.[18] However, the guard in "Sophisticated Lady" cannot fill the boots his social role dictates, and he experiences a devastating sense of failure, which is displayed in the following encounter:

> "Good afternoon." On the girl's long, delicate fingers there is a wedding band. "I've brought some clothes for Cuperto ... He's getting out today."
> He can't believe what he's hearing! Cuperto is a criminal!
> There can't be any possible relationship between him and this young lady with such refined manners, who is so foxy, who is indeed a sophisticated lady.
> "That's a matter for the sh-sh-sheriff ... G-g-go in that door. He's r-r-right in there." (57)

A third reason for her poise and self-confidence is that Sophisticated Lady is inventive, a quality that enables her to function as a trickster figure like Anancy. The wedding band creates the impression that she is the criminal Cuperto's wife, although it is suggested in the outcome of the story that she is his sister. This illusion helps divert the sentry's attention from the woman's backup—an anonymous black man:

> Perhaps making fun of him on the sly, she thanks him and moves toward the door. The guard's eyes devour her fine cinnamon skin, his lips hang partly open, a savage delight gleams from his frightened eyes. He trembles. Someone has touched him on the back. He turns around only to come face to face with a tall, athletic-looking black man. He comes crashing down from his ecstasy.
> "What you lookin' at so hard?"
> Total bewilderment. Blood rush.
> "Don' look at that woman twice if you wanna keep on livin'." (57)

As observed in the following commentary, "Sophisticated Lady emerges victorious, for the man is so taken off guard that he is

---

18. In Stephen Spielberg's movie adaptation of Alice Walker's *Color Purple,* the character Squeak is raped by the sheriff or a prison guard when she goes to visit Sophia in jail.

totally unaware of her companion, who symbolizes the black phantom that lurks in the Euro-American male psyche. The litmus test: How would the guard have reacted had the man approached him first? Together the two reenact a time-tested survival ritual, playing the trickster, with the added aura of 'dropping the pigeon' here (she is the decoy, he the hit man)." No matter what the language, the use of the trickster figure—whether the African Tortoise, the African American B'rer Rabbit and Signifying Monkey, or the Caribbean Anancy the Spider—is universal in African diaspora literature because of the shared vision of history and ethnic memory of African-descended peoples in the New World.[19] The reader who is aware of that history already knows the rest of the story, for it is an age-old blue melody of heartache, trouble, oppression, and disruption—symbolized by the storm clouds and chilly, dreary atmosphere in the opening scene of "Sophisticated Lady"—but it is also a song of resilience, survival, and triumph. Whether Cuperto has committed an offense that requires incarceration is less certain than his perceived guilt in the eyes of the society. Hence, Duncan uses color sparingly in this vignette, but it is enough to accentuate the central conflict. Cuperto's blackness, captured in the athletic figure of the mysterious specter who appears and vanishes almost magically, is a challenge and affront to whiteness, reflected in the looming, antiseptic prison walls. This stark contrast reinforces the prevailing attitude that black people are always on the wrong side of the law. By donning a white cape, Sophisticated Lady simply takes the white supremacist ideology and turns it on its head, but she also hoists it upon her shoulders. In doing so she evokes Zora Neale Hurston's "mule of the world" metaphor as a sign for the black fe-

19. Martin-Ogunsola, "Translation as Experience/Experiment," 46; Gates, "Blackness of Blackness," 286–87. Mosby informs us of the following: "One of the most frequently retold African-derived oral traditions in Afro–Costa Rican literature is the Anancy story as it has taken shape from West Africa to the West Indies to Costa Rica. The Anancy stories, also called 'Annancy,' 'Ananse,' 'Anansi,' or 'Nancy' stories, are the best known of these orally transmitted tales and tell of the exploits of the cunning, crafty, and sometimes cruel spider of the same name. The Anancy tales have been passed from the Ashanti people of West Africa and diffused throughout the West Indies, becoming part of oral Caribbean culture during and after slavery. In the journey from Africa to Central America, Anancy transformed from a demigod to a symbol of cultural maroonage. The Anancy stories or tales of 'Hermano Araña' ('Bredda Spider' in Creole, 'Anancy' or 'Brother Spider' in English) usually present the spider involved in some form of trickery" (*Place, Language, and Identity*, 35).

male. Consequently, the contrapuntal repositioning of the black/mulatto protagonist as a symbol of refinement ("delicate fingers") and the guard as a representative of crudity ("savage delight") reverses the poles of the "civilization/barbarism" trope associated with the white/nonwhite dichotomy in the Eurocentric imagination. This reversal plays into the Eve/Hagar paradigm, for her individual performance transcends societal expectations.

One could easily call the tapestry "Portrait in Black and White," but it would not be as highly charged. Moreover, a literal translation of the title, "The Woman in the White Cape," suggests that the character's body is foregrounded. However, the epithet "Sophisticated Lady" gives her an identity and a more heroic stature in the epic battle of wits between the powerful and the powerless. Furthermore, my use of the Duke Ellington tune as the story's title recognizes the writer's appropriation of the technique of improvisation to define the character. Sophisticated Lady does not have to compromise herself, and lest one is tempted to dwell on her physical attributes, the author couples her beauty with a confrontational stance (Eve/Hagar metaphor), as depicted in the opening scene when she approaches the jailhouse door: "The guard looks at her, his eyes glued to her fantastic body. He tries to avoid such an open indiscretion, but his eyes come back to feast again on her exquisite physique. He looks her up and down until his gaze rests on her face. For an instance his glance is held spellbound by the defiant look of this mysterious beauty. But her glare blinds him. He lowers his eyes" (55, 57). Author bell hooks refers to the act of staring down as the "oppositional gaze," through which one who is positioned as weak or powerless is able to prevail.[20] Furthermore, Sophisticated Lady's rebellious posture makes a difference between a feminine voice, or one that casts the female as object, and a feminist/womanist voice, or one that allows her to speak as a black subject. This story depicts an Eve/Hagar figure who successfully navigates a sea of sharks—race, gender, and class—and the womb/tongue metaphor is played out through her silent but potent oppositional gaze.

Race/color and class/caste are not defining aspects of characterization in "The Watchman's Light." Tradition has it that the ghost-victim of a train accident guards the railroad tracks leading into

20. Hooks, *Black Looks: Race and Representation*, 115–31.

town at night, but a group of young Turks is determined to prove the elders wrong. After one delightfully unsuccessful excursion, the schoolboys return to the battlefield with their teacher Miss B(arrantes), who intends to use the occasion to teach a lesson to her "superstitious" students. However, the General and her makeshift army of disciples are ultimately routed by the supernatural presence, and the mystery remains unsolved.

Like other women characters in *Dawn Song*, Miss B illustrates sundry qualities of the Eve/Hagar mold in that she is smart, resourceful, and independent, but she is also proud, obstinate, and overconfident. In addition, she represents the dilemma of the Western-trained educator caught between diametrically opposed value systems. The science she teaches is based on an acceptance of Cartesian logic, whose basic premise is that every aspect of reality in the universe can be proved or disproved. According to this essentially Eurocentric ideology, anything that cannot be verified empirically falls within the realm of magic or superstition. In effect, "the conflict between the scientific approach and the magical one such as it is presented in *The Four Mirrors* and 'The Watchman's Light' is essentially ideological and one of opposing world views." On the other hand, Edward Kamau Brathwaite addresses this systemic clash in terms of its generic origin in precolonial Africa, where each culture resided within a religious network as an organic whole. "In traditional Africa, there is no specialization of disciplines, no dissociation of sensibilities. In other words, starting from this particular religious focus, there is no separation between religion and philosophy, religion and society, religion and art. Religion is the form or kernel or core of culture." Thus, religion is a signifier for a whole cultural complex in spite of the disintegration imposed on African cultures by the slave trade and the plantation structure. A critical construct like magic realism, so popular in Latin American literature during the 1960s and '70s, is an artificial approach to the study of Afro-Hispanic fiction because it does not take into account the underlying unity of the material and spiritual spheres that Afrocentric philosophy acknowledges.[21] Afro-realism, or the reconstitution of multileveled realms of truth as they impact every-

21. Ian Isidore Smart, "Religious Elements in the Narrative of Quince Duncan," 29; Brathwaite, "African Presence," 74; Smart, *Amazing Connections: Kemet to Hispanophone Africana Literature*, 7.

day life, underlies the mystery. Seemingly, in "The Watchman's Light" the unbroken circle of elders and children is threatened by Western science, an approach that is not indigenous to their culture. However, the surprise outcome of the story routs that menace.

Duncan places the Educator in an assertive mode, which goes against the grain of black and female characterization in hegemonic discourse. Because there are no references to physical traits, Miss B's race is indeterminate. During the early period of Antillean re-settlement in Costa Rica, it was common for British teachers to be brought from Jamaica for primary education in Limón Province, and the Protestant denominations played a significant role in that process.[22] The only hint of a close-knit relationship is the students' use of the word *niña*, an affectionate term or title of respect for Miss Barrantes. It seems to be an expression of endearment for a close member of the community rather than an outsider, but it does not indicate any preoccupation with race/color or class/caste.

Concerning the Eve/Hagar paradigm, "The Watchman's Light" centers on the dominance of mind over body, specifically tongue over womb in this case. The Educator is ensconced on the bedrock of data, facts, and formulas that will undoubtedly prove the correctness of her theory: that there is a logical explanation based on empirical evidence for the so-called mysterious light. Forewarned (but not forearmed), the General proceeds to lead her ragtag army of male children back to the site where they have a humorous encounter with the lantern-bearing ghost/man. However, when the apparition confronts the group, Miss B reverts to a traditional male-female relationship in that she allows the oldest student to take the lead, thus protecting her:

> "Stop, you all," she commanded after about 90 feet; "I'll go alone."
> "But, Miss B..."
> "Don't worry..."
> "I'll go with you," said the oldest. "Please let me go."
> "All right, come with me, but only you."
> She believing in her own knowledge, he believing in her, both advanced with flashlights extinguished. A Paternoster escaped from the Educator's lips. It was not enough, for which reason she stuttered a Hail Mary too. After that, together with

22. Meléndez Chaverri and Duncan, *El negro en Costa Rica*, 127–30.

her faithful disciple, she broke out running in the semidark-
ness of the night. Behind them at a distance, the other pupils
drifted along. (85, 87)

Like the Western mind-set she represents, Miss B's conviction is
that science is progress (right) and superstition is backwardness
(wrong), but that false dichotomy becomes her undoing, and it un-
ravels the boys, too. The tables are turned, and the character is
driven toward the pole of fear and submission rather than courage
and aggression in the Eve/Hagar paradigm. The response of the
omniscient narrator is a belly laugh, a major trope in Duncan's
fiction that is associated with the African trickster figure, the dual
deity Legba/Cuminá.[23] In "The Watchman's Light" Miss Barrantes
functions as a mentor to the young men, a part usually played by a
male figure in traditional societies. However, her blind faith in science makes her just as vulnerable to defeat as any male character
who refuses to admit that he cannot reconcile conflicting realities.
The outcome of the story is gender neutral with respect to the Eve/
Hagar principle, for the watchman's light holds the key to the mystery, but it is not accessible to Miss B or the boys. The implication
is that some things are best left alone. Thus, the Educator/General's
comical about-face indicates her decision to do that very thing.

"Two Roads" is an antiphonal interlude that connects "The
Watchman's Light" and "A Letter" in *Dawn Song*. Moreover, the
sketch represents Duncan's modulation into another key of the
Eve/Hagar melody, perhaps here into a drum song. The dialogical
nature of this vibrant portrait is not readily apparent, for only the
voice of an old woman, represented by a wrinkled black face, is directly audible. However, the reader becomes the interlocutor as he
tunes into the fifteen-year-old first-person narrator/character's interior monologue. In the story antithetical correlatives are expressed
in a series of pairings: capital city and province; education and illiteracy; middle class and poverty; Spanish and English; high road
and low road; equality and inequality; and love and hate.

Paulette Ramsay observes that "Two Roads" is an illustration of
"the idea of the ancestors intervening in the lives of the living to

---

23. Smart, *Amazing Connections*, 5–7.

influence them in the direction that their lives should take."[24] That is, the teenage boy signifies a new generation of Afro–Costa Ricans, and the old lady symbolizes the *samamfo*, a word that is not actually used in the text but is suggested by the context. Filled with dignity and wisdom, but also refined through suffering and tribulation, the disembodied voice has a story to tell: in order to succeed, the youngster must leave the province (Limón) for the capital city (San José). Even if he does not understand or want to hear it, the elder's tale must be told, for in doing so she passes the torch to a new generation—his: "I stopped here by the roadside, to tell my race . . . to tell my peoples that only by bein' better will they get the equality they want so badly. Whoever work, let him be the best. Whoever study, let him devote hisself entirely to it. And, above all, my son, love, love a lot" (91).

This resonant ancestral voice is the vital link between forebears, descendants, and future progeny and, thus, serves as the support system the youngster will need to succeed. The English translation of the vignette takes poetic license by employing a vernacular language lyricized by Duncan's deft placement of rhythmic repetition, use of oxymoron, zero copulative, lack of temporal markers for the third-person singular, and percussive attack. It is music to the culturally sensitive reader's ear, but the young character seems deaf to it because he is more focused on externals—how he looks, what he will wear, what things he lacks—than on her words. Nevertheless, a seed is planted in his consciousness despite his haste to depart from the mud hole, which is a metaphor for the penury in which they live. "Two Roads" brings to mind Langston Hughes's poem "Mother to Son," in which the people's existence in the attic is contrasted to high society's life on the crystal stair. Both Duncan and Hughes illuminate the spiritual richness contained in the dark tower of African-descended cultures, but they are also aware of the harmful potential of the blinding light (material affluence) on the stairway. In "Two Roads" the young Limonese character's determination to rise by his bootstraps in the capital city will be confronted by the metaphorical question: "Can anything good come out of Nazareth?"

24. Ramsay, "The African Religious Heritage in Selected Works of Quince Duncan: An Expression of Literary Marronage," 36.

The elderly woman is a Hagar figure and an Eve archetype—a giver of life, griot, tradition bearer, and herald of a new day (a dawn song). Again, a description of physical features is not prioritized over characterization in the story, for blackness is a symbol of wisdom, spirituality, and redemptive suffering, not the mark of oppression. From a Eurocentric point of view, the persona in "Two Roads" is a poor, ignorant old colored woman, like the character Marimorena in "Pregón de Marimorena" (Marimorena's cry), a poem by the Afro-Uruguayan Virginia Brindis de Salas. It is not certain whether the youngster in the story sees his elder in that light, but his youth blinds and deafens him to the significance of her words. In conjunction with the youth/age antithesis, Duncan employs ambiguity to deconstruct another fundamental dialectic: progress in the city versus stagnation in the provinces, or Domingo Sarmiento's classic "civilization versus barbarism" argument. That is, the narrator/character realizes the importance of migrating to the city to improve himself, but he is not yet aware that many of the values he has gained from his provincial culture will help sustain him in the new environment. That is why the old lady admonishes the young man to combine formal education with hard work and love, as well as other values instilled in him from his nurturing community. Ramsay concludes that "the author's use of the *Samamfo* fully demonstrates the abandonment of traditional Western sources or forms for the use of the African religious heritage to give expression to his message, thus providing a bold example of literary marronage."[25] Not only does the female persona's role as guide, counselor, and nurturer direct the young man's attention toward a holistic concept of life that includes both poles—civilization and barbarism, or material success and pristine values—but it also reinforces the Edenic equilibrium between mind/spirit and body/womb. In short, it is the Eve/Hagar principle regally dressed as the *samamfo*.

Among the selections in *Dawn Song*, "A Letter" is the most carefully wrought and delicately sketched in terms of characterization. In effect, the protagonist, Miss Spence, is a blowup of the anonymous old lady in "Two Roads." Toughened by years of hard labor, great physical deprivation, and overwhelming responsibilities, Miss Spence evokes Hagar in her sojourn in the wilderness.

25. Ibid., 37.

Moreover, she is placed in the mode of Eve in that she is the loving grandmother or surrogate mother of eight youngsters, seven of whom live with her. Miss Spence is an anchor in her family and community, even though she does not meet the approval of some of its members. The layered portrait of this female character unfolds in accordion-like fashion in "A Letter," radiating with the themes of agape love, redemptive suffering, survival, and triumph.

The first image of Miss Spence is that of a street vendor who hawks her wares diligently to earn her daily bread by the sweat of her brow: "Yucca, yucca, yucca, *bofe*...fish...*bofe*...fish...meat patties...patties...patties..." (111).[26] However, the staccato rhythms and shouts with which the woman punctuates the torrid atmosphere of the town belie a world-weariness. As she trudges home after a hard day's work, her public face segues into a private domain when Miss Spence recalls her daily drama of trekking to the post office only to be met with hostility from the flippant Lippo. The appropriately named male/mail clerk cannot see past Miss Spence's wrinkled black face, disheveled hair, hanging apron, and peeping-toe shoes. In effect, the society's aversion for the likes of Miss Spence is channeled through Lippo, and in one of the most lyrical passages of Latin American prose fiction, Duncan deconstructs the woman's rag-doll image:

> Cruel, almost inhuman, a voice tears into her: "No, Miss Spence, there're no letters for you today."
> The wind picks up the voice, playing with it. The wind nails the savage fist of its laughter. Too heavy for the air to sustain, the mockery is dashed against the rocks. The echo catches the story and smears it in the old lady's ears, eyes, nostrils and mouth: "No, Miss Spence, there aren't any letters for you today: there'll never be any." But with all that, she kept the faith. (111, 113)

Through the blue-note street cries and prayers she constantly utters, her courage, and her faith, Miss Spence is transformed from one of the wretched of the earth into a model of lifemanship for future generations. This magnificent transformation is especially significant when contrasted to one's first impression of her. Miss

26. See Martin-Ogunsola, *Best Short Stories*, 289. *Bofe* are the lungs of sheep or hogs.

Spence goes against the grain of the canonical ideal model of womanhood (Gisella) because she is neither pretty nor young nor white. From the hegemonic point of view, she is offensive at best, useless at worst. Nevertheless, her hidden gifts shine like diamonds within the context of home, where she works diligently and lovingly to rear her grandchildren: "They were bone of her bone, her son's flesh and blood" (119). Miss Spence proudly rejoices when her own man-child finally sends a letter with a hundred-dollar bill enclosed: "'My boy!'" That's what she would say to those who were quick to point out her son's faults: "'My boy. Y'all gon' see what he capable of'" (121). Moreover, the woman's faith in God is renewed, and her abundant spiritual wealth remains intact, a "possession" that lifts her out of the *cieno* (the cesspool referred to in "Two Roads") up to a higher plane. It is not a matter of being content with material deprivation, but a matter of not allowing the lack of things to stifle her desire to live each day joyfully. Miss Spence's neocolonial condition closely links her to the historical Hagar, for the latter's experience of oppression in ancient Egypt has been replicated through the ages in the various communities of the African diaspora. Rosalyn Terborg-Penn expands the concept of diaspora to include women on the African continent as well:

> African women were removed from their local areas and taken to places outside their kinship network, and often they went to societies foreign to them in language, customs, and environment. As a result, the majority of men enslaved during this period were dispersed throughout the Western Hemisphere, while the majority of women enslaved were dispersed throughout the African continent. Consequently, the disruption and alienation that most men experienced with enslavement throughout the diaspora, women experienced on the continent of Africa.[27]

Although protagonists of strong religious conviction like Miss Spence have been celebrated in the oral and written literature of African-descended writers, her importance as a heroic figure has not been recognized. Neither has that of other anonymous women of color, and ironically it took the publication of a book by someone like Hillary Rodham Clinton to insert into the Euro-American

---

27. Terborg-Penn, "Slavery and Women," in *Women in Africa and the African Diaspora: A Reader*, ed. Rosalyn Terborg-Penn and Andrea Benton Rushing, 218.

consciousness the meaning of the traditional African proverb "It takes a whole village to raise a child." Of course, the book appropriated and commercialized a culturally specific linguistic form, but the pithy expression reflects the values of many cultures where women daily undertake the job of caring for the members of a given community, including "motherless children." Miss Spence does her job(s) quite well in spite of her lack of resources. Lest one is inclined to perceive her as a stereotyped Madonna figure, the author deconstructs that image, too, by depicting her as a breadwinner who also plays the lottery *religiously*. Duncan's constant juggling of multiple and sometimes contradictory images is a technique that rescues his work from sentimentality and male chauvinism. Consequently, "A Letter" might not be written entirely in the womanist mode, but the voice of the black female as subject emerges in its protagonist through the Eve/Hagar principle.

As its title indicates, *Dawn Song* ends on a positive note in that the last story explores the benefits and disadvantages of the extended family, which constitutes the cornerstone of the African value systems transplanted to the Americas. Like Myra in "Dawn Song," the anonymous women in "Sophisticated Lady" and "Two Roads," and Ruby in "A Gift for Grandma," Miss Spence in "A Letter" represents the kind of spiritual and physical wholeness attainable when the positive aspects of the Eve/Hagar paradigm are operative. Miss Barrantes the Educator in "The Watchman's Light" is the only character treated who does not strike this balance. Nevertheless, all of the figures in one way or another manage to assert themselves, to be enterprising and industrious, and to exercise courage and compassion even when they are afraid or discouraged. They also assume numerous roles—wives, mothers, grandmothers, actresses, street vendors, singles, sisters, prophets, counselors, and educators—and in those capacities they are agents of change, just as Eve and Hagar were in their time. In each of the stories, the characters are broadly sketched, but they come alive through the Eve/Hagar principle. They are intimations of female characterization in subsequent fictional works by Duncan.

Before 1948 the Atlantic Coast enclave that constituted the sociohistorical and cultural context for the preceding stories was a kind of "comfort zone" for West Indians, who saw the Hispanics of Costa Rica as a poverty-stricken, culturally inferior group of people who could not run their own country. Although most families were workers on banana plantations or the railroad and as such were subject to the control of neocolonial enterprises like the United Fruit Company, they helped the latter to forge a British colony in Central America with all its concomitant pride and prejudice.[28] This ethnocentric and linguistic mutual exclusivity divided Costa Rica into almost opposing camps of the Caribbean coast and Central Valley, even though there were whites on the coast and blacks in San José. However, de facto segregation discouraged internal migration from coast to highland because the town called "Turrialba was the train station where the black West Indian crew disembarked and the white Hispanic crew members boarded, marking a symbolic 'border' between the 'black coast' and the 'white Central Valley.'" The first and second generations of West Indian immigrants, who are portrayed in *Dawn Song,* were content to have their own lodges and burial societies, English-language newspapers, denominational congregations with imported preachers, parochial "English schools" with imported teachers, and products from Jamaica, England, or other parts of "Grand Britannia" to ease the pains of life in a tropical inferno.[29]

After the promulgation of the new Constitution in 1949, the rights of citizenship, including enfranchisement, were extended to West Indian blacks and their children and grandchildren born in Costa Rica. This act, in turn, opened the doors to increased internal movement from coast to highlands, and it increased opportunities for jobs and higher education in San José. Thus, the "important event of enfranchisement marks the transition from West Indians who remained 'foreigners' even after several generations in the country to Afro–Costa Ricans. The transition was both generational and cultural, with each generation experiencing its own conflicts and transformation of identity." The first generation was Afro-Caribbean and was temporarily in Costa Rica only to "civilize" it and then return home. The second generation was rootless in spite of being born in the country. Moreover, its members had been socialized by their elders to reject the national culture in favor of a past with which they could identify only vicariously. The third and

28. Lorein Powell and Quince Duncan, *Teoría y práctica del racismo,* 55–56; Meléndez Chaverri and Duncan, *El negro en Costa Rica,* 3.
29. Mosby, *Place, Language, and Identity,* 14; Powell and Duncan, *Teoría y práctica del racismo,* 54.

subsequent generations were and are Spanish-speaking with the same rights and privileges as "white" Costa Ricans. Although their "navel-strings" are buried in the nation, which is a Creole expression for belonging to a land by virtue of one's birth, they have had to face strong resistance to their inclusion in the dominant culture.[30] Integration into the national life implied the hispanization or rejection of traditional cultural values, which often led to fragmentation, chaos, and conflict within the Afro–Costa Rican community. Their efforts to build a new home, speak a viable language, and forge a new identity in Costa Rica is a multifaceted transformative process that Duncan portrays in his second collection of short stories. Through the Eve/Hagar principle seen in the female figures from the period of transformation, the impressions of an authentic womanist voice in *The Pocomía Rebellion* are first struck in *Dawn Song*. At the same time, the author inserts a real black presence (Afro-realism) into the Costa Rican and Latin American canon that the Eurocentric discourse ironically perceives as an exotic entity. Nevertheless, the effects of Duncan's literary finesse on the national and continental consciousness would not be obvious until the end of the decade.

30. Mosby, *Place, Language, and Identity,* 17, x.

# 2

## WOMANIST FOOTPRINTS IN
### *The Pocomía Rebellion*

*The Pocomía Rebellion* (1976) contains stories based on historical events that cannot be substantiated by written records. Thus, these accounts are colored by the myths and legends of the Afro–Costa Rican oral tradition. Like the characters of *Dawn Song,* those of *The Pocomía Rebellion* struggle against oppression, and the strategies they devise are as ingenuous as they are necessary although sometimes violent. In fact, the title story sets a tone of rebellion for the entire collection of eleven stories, in six of which women characters are significant: "The Pocomía Rebellion," "Go-o-o-o-al!" "Family Ties," "Little Boy Blue," "The Legend of Joe Gordon," and "Ancestral Myths." As mentioned earlier, the Antilleans had formed a majority in a relatively isolated area of Costa Rica during the early period of migration, but they were regarded as undesirable foreign nationals who competed with citizens for jobs.[1] Except for the title story, the selections from *The Pocomía Rebellion* illustrate events that happened during the middle period (1950s to 1970s) of Antillean residency in Costa Rica when there was an emphasis on integration into national life. Furthermore, through the Eve/Hagar paradigm, the womanist footprints of the collection's female characters begin to break through the cracks and crevices of the national myth of white supremacy.

As a first step toward inclusion, West Indian blacks obtained citizenship in 1953 as a result of the post–Civil War legislation enacted by the Figueres administration.[2] In addition, Afro–Costa Ricans

---

1. Purcell, *Banana Fallout,* 43–44. See also Lisa E. Davis, "The World of the West Indian Black in Central America: The Recent Works of Quince Duncan."
2. Purcell, *Banana Fallout,* 48.

were required to send their children to the Spanish-speaking primary schools built in Limón Province for the first time. Those students who wished to further their education were encouraged to attend secondary institutions and eventually the Universidad Nacional
in San José.[3] Despite these changes, black Costa Ricans still experienced economic exploitation and social rejection because of an
influx of Spanish-speaking natives into Limón Province and other
regions of the Atlantic Coast.[4] *The Pocomía Rebellion* illustrates
some of the major conflicts that inevitably developed from the national government's efforts to find a place for English-language
Caribbean-heritage black people in a Spanish-speaking society that
defined itself as "white." In spite of the strong education and work
ethic of West Indian culture, the new citizens found that they were
essentially a people without a history from the perspective of the
hegemonic discourse. Consequently, Duncan's fiction addresses the
need to educate the general population of "Ticos" about the Afro-
Caribbean presence in their midst. We have seen how white Costa
Rican writers like Carlos Luis Fallas, Fabián Dobles, and Joaquín
Gutiérrez tended to stereotype black culture. At the same time, there
was a first generation of West Indian writers-in-exile, like Alderman
Johnson Roden and Dolores Joseph, who began to deconstruct the
national discourse. However, their works did not have any impact
on the dominant ideology since they wrote in English and did not
publish all their writing. It was left to members of the "nowherean"
group, like Eulalia Bernard and Quince Duncan, to begin reconstructing their denigrated heritage.[5] Through the lens of the Eve/
Hagar paradigm, a more pronounced black female subject begins
to emerge in Duncan's second collection of short stories.

   "The Pocomía Rebellion" is a fictionalized historical narrative
about the revolt of the Pocomía Brotherhood in the early years of
the twentieth century. The anthropologist Leonard Barrett employs
the term *Pukumina* to refer to this religion. "Pukumina is a corrup-

3. Meléndez Chaverri and Duncan, *El negro en Costa Rica*, 135–37.
4. Purcell, *Banana Fallout*, 45.
5. Mosby, *Place, Language, and Identity*, 9, 32–74. Bernard and Duncan are
part of overlapping second- and third-generation writers born in Costa Rica but
socialized in West Indian culture. She was born in 1935 of Jamaican parents, and
he was born in 1940 of Jamaican parents, but his grandparents were also from
the islands (Jamaica and Barbados). Concerning Duncan's ideological stance, see
Donald K. Gordon, "The Socio-political Thought and Literary Style of Quince
Duncan," 27–31.

tion of the name of the old ancestor cult Kumina.... And Pukumina
has, in turn, been corrupted in Jamaica to 'Pocomania'—'a little
madness.' The peculiar behaviour of the cultists, their dancing, possession and speaking in unknown languages may appear to the outsider as a slight 'case of madness.'" The Pocomía group practiced a
form of neo-African religion brought from Jamaica to Limón with
succeeding waves of Antillean immigrants. Moreover, it was syncretistic in that it combined in its ceremonies Protestant hymn
singing, selected scriptures, and other sacred songs, along with the
use of altars, special objects, and, sometimes, animal sacrifices. During their rites its adherents danced in a counterclockwise fashion to
the beat of drums, and they were "possessed" by spirits. It was
also alleged that they used drugs to induce a state of euphoria. Because there were well-known sorcerers among them, outsiders
thought that the Pocomía disciples worshiped the devil. However,
in its heyday the sect constituted a small group within the black
population of Limón Province. Presently, Pocomía has all but dis-
appeared from Puerto Limón, although there may still be pockets
of activity in the rural areas of the coastal province. Paulette Ramsay
gives a unique slant on Duncan's use of the word *Pocomía,* which
she cites as an example of the literary marronage characteristic of
his fiction. She comments that "the avoidance of the commonly
accepted term 'Pocomania' seems to be the author's method of over-
throwing the racist attitude with which the Afro-derived form has
been viewed, even before it was transplanted to Costa Rica."[6] In
accordance with the rebellious tone of the stories, the Spanish form
*Pocomía* will be used in this study.

The title story portrays Jean Paul, a Santa Lucian immigrant,
and Mama Bull, high priestess of the Pocomía sect, as "cotagonists."
Jean Paul seeks help from Mama Bull in order to take revenge on
the banana company he feels is responsible for his brother's untimely
death. (The latter perishes when a rafter from a railroad bridge
crushes his chest.) From that tragedy Jean Paul soon realizes that
management is insensitive to the needs of its workers: "At the
gravesite Jean Paul spoke to the other workers. He made them see—
as tears streamed down his peasant face—the fundamental injustice

6. Barrett, *Soul Force: African Heritage in Afro-American Religion,* 82; Meléndez Chaverri and Duncan, *El negro en Costa Rica,* 121; Ramsay, "African Religious Heritage," 33.

of his brother's death; and he called on them, he called on his friends to declare a total strike, to force the Company to concede to the workers' demands."[7] Besides heartache, Jean Paul is sorely disillusioned by the cruel reality to which his dreams have been reduced, especially when he remembers the false promises of the recruiters who came to his island country: "'Plenty money, plenty fruit, good government benefits. Nice people, but a little backwards. No resistance to colonization. Land while you're in Costa Rica and a boat to return home whenever you like'" (123, 125). In "The Pocomía Rebellion" the technique of an omniscient narrator is combined with a third-person character/narrator so that the reader can be informed of details of the story while maintaining an emotional distance. This is a technique designed to replicate the "objective style" of historical documentation.

The Pocomía ritual is reenacted in terse fashion—incessant drumming, incantations, and dancing led by Mama Bull, who dresses the altar and serves as intermediary between the believers and their ancestral god, Otto.[8] However, there are enough essential elements to suggest the importance of this mythology—this system of beliefs, attitudes, values, and practices—as a unifying force for the group. For example, the ceremonial dance and possession of the "saints" has a timeless quality:

> They circle counterclockwise; they grunt their beautiful dark song, with words that make even the bravest of Jamaicans tremble. Bare-chested men, bare-breasted women. Agile-legged men and women. Drumming with Western rolls. African meanings. Caribbean cadences. Sweaty haze on bodies that fall for hours into a cataleptic state. Fleeting lament of an owl that crosses in the air with the burden of death etched on its forehead. Disturbing symphony that surges from the depths of one's bones, tremulous voice, fear in the virginal jungle. (129, 131)

The above passage illustrates that Africa, Jamaica, and Limón are perceived as points on the same continuum along which the *samamfo,* or spirit of Africanity, moves. Through the Pocomía ceremony, the members of the sect fortify themselves spiritually in

---

7. Martin-Ogunsola, *Best Short Stories,* 125, 127. All subsequent quotations will be cited parenthetically.

8. It is not clear why Duncan uses the German name "Otto" for an African deity. Perhaps this is a tongue-in-cheek tactic.

preparation for the strike/revolt, for as Jean Paul muses: "It was now time for protest. Time for arms down at yo' sides, for work slow downs, for sabotage, like on the old plantations. Like his great-grandfather would 'a done. The workers live off Company credit and spend up they salaries at the commissary 'thout realizin' it. It was time for action" (129). Religion as a maroon narrative is the key to confronting exploitation, and the figure of Mama Bull rises to display the most aggressive elements of the Eve/Hagar principle.

Mama Bull dominates the Pocomía rites. She is called "Mama," an affectionate term for "mother" that underscores her Eve-like or matriarchal functions—the nurture, guidance, and inspiration of the young. Thus, her bare beasts are a sign of maternity, not sexuality, for they emphasize her figurative role of giving sustenance through milk. On the other hand, the priestess exudes sensuality as she encourages her disciples to engage all their senses during the ceremony. Such is evident in the evocative imagery of the passage: a circle that moves in a counterclockwise fashion (visual), grunting and drumming (aural), a sweaty haze that envelops the believers (olfactory, tactile, and gustatory), and, as usual, dark song (visual and aural). Both traditional and neo-African religious traditions had respect for male and female leadership, using "priests or priestesses as the main functionaries." Furthermore, the drum is a primary system of communication in all aspects of African cultures, but especially in religious ceremonies involving spirit possession, and it is a universal symbol of community.[9] Mama Bull functions as spiritual leader of the group and intercessor between the earthly and supernatural spheres.

On the other hand, the term *bull* suggests masculine qualities—aggression, strength, and virility/procreation—all of which the priestess exercises in her official capacity. Through utilizing such, the seed of rebellion in Mama Bull is "implanted" in her children, who get fired up to undertake their mission. One of her disciples shouts: "We gon' do what Mama Bull say, 'cause Mama Bull beautiful like Otto, the ancient god of our ancestors. He almighty God that come back to every ceremony to end all evil. He Cuminá who return and dance with the believer's body. He the word that end all yo' enemy's evil, the word that must be heard. The final word" (131). The Pocomía worshipers carry on as planned in spite of their uncertainty

9. Barrett, *Soul Force*, 30, 25.

about the loyalty of the Jamaican brothers, for as one member points out: "They black like us" (131). Nevertheless, the inevitable happens. The scheme is discovered, the sect ruthlessly hunted down, and its members executed one after another by the Civil Guard from San José "under the command of a Captain Castro or Pérez or López" (133). Oral history is imprecise about details. As expected, Mama Bull and Jean Paul, the Pocomía "generals," are the last to be captured, and they refuse to be taken alive. In fact, the priestess resists in an epic battle with the authorities. Like Hagar, Mama Bull is androgynous in that she performs both female and male tasks when the situation calls for it. In the wilderness, Hagar has to find a way to care for her dependent child in spite of her fear of failure and her dejection at exile. In her position as intermediary between the community of believers and its deity, Mama Bull must devise a plan to redress the injustices of a neocolonialist system that perceives her "children" as expendable. Even though the incidents of the story stem from Jean Paul's clash with civil authority, there would be no tale without Mama Bull since the revolt is named for the brotherhood she leads. Thus, the elder woman's significance is doubly highlighted in the tragic denouement of "The Pocomía Rebellion": "Mama Bull is tender as a mother hen with her children, but a wildcat when facing her enemies. The story goes that she was the last victim of the Pocomía rebellion, and that when she died in the violent jungle in the sun that charred her skin, she cursed all the Jamaicans in Limón" (133). In short, "the portrayal of Mama Bull through the image of the panther, an animal associated with fierceness, suggests the belligerent spirit of the god by which she is possessed and, by extension, the ability of the group to defeat the enemy."[10] Unfortunately, the Pocomía brothers lose this battle, and Mama Bull is embittered at a defeat caused by the lack of solidarity. In fact, she feels especially betrayed by the men who let her down (the Jamaicans), and this treachery is poignantly conveyed in the storyteller's double-edged commentary on Jean Paul's final destiny: "They say that he was 'offed' by a Negro" (133). Nevertheless, losing one battle does not stop the struggle.

Betrayal and docility notwithstanding, the Pocomía rebellion is important in Costa Rican history because it represents an early freedom movement for African-descended people that features two

10. Ramsay, "African Religious Heritage," 34.

culture heroes/martyrs: Jean Paul the activist and Mama Bull the guardian of religious traditions. We are informed that the Pocomía revolt was a real uprising carried out by a group of French-speaking Antillean workers, who demanded a boat to return to their country. Moreover, it represented the first violent confrontation between angry black laborers in Limón and the police from the Central Plateau region, who carried out a series of bloody reprisals in 1910.[11] Through literary marronage, or the use of the Eve/Hagar paradigm to cloak Mama Bull and Pocomía as a metaphor, Duncan depicts characters that historically resisted oppression, thus contesting a national discourse based on white supremacy. Consequently, he inscribes a text of blackness in the canon.

"Go-o-o-o-al!" is the story of an identity crisis suffered by the main character, Guabo Brown, a soccer player on the neophyte Sonora team coached by Aleluya Rodríguez, and Guabo's close buddy Melico Pérez, who serves as his double. However, the tale also features Guabo's sister Aracely, who is a key figure in this drama of othering, self-hatred, and rejection and who embodies the Eve/Hagar paradigm. Their dramas are two sides of the same coin. Like numerous racially mixed persons in Latin America, Guabo and Aracely belong to a rainbow extended family that is the result of the five hundred–year blending of African, Amerindian, Asian, and European phenotypes in the New World. Because the Browns (note the surname) are ambivalent toward the dominant discourse, they experience the double consciousness of outsiders who yearn to be accepted into a society that regards them with amused contempt and pity. Although Guabo and Melico have achieved a certain level of formal education, it has not helped them to progress as they had hoped. Consequently, Guabo broods over his dilemma as he rides the city bus to the national stadium, where he is scheduled to play in a soccer championship game that will determine his future with the up-and-coming Sonora team: "To eat or not to eat. No more, no less. That's the real question. Because a long time ago, others defined my being; underdeveloped, Afrolatin-indigene, black among whites, white Indian among blacks, white Negro among indigenous people, but in any case, underdeveloped, a bum" (165). The above rendition of Hamlet's soliloquy is doubly parodic, for it

---

11. Powell and Duncan, *Teoría y práctica del racismo*, 73.

deftly plays on the Euro-American and African-diaspora traditions that coalesce in Duncan's fiction. Through a "writerly" response to Western/European discourse, Duncan respectfully enters the ongoing dialectic with Shakespeare, scion of English literature, and the circle of writers for all time. When the ball is passed to the Costa Rican author, he ups the ante with a "speakerly" dribble. That is, Guabo's soliloquy becomes a signifyin(g) pastiche that imitates the rhetorical form of Shakespeare but fills it with an incongruous content, in this case the concrete conditions of Afro-realism. To survive or not to survive in an inferno of racism, macho posturing, and caste is the burning issue. Since existence precedes essence, one must eat before he can do anything else. On an immediate level, the allusions to race and class contextualize Guabo Brown as a tragic mulatto in Latin American literature, a character whose bitterness reflects that of historical figures like the Cuban-born poet Juan Francisco Manzano. Although Guabo has tried to play by the rules of the game, it has not helped him to gain access to wealth, status, or acceptance. He is too black to be white and too white to be black, a misfit. On a broader plane, the story highlights the dilemma of the black athlete in the Americas, whose last hope of overcoming racism and breaking out of a caste system has been tied to the compensated exploitation of his talents. Coach Aleluya (Praise God!) Rodríguez expects his star players, Guabo and Melico, to perform miracles by leading their rookie team to a victory over the undefeated Saprissas. Thus, both men are under a great deal of pressure to excel as sports figures and to "stay in their places" at the same time. Afro-realism— the concrete circumstances of their lives—makes Hamlet's philosophical ruminations pale in comparison.

As the Sonora players file onto the turf, a rival fan challenges a Saprissa player with an oblique insult to Guabo: "'Marvin,' he heard someone say, 'stomp that nigger'" (171). At that moment, the protagonist experiences a crisis of nerves and yearns for the presence of his brother Martin, for Guabo realizes the importance of family support in the face of adversity: "That would have given him greater courage. On the other hand, the one who was there was Aracely, his youngest sister, with her flat nose and thick lips. It was incredible that she was successful as a prostitute. But he knew that things were going well for her. She was black and, precisely because of that, exotic in a society of whites. Her success rested on such. Men are usually very curious when it comes to sex" (171). The

Brown family's contempt for Aracely, which is but a reflection of its own self-hatred, feeds into the central conflict of "Go-o-o-o-al!" and allows the focus to oscillate between Guabo's struggle to meet the unreasonable expectations of an ambitious manager and ambivalent public and Aracely's fight to survive in a racially and sexually exploitative environment. Guabo abhors his sister and seeks to vent his rage on her at every opportunity. For example, he recalls the time Aracely showed up uninvited at his wedding reception and their family's reaction:

> Rita, their oldest sister, became hysterical. "Who invited you here?" she asked her furiously.
> "I only came to meet my brothuh wife. They told me she blonde with blue eyes, but me, I didn't wanna believe it. Don't she know he black?"
> "He's not black," Rita answered deeply perturbed. "He's colored. One grandfather's Irish and the other's from York."
> "He black," Aracely retorted laughing, "and his wife Indian."
> "Show some respect."
> "She Indian, a Indian with dyed hair. Why don't our dear brothuh look for a pretty woman?"
> "Aracely, people can hear you..."
> "I hope they do hear me: she a Indian, a ugly one with dyed hair. She probably got false titties too." (173)

Grabbing Aracely by the hair and ungallantly escorting her to the front door, Guabo literally ejects his sister from their midst, and his buddy Melico invents the myth that she had been adopted by their mother after the other children's father had died. Like Eve and Hagar, Aracely is cast out. She, in turn, dissimulates her wounded feelings by expressing disdain for them and by vowing to cheer for the rival Saprissa team on Saturday.

At first, the young men seem impervious to remarks about their race by the sports announcer: "the ball rests on Sonora's turf; Referee Luis Cuevas adjusts the whistle in his mouth and deeply inhales; the ref's whistle blows, the games's startin', attention devoted fans, Guabo's movin' the ball, he passes to the colored boy Pérez, who centers it" (175). However, Guabo and Melico gradually become consumed by an emotional inferno when they realize how difficult it is for them to win the match in the face of such hostility. For them, winning is ultimately a question of eating or not eating. To compensate for their fear and discouragement, the soccer play-

ers practice one-upmanship toward Aracely, by ridiculing and os-
tracizing her at every opportunity. In fact, "Go-o-o-o-al!" shows
how Guabo's sister becomes the scapegoat for the individual and
communal identity crises, which is often the destiny of the unmis-
takably black female in the Americas. So many dark women go to
pitifully extreme lengths to whiten, lighten, or otherwise make themselves "beautiful" according to the Eurocentric somatic norm.[12]

The Eve/Hagar principle reveals a woman off balance in "Go-o-
o-o-al!" Aracely acts out her own self-abasement by resorting to
the kind of lifestyle that makes outcasts of females in all societies—
prostitution. In fact, that particular trade is associated with very
dark females in many neocolonial regions of the world, where the
invention of race and its stigmatization based on color have historically made it difficult for women with deep melanin pigmentation
to find gainful employment outside the home if they are not wealthy
or educated or both. Unlike the works of writers like Allende,
Borges, Cortázar, and García Márquez, who, more often than not,
portray black female characters in stereotypical roles, Duncan's
stories situate characters like Aracely, who struggles to define herself
within the specific sociohistorical context of racism, sexism, and
caste in postcolonial Costa Rica. Therefore, the poignancy of her
contradictory response is highlighted at the end of the story as she
celebrates Sonora's (her brother's) victory with tearful joy and relief:
"Outside a black woman who was crying waited to embrace and
kiss the hero. 'Thank you,' Aracely Brown murmured, 'thank you,
Virgin. Thank you...Thank you'" (177).

"Go-o-o-o-al!" gives a different twist to the theme of the tragic
mulatto by depicting the complex psychoemotional dynamics of
the Brown family not only in terms of color/race, but also in terms
of gender/sex and class/caste. Guabo negatively defines himself by
what he does not want to be (black) or by what he is not (white).
Moreover, he tries to come as close as possible to achieving the phe-
notypic ideal by marrying a woman with obviously indigenous features, who also tries to "pass." The game of negotiating difference/
otherness is dramatically brought to the fore at Guabo's wedding reception, which a literal translation of the story's title ("The Game")
would convey. However, soccer is a sport that relies on mental strat-
egy rather than brute force. Concerning that point, Aracely has the

12. Richard L. Jackson, *The Black Image in Latin American Literature*, 7–9.

upper hand, but the Eve aspect of the paradigm reveals itself in the most negative sense through the femme fatale model of misogynist tradition. Like Hagar, Aracely embraces her shadowy position, but she castigates herself by choosing the self-destructive lifestyle of a street woman. Instead of breaking with her family for good, she visits them from time to time because she needs their malice to reinforce her low self-esteem, which is the only form of love she feels she merits. For their part, the superstars Guabo and Melico achieve a Pyrrhic victory because they receive the material rewards (money and fame) for winning the soccer match, but that does little to compensate for their anguish at being ostracized. On the other hand, the calibanesque Aracely experiences a degree of triumph in that she offers an unreciprocated love to those who abuse and spurn her. There is a traditional African American spiritual that underscores Aracely's blues: "I've been 'buked and I've been scorned." Consequently, the womb/tongue metaphor is manifest in Aracely Brown, who gets caught in the body trap while proclaiming with her tongue a truth her family denies. Only in this sense does she score the one true goal in the game of life, which makes her the real hero of the story.

Through the contrapuntal drama between Guabo and Aracely, and through the repetition and inversion of the Eve/Hagar paradigm, "Go-o-o-o-al!" dramatizes what have been identified as two master symbols of ideology in Latin America:

> Race is a powerful ideological concept in modern Latin America and the Caribbean. In Spanish-, Portuguese- and French-speaking republics today we find two nationalist ideologies of racial culture: *mestizaje* (racial mixture) and *négritude* (blackness). *Mestizaje,* the ideology of racial intermingling, is an explicit master symbol of the nation in all Latin American countries. *Négritude* is a concept that denotes the positive features of blackness among "black" people. In the Americas only Haiti has adopted an explicit nationalist ideology of *négritude*.[13]

Moreover, scholars point out a third ideological sign in their discussions of race and class:

> Competing with *négritude* in black communities is another master symbol of ideology: *blanqueamiento*—somatic, cultural,

---

13. *Report on the Americas: The Black Americas, 1492–1992,* 18.

or ethnic lightening to become increasingly acceptable to those classified and self-identified as "white." Although not often recognized as such, the ideology of "whitening" is an unconscious psychological process that accompanies the economic state of underdevelopment in the twentieth century. Essentially, *blanqueamiento* accepts the implicit hegemonic rhetoric of the United States with regard to "white supremacy," and often blames those classed as black and indigenous for the worsening state of the nation.[14]

Whitening is also perceived as a form of ethnic lynching because it is primarily based on the rejection of Africanity.[15] Thus, Guabo's soliloquy at the beginning of "Go-o-o-o-al!" shows just how aware he is of the society's perception of him as "underdeveloped." This underscores the fact that Latin American nations seek to whiten, lighten, or erase those features of the African heritage that do not enhance their image abroad, otherwise known as "making progress." Often, Africanness is camouflaged as "Spanish," "Indian," or something else, except for stereotyped cultural expressions from religion, folklore, music, and sports. Therefore, the discourse sustained by the media and educational curricula, and supported by the economic, religious, political, and social institutions inherited from Spain—in short, every possible means of perpetuating the myth of white superiority and black inferiority—refuses to acknowledge the positive value of the African contribution to Latin American culture. This constitutes a psychoemotional identity crisis of continental proportions, which is articulated by Duncan in the following passage:

> That dream, that old dream of being the pure descendant of a *criollo,* of being the son of Europeans born in America, is the Eurocentric complex, the inability to accept oneself as he is and to come to grips with his mixed heritage. Moreover, it is a situation of alienation in which there has been an overestimation of the European contribution almost to the exclusion of other significant ones, which results in a very biased presentation of Latin American societies in favor of European history.[16]

14. Ibid.
15. Jackson, *Black Image,* 1–4.
16. Duncan, "Black Images and the Eurocentric Complex in Latin America," tape 1, "The Birmingham Talks."

In short, "Go-o-o-o-al!" illustrates how the dragnet of "Euracism" plagues Latin America, keeping African-descended people and others of color in situations of incredible poverty and emotional turmoil.[17] Furthermore, the Eve/Hagar paradigm calls attention to this pathological phenomenon in the lives of women and children who are, more often than not, its most unfortunate targets.

"Family Ties" is the lyrical account of the loss of innocence by four orphaned adolescents whose destinies have been intertwined with that of a surrogate mother since infancy. As the omniscient narrator informs us, "They had the ties that bind from the cradle" (181). Pablo and Paco are brought to Mama Drusilda when they are babies, and she nurses them after her own dies; Andrea enters the household at age four, and Lucho soon follows. At first, the children function as one—eating, sleeping, bathing, and playing together wherever their hearts desire. As they grow up, Andrea is scorned and ridiculed by the neighbors, who call her Macho-macha (She-Man), because she is the only girl in the band. However, her relationship with the boys is purely fraternal. Mama Drusilda, a humble, kindhearted woman, is the epitome of the Eve/Hagar prototype because she is the nurturer and provider, although she inhabits the lowest rung on the social ladder and expects little from life. Conversely, Mama Drusilda gives much to the "haves" and the "have-nots" in her attempt to find a reason for being.

The story begins in media res at the point when the four kids have to make a crucial decision—whether to go their separate ways:

> "I don't feel like goin' on this way. I'm splittin'..."
> "You was born marked, Paco, like a leper. Remember."
> "I ain't no cow..."
> "Paco," like the sweet fragrance of a flower, her voice draws wave upon wave of magic.
> "I ain't marked," he said in a lower tone. "I ain't no animal. Tha's all." (181)

Through the technique of blurred voicing, Duncan shows the oneness of mind and singleness of purpose that have characterized the youngsters' relationship from the beginning:

17. Teun A. Van Dijk, *Elite Discourse and Racism*, 5. Apparently, Van Dijk coined this term.

> "We have to decide now."
> "That's what I say. I'm bored."
> "But I don' understand you guys."
> "What don't ya understand?"
> "Just for somethin' like this . . . like this . . ." (189)

By contrasting blended first- and third-person character/narrators with an omniscient narrator, the author enables the reader to experience the children's forlornness. "But one day the gentle magic of their first state had to be broken. Leticia came to Balmoral Street to look for Ma' Drusilda. You know, it hurts to lose what was ours. It always hurts" (183). There is a personal touch associated with this sense of loss. The danger that the teenagers discern from the arrival of this strange creature out of nowhere leaves them sweaty, speechless, and inert. Furthermore, Lucho, Andrea, Pablo, and Paco soon learn that *they* are the "Nowhereans" from the perspective of the dominant culture.

Leticia, the blonde, blue-eyed rich girl from Felipe Segundo Street, does indeed invade the orphans' world to repossess *her* Mama Drusilda as a live-in domestic for her family's household. This incident provides the catalyst for the children's crisis of identity:

> Shame entered their street through blazing lights that warily split open the silence, slowly rocking and rolling upon stone after stone, like a shining white serene monster so alien to the place's abject poverty. The children felt humiliated in their own neighborhood. They definitely tried to hide their chagrin. This was *their* street, filled with left-overs, bad odors, anxieties, and an iguana pasture in the background. . . .
> Lucho experienced his first sense of uprootedness; soon his street was not the everyday street he used to know. (183)

Prior to Leticia's arrival in their neighborhood, the foursome is only vaguely aware of a different way of life, but such knowledge does not affect them because they are content. However, when Ma' Drusilda decides to work for Leticia's family again, Pablo, Paco, Andrea, and Lucho are dumbfounded since her decision is tantamount to desertion. Even more disconcerting is the change in attitude and behavior the kids see in their surrogate mother, who becomes submissive, apprehensive, and conciliatory in Leticia's presence. In response to the girl's inquiry about their "mom," Lucho resists, but

Ma' Drusilda rebukes him from inside their shanty, shouting out the girl's name with awe and respect:

> "Leticia!" Ma' Drusilda's voice prevented him from answering with some insolent remark like, Who you think you is, Santa Claus or somethin', expectin' peoples to know you. "Leticia, what you doin' heah, honey?"
> Ma' Drusilda's voice contained an element of fear that Lucho could not quite understand. (185)

After their mama departs, the four adventurers go in search of her, and this quest begins to unravel their relationship because they are not prepared to deal with the discrepancy between their lives and the opulent world on the other side of the tracks.

In the opening scene of "Family Ties," Pablo, Paco, Andrea, and Lucho attempt to recover from the severe culture shock of visiting Leticia's affluent household and basking in the condescending limelight of her family, who buys them new clothes, shoes, and other things. From this experience, it soon becomes apparent that they cannot return intact to their original state. Besides, Mama Drusilda, their center of gravity, is no longer there. Their "eviction" from Eden repeats the Eve and Hagar patterns, even though it appears to be self-induced. Nevertheless, when one considers that poverty is often the driving impetus behind the forced relocation of numerous people, there is no real choice. Although the old woman makes occasional visits to their hovel, she is basically at the beck and call of Leticia's family to earn her living. Thus, the confusion and uncertainty of her life negatively impact the children. In essence, Mama Drusilda's dilemma reflects the precarious situation of numerous poor, marginalized females of color in North, Central, and South Americas.[18] From the nameless Cuban *lavandera* (washerwoman) in Nancy Morejón's poem "Richard Brought His Flute" to the street vendor in Virginia Brindis de Salas's lyric "Marimorena's Cry," from Duncan's Miss Spence ("A Letter") and Cubena's mythic Felicidad Dolores (in his novel of the same name) to the Brazilian writer Carolina María de Jesús, poor, working-class black females as well as their literary counterparts are in a constant state of emergency, invisible to the higher echelons of their respective societies because

---

18. Duncan, *Cultura negra y teología*, 30–34.

people *choose* not to see them. They are truly the many faces of Eve and Aunt Hagar's daughters in the New World.

Now poor, oppressed women are not necessarily black, that is, persons who identify themselves as African-descended. However, they are almost invariably women of color, and the degree of their suffering is, more often than not, measured by the amount of melanin in their skin. There is no indication of the racial/ethnic origin of the characters in "Family Ties," but race would undoubtedly intensify their marginality. In a metaphorical sense, black is the color of their suffering, and this reality is embodied in the Eve/Hagar figure of Mama Drusilda. At the end of "Family Ties" Paco and Lucho prepare to "hit the streets," Andrea is embittered, and Pablo withdraws. *Miss* Drusilda, as the narrative voice refers to her with respect, is left to grieve over their breakup as a painful reminder of their rite of passage through her household: "Miss Drusilda wrings her hands. With her very last glimpse of them drowned in tears, she muses while the skylight sinks into the horizon and Lucho's wet eyes begin to dry" (191). In short, the struggle of this tired, dispirited woman to maintain a home for the four orphans has ultimately failed.

Despite her unequal battle with overwhelming sociohistorical, political, and economic forces, Mama Drusilda is heroic (like Miss Spence) because she is motivated by her love and desire to create a family and home for the children during their tender years. That is why a symbolic translation of the story ("Family Ties") carries more weight than a literal one ("The Meshing"). Furthermore, its open ending suggests that at least Lucho has the possibility of escaping the mark of oppression to which Pablo earlier refers: "You was born marked, Paco" (189). In the first place, Lucho is the most determined of the gang of teenagers (his name means "I fight" in Spanish). Second, he has managed to pick up a modicum of literacy: "They never learned to write anything more than their names. But Lucho could read well" (181, 183). Third, he has backbone and self-confidence: "Lucho's wet eyes begin to dry" (191). Like Hagar does for her son, Ishmael, Mama Drusilda has planted a seed in Lucho that others will water but that he will develop according to the possibilities life offers and the choices he makes.

Making the right decision constitutes the basis for the central conflict in "Little Boy Blue," the portrait of a twenty-four-year-old anonymous protagonist who tries to avoid responsibility for his (mis)behavior. The drama unfolds when the student informs his parents, Santos and "Mama," that he has impregnated a young woman named Lupe and wants to legitimize their relationship through marriage. The primary "action" of this vignette involves the clash of wills *(las voluntades)* between the parents, who want their son to complete his formal education, and the youth, who feels obligated to give the baby his family's name: "There are some decisions made without much complication. Not only is there another life to be considered, but also a sense of honor. And that is very important. Marry her. That's all" (207). The second level of conflict relates to the student's inner struggle to choose between his responsibility for a family and his enjoyment of a dependent status at home. Thus, a literal translation of the title (Good intentions) does not convey the protagonist's immaturity as well as the nursery rhyme.

The humor of "Little Boy Blue" emerges when the reader perceives the discrepancy between the character's noble intentions, evident in the pontification of his opening remarks, and his cowardly conduct, overheard in the following interior monologue:

> They've finally stopped the bleeding. Santos is at my side now. My mama's fondling my hair. They've begged me to forgive them. They've talked about allowance money for the baby. I remember Santos's voice in the clear dark of my childhood dreams. I remember my mama's breasts in my little mouth. And once I come to my senses here in my parents' house, I realize that I'm not gonna get married to Lupe next Thursday evening at 7:30 like I had planned to, because my daddy's calling her up on the telephone to tell her "no." (211)

Although Lupe and her unborn child are unseen parties in this drama, they are nevertheless important as splinters of the Eve/Hagar model, which privileges marriage or concubinage, childbirth, mothering, and nurturing. Like many gullible females who succumb to the multitude of "Baby, I love yous," Lupe has to deal with choices for two lives instead of one. Moreover, the likelihood is that she does not have as much formal schooling as her boyfriend, whom she probably considers a "good catch." Therefore, she will have a difficult time coping with all the challenges of single parenthood, unless she has strong support from both families. The fact that Lupe "appears" in the story only through the words of the male protagonist underscores her invisibility, which is a function of her race, gender, and class. Similar to Eve, she has succumbed to curiosity, pride, and rebellion. Like Hagar, she becomes the victim of her own dependence, submission, and passion. As an ironic twist to the vignette, the name Lupe, a shortened form of Guadalupe, evokes the Virgin Mary figure, or the patron saint of Mexico. However, it also parodies the young woman's condition, for she may be a Madonna, but her unborn child is certainly not the result of the Holy Spirit. Without the legal protection of marriage, Lupe and her baby will be at the beck and call of a merciless society.

The protagonist of "The Legend of Joe Gordon" finds himself on the wrong side of the law precisely as a black male laborer. The tenth narrative in *The Pocomía Rebellion,* the story is a literary rendition of Afro-realism—the historical reality of migration and resettlement of Antilleans from the West Indies to the Atlantic Coast of Central America. It is clear that Joe Gordon is the culture hero of the community of banana plantation workers and their families in Limón Province, for he openly challenges the company/management on behalf of the people. Less evident, however, is the Eve/Hagar paradigm in the person of Gordon's anonymous wife.

Like the Eve archetype and the character Lupe in "Little Boy Blue," Gordon's wife is there for his benefit. This is obvious from the beginning to the end of the story in the woman's terse remarks to her husband. In one scene she is his sounding board: " 'The important thing,' he said, 'is not what's happenin' to me. That's not it. The important thing here is I've discovered that . . . there's laws. There's rules.' 'What kinda rules?' " (219). In another, this ghostlike character serves as cook and pacifier to a depressed husband: " 'I don' wanna eat.' The steam freely escaped from his favorite gruel. 'It's gruel,' she insisted, 'plantain gruel' " (219). When Gordon decides to seek revenge for being fired unjustly from his job, his spouse subtly counsels him against acting too rashly: "But suddenly the money was not important——he needed a horse, bullets, and his old shotgun. 'That's a pretty horse,' his wife said when she saw him trot into the patio. 'Is it John's?' 'It's mine.' 'Yours? And . . . what you want it for?' " (221). After this, Gordon's wife is silenced and maintains a low profile, just like the post-Edenic Eve and the exiled Hagar: "His wife did not ask any questions when she saw him leave, but simply resigned herself to waiting" (223). The woman's docility leaves her open to victimization by the authorities, who harass and intimidate her, as well as some members of the black community, who, in turn, accuse Joe's wife of conspiring with the officials to capture the black Robin Hood.

In essence, Gordon's wife is cast in the feminine mode, or the conventional way of representing women in male texts, "using the language, images, rhetoric, and literary conventions that mirror patriarchal visions of female experience." That is, the feminine mode "reinforces, through appeal to sentiment rather than to intellect, conventional images of women as nurturers who inhabit domestic spaces; which underscores the sexual and reproductive roles of females; and which dichotomizes women, idealizing them as virgins and goddesses or denigrating them as whores and witches."[19] From the perspective of the black community, who adores Joe Gordon and considers him a Christ figure, his spouse is guilty. In her despair over the misreading of her actions, she commits suicide: "Joe Gordon's wife threw herself into the sea with stones tied to her feet, and that year the Banana Company's sales increased tremendously" (247). This is the voice of the omniscient storyteller, who provides "the factual version." On the other hand, a second and more subtle omniscient voice embedded in the narrative implies that Gordon's wife is the victim of her own despair (the hidden drama behind the facts), and that the real culprit is an unnamed mulatto who wants to return home to Jamaica:

> Finally, one day a man reported to the superintendent's office. He was a light-skinned Negro who wanted to go back to his country. People later found out that flowers blossom on the third day. So, the night Gordon was caught at home, nobody was surprised, and they even say that it was in part due to his wife's silent complicity because she was tired of his shenanigans. But people also say that the little yellow man was the real culprit, that he had promised only to injure Joe, collect, and leave, while the hero suffered the metamorphosis of his resurrection. (245)

This double-voiced discourse splits into parodic narration and internal polemic, thus presenting variant versions of the tale that contest one another.[20] Through the use of ambiguity, it is clear that Gor-

19. DeCosta-Willis, "Afra-Hispanic Writers," 251.
20. Mikhail Bahktin, "Discourse Typology in Prose," 187, quoted in Gates, "Blackness of Blackness," 295.

don's wife is neither virgin nor goddess, neither whore nor witch, but a quiet, pensive woman who is also an ordinary human being under extreme duress. For this reason, she is an Eve/Hagar figure who cannot be pigeonholed in the feminine mode, although she is not the womanist type, either.

"The Legend of Joe Gordon" fictionalizes historical events that are part of the narrative tradition of black Costa Rica. Other than "The Outlaw," a poem about Joe Gordon by Alderman Johnson Roden, the legend exists in many oral versions.[21] Moreover, Duncan's story is one of the few written accounts by a black writer about the dominance of the United Fruit Company in Central American countries, which were labeled with the pejorative epithet "banana republics." Although Gordon's role as a legendary figure is highlighted in the story, his wife's importance is not to be minimized, for there were many such women who provided support for the famous as well as the infamous. In fact, heroes stand on the shoulders of everyday people, many of whom are females of color, and this is a truth that the stories of *The Pocomía Rebellion* consistently call to our attention in the characters' incarnation of the Eve/Hagar principle.

Women don multiple masks of the Eve/Hagar paradigm in "Ancestral Myths," the last selection in *The Pocomía Rebellion*. In this tale Duncan broadens his focus to include the impact of colonialism on the traditional cultures of the African continent, and he dresses this reality in the allegorical contours of a clash between the ancients and moderns—between gold and silver. The most prominent female at the beginning of the story is the Princess, young bride of the Heir-Prince to the throne of Kumasi. Despite her youth, the Princess is a strong figure, who resists the attempts of the usurper Omowa to take over the throne after the latter kills her husband. The voice of a griot celebrates the Eve/Hagar qualities of strength, courage, and assertiveness in the women of Kumasi: "The women of Kumasi are real women, like November rain is real rain" (261). Once the Princess becomes Queen, she continues to rule according to precolonial traditions. When the invaders abscond with the Golden Stool, the Ark of the Covenant of the Ashanti people, she makes a valiant attempt to recover it, and a bitter war ensues.[22]

21. Mosby, *Place, Language, and Identity,* 50–52.
22. Diop, *Cultural Unity,* xiv–xv.

However, the Europeans eventually force the Queen to become a puppet: "The ambassador-subjects of his most sovereign and exalted Majesty, protector of Kumasi, imposed only one condition on us: that our queen substitute all gold decorations in the royal palace for silver ones, and that they cover the gold rug with fine silver linen" (261, 263). In the face of raw power, the Eve/Hagar traits of humility, powerlessness, and acquiescence begin to replace the Queen's former daring, strength, and pride.

During the colonial period, tradition, symbolized by gold, is replaced by modernization, represented by silver. At this point Lucy (light?), daughter of the Governor (Germanson I), begins to wield a strong influence in the cultural affairs of the nation, and through her Eve-like characteristics of curiosity, ingenuity, and persuasiveness, she insists that silver replace gold as the official sign of "civilization" in Kumasi. The success of this radical change is due to the false reflections of light from the invading cultures, as well as their co-optation of the native elite, who are sent to various European metropolises to learn Culture. One cannot underestimate the role of the spouse in fortifying the position of the "colored intellectual" vis-à-vis the clash between gold and silver:

> The Doctor's wife had been trained in Paris, so she spoke perfect French. On his part, the Doctor had an ample knowledge of Latin, apart from English, which he mastered to perfection. In addition, between the two of them they spoke a few primitive dialects. Those were sufficient reasons for the Governor to send them to represent their country on the Council of Protectorates with its seat of power in the Metropolis. There the Doctor was set up as the official spokesman of his people, and whatever he said was the Kumasi people's word. (273, 275)

Just as in "The Legend of Joe Gordon," women are secondary characters in "Ancestral Myths," but they are essential to its development and denouement. For one thing, the voice of the anonymous narrator, who plays the role of different characters depending on the era, is tinged with irony as it articulates the dialectic of civilization versus barbarism. When the narrator is the Doctor, he and his wife learn French, the language of "high culture"; English, the language of modern empire; and Latin, the tongue no one speaks anymore, but they also know a "few primitive dialects." For another, his spouse's actions are conflictive because she tries to dissuade her husband from reclaiming his true heritage, that is, from painting small circles of gold as a clandestine activity: "His wife was against art, considering it a dangerous pastime" (275). When the Doctor deserts the silver world to join the struggle for Kumasi's independence, his wife returns to the homeland only after the smoke has cleared, and then becomes a fanatical supporter of the new regime under the Partido de la Liberación Aurea (PALA). Unfortunately, her Hagar-like boldness, enterprise, and hard work drive her to extremes, and she betrays her husband: "My wife denounced me to the Art Commission. Now converted into a fanatic of the new regime, she succeeded in having me condemned for turning away from the Samamfo's Spirit. And after losing my position on the Central Committee of PALA, I went to serve my sentence: to paint 700 suns of pure gold under my wife's vigilant eye" (281).

In the wake of the postcolonial order, the Doctor and his wife must acknowledge that they are the product of two worlds—the gold and the silver—and that both must be painted: "My agony was not sufficient, neither the multiple interpretations given to my picture. It was not enough to demonstrate that we were no longer children of one Samamfo, but a hybrid of two" (281). In short, "Ancestral Myths" is similar to "The Legend of Joe Gordon" in that it depicts Eve/Hagar figures in supportive positions that are essential to the outcome of the story. However, "Ancestral Myths" differs in that the Queen, Lucy, and the Doctor's wife are not invisible like Joe Gordon's wife, even though they do not carry names as a sign of their personhood. It is significant that the only woman with a name (and an identity) is the European Lucy. The African females in "Ancestral Myths" represent historical types in the pre- and postcolonial epochs. According to Filomina Chioma Steady, these women played specific economic, political, and social roles that allowed them a measure of independence and autonomy. Therefore, they could develop self-reliance and networking through their means of production (farming, trading, cooperation, and distribution) and reproduction (marriage, childbirth, and shared mothering).[23] The telling of myth involves an allusion to archetypes/prototypes, which allows the Eve/Hagar paradigm to reinvent itself over time and space. Consequently, because the specific names and identities of these ancestral warriors were lost during the Middle Passage, it is

23. Steady, "African Feminism," 6–7.

fitting that the black female characters in the story remain anonymous. Nevertheless, they are no less heroic.

In "Ancestral Myths" the Eve/Hagar paradigm is manifest in the lives of the Queen and the Doctor's wife, who represent the times when male and female functions were complementary and interdependent in the movement from autonomous precolonial states to colonized enclaves and, subsequently, to postindependence nations. The young Queen is an Amazon-like character who resists both European and African male chauvinism when Omowa the usurper tries to take her body and throne. As she ages, however, she is overwhelmed by the power of the European monarchy/patriarchy, and her strength falters. Conversely, the Doctor's wife in a later era has authority and influence probably because of her experience abroad, but she cannot apply them wisely because she has bought into an alien (silver) value system. Duncan utilizes image reversal in the gold/silver dichotomy by equating gold with precolonial Africa and silver with modern Europe. Yet Africa is neither lionized nor Europe debunked in "Ancestral Myths"; instead, they are presented as changing realities that must be dealt with by each generation of intellectuals. This is the meaning of discovering one's roots and routes in Afro-realism. Consequently, questions of self-definition and identity that emerge from the lives of specific individuals, communities, and nations are related to the global restructuring of continents during the modern era.

The stories of *The Pocomía Rebellion* are excellent examples of literary marronage because they appropriate archetypes, icons, myths, and symbols from the African-derived oral traditions of Costa Rica.[24] Moreover, the author creates a new language by blending standard and vernacular variants of Spanish, Caribbean-inflected English, and words of African origin. The most outstanding example of a neologism is the word *samamfo,* a term that Duncan discovered while perusing a book on African culture. He states that "I couldn't find any way of expressing this in either Spanish or English until I ran across that term *samamfo,* which said exactly what I wanted to say."[25] It is the perfect word to convey those as-

24. David T. Haberly, "The Literature of an Invisible Nation," 134–37.
25. Duncan quoted in Ian Isidore Smart, "The Literary World of Quince Duncan," 290.

pects of the African heritage that the machinery of Western civilization did not destroy, and it is the consummate expression for the reconstructed word on which Afro-realism is based.

The various manifestations of the Eve/Hagar principle in the female characters of *The Pocomía Rebellion* elicit ambiguous reader responses. For one thing, it is relatively easy to place women like Mama Bull (priestess), Aracely (prostitute), the Queen (royalty), and the Doctor's wife (intellectual) into the Eve/Hagar paradigm because of their strong inclination toward womanist postures. These figures are aggressive, daring, curious, independent, and, above all, rebellious. On the other side are characters like Mama Drusilda (live-in domestic), Lupe (unwed mother), and Joe Gordon's spouse (housewife), who are passive, submissive, fearful, and vulnerable, but who also fit into the mold. The contradiction resolves itself in paradox, for the Eve/Hagar paradigm embraces the temporal and spatial circumstances of the bearers. Sometimes they are balanced, sometime not. By impressing the footprints of black female subjects within the national discourse, *The Pocomía Rebellion,* through the Eve/Hagar paradigm and other significant tropes from the black cultural matrix, is an outstanding example of contestatory and revisionist literature, achieving stylistically in his short fiction what *The Four Mirrors* would do in the new Latin American novel.[26]

26. According to Mosby, Duncan, like most African Hispanophone writers, was omitted from Raymond L. Williams's two literary studies, *The Postmodern Novel in Latin America* (1995) and *The Modern Latin American Novel* (1998). I agree with her that this omission is unfortunate, since Duncan, "informed of world literary movements, connects a technically inventive writing style with a serious treatment of ethnic and national identity. His innovative narrative experiments alter the logical order of time and space, frequently incorporating leaps between present and past, flashbacks, flash-forwards, and dreams" (*Place, Language, and Identity,* 122). However, the postmodernist worldview is incompatible with Afro-realism, a theory and praxis that dig into the roots of the black cultural matrix and extract intrinsic models that build on African-diaspora experiences. Postmodernism eschews meaning and completeness. Duncan's literature wrests healing out of apparent meaninglessness and restores a sense of wholeness to fragmentation. Consequently, black writers might appropriate the techniques of postmodern literature, since all artists borrow from diverse sources. Nevertheless, the vision projected by all of the "post" theories is ultimately antithetical to the explication and elucidation of African-diaspora literatures.

# 3

# A Tale of Two Wives in
## *The Four Mirrors*

Of the novels penned by Quince Duncan during the 1970s, the theme of *The Four Mirrors* (1973) is the most familiar to a North American audience because it reminds one very much of Ralph Ellison's *Invisible Man* (1952). This is not to say that Duncan's work is derivative, but that the issues of invisibility and identity are present wherever African-descended writers are found in the diaspora.[1] As in other areas of the New World, race, gender, and class in Latin America are invariably linked to questions of identity, power, and authority. Thus, the social hierarchies of the Spanish-speaking countries have historically determined the development of an elitist, exclusivist discourse and canon. *The Four Mirrors* presents the dilemma of Charles McForbes, whose severe psychoemotional crisis causes him to go blind temporarily until he begins to come to terms with himself, that is, with his position as a black man in a "white world." It has been established elsewhere that "Duncan's character incorporates the double consciousness and sense of duality classically articulated by Du Bois in *The Souls of Black Folk* (1903), for McForbes' quest for an identity with which he can be comfortable illustrates the ongoing battle of the 'two warring forces in the one dark body.'" This individual crisis might also be seen as "a metaphor for the formation of a new cultural and national identity" that reconciles

1. Smart, "Literary World," 281–84. In this interview Duncan talks about some of the writers who have had the strongest impact on him. They include James Baldwin and William Faulkner from the United States, and Gabriel García Márquez and Mario Vargas Llosa from Colombia and Peru, respectively. In addition, Duncan's fiction has emerged within the context of a host of twentieth-century writers in Costa Rica: Fabián Dobles, Carlos Luis Fallas, Joaquín Gutiérrez, Abel Pacheco, Alfonso Chase, Laureano Albán, Yolanda Oreamuno, Carmen Naranjo, Eulalia Bernard, Shirley Campbell, and Delia McDonald, to name a few.

the hegemonic Spanish culture of the Central Valley with the marginalized West Indian culture of Limón.[2] However, the unfolding of the Eve/Hagar paradigm in relation to McForbes and his two wives—Lorena Sam and Esther Centeno—reveals that the protagonist's identity is still ambiguous at the end of the novel and that a hybridized cultural and national identity is yet to be shaped.

Edwin Salas Zamora's discussion of *The Four Mirrors* enables one to understand a stylistically challenging novel that falls within the genre of the new narrative in Spanish American literature.[3] Charles McForbes, a mulatto descendant of Jamaican emigrants to Costa Rica, is a small landowner and part-time minister in the town of Estrada, Limón Province. When he is about nineteen years old, Charles marries the brown-skinned Lorena Sam, daughter of Mr. Sam the obeah man, or one who practices a traditional neo-African religion. In southern black culture of the United States, a figure like Mr. Sam is called a "two-headed man" and his beliefs "hoodoo" or "voodoo." Charles and Lorena have been married five years when she is struck down by a malignant spirit known as a *dopí* (duppy).[4] With the help of family and close friends, McForbes tries to revive his wife with a medicinal counterpotion, which is suggested to him in a vision and to Lorena in a dream by their dead fathers. When that does not work, Charles allows Clarita de Duke, a local nurse, to give Lorena an injection, but the health care worker insists that he take his wife to a hospital in San José. Charles commutes from the province to the capital, trying to keep up their home and work their land while caring for his ailing spouse. However, the doctors, including Charles's future father-in-law, Lucas Centeno, cannot find a cause or a cure for Lorena's illness, and she dies. The grieving widower goes on a womanizing binge for several

2. Martin-Ogunsola, "Invisibility, Double Consciousness, and the Crisis of Identity in *Los cuatro espejos*," 9; Mosby, *Place, Language, and Identity*, 136.

3. Salas Zamora, "La identidad cultural del negro en las novelas de Quince Duncan: Aspectos temáticos y técnicos," 380–81.

4. The word *duppy* does not appear in an American English dictionary, but it is widely used in Jamaican Creole to mean "an evil spirit." Mosby documents this in *Place, Language, and Identity* (140). In addition, Núñez elaborates on this meaning in *Dictionary of Civilization:* "*Duppy* (Afr.), in the West Indies, a ghost or spirit attached to every person, child or adult, throughout his life. Even after death, a duppy is capable of returning to aid or harm living beings, directly or indirectly. Among black slaves, and even today among blacks, the duppies are feared but not worshipped. At some black wakes, there is a ceremony designed to catch duppies and lay them to rest" (168–69).

years, but finally leaves Estrada for the capital. There he earns a doctorate in English literature, renews his friendship with Centeno, marries the latter's daughter Esther, and settles down in great contentment. Or so it seems.

In the opening scene of *The Four Mirrors*, Charles and Esther McForbes are asleep in bed after having attended a lecture, "Racial Minorities in Costa Rica," at the National Theater that evening. The Eve principle emerges in two similes—woman as man's anchor and woman as the net/rope with which man gathers/ties up the loose ends of his life—as Charles makes love to the dormant Esther. Later, the protagonist wakes up in anguish in the wee hours of the morning, convinced that he is going blind because he cannot see himself in the bathroom mirror: "Then I looked into the mirror. A man with disheveled hair, dressed in blue pajamas, appeared in front of my eyes. The image lacked something" (Entonces miré el espejo. Un hombre de pelo desordenado, vestido de pijama azul, apareció frente a mis ojos. Algo le faltaba a la imagen).[5] McForbes's strong sense of alienation is indicated by the sight of a nonspecific being (a man) who looms before his eyes as if summoned by some external force. After several comic attempts to see himself by rubbing his face violently (as if he is trying to erase his color), he concludes that he really is blind: "An inexplicable blackness buried my face in the night" (Una inexplicable negrura sepultaba mi rostro en la noche, 10). This drives him to seek professional advice from an oculist and friend, Agustín Pineres. The latter, in turn, refers Charles to a psychoanalyst named Díaz, but this only complicates matters. Thus begins the protagonist's odyssey in search of himself, an act that takes him on a three-day trek through the streets of San José with a one-day trip to Estrada. Charles tries to rekindle the sparks with some of his former paramours, but he flees back to Esther. The San José–Limón–San José axis undergirds the structure of *The Four Mirrors*, which makes the novel a tale of two cities. Although the protagonist begins to see his brown face (true color) at the end of the novel, he still has not resolved the dilemma. Thus, one of the keys to understanding the character is by analyzing his emotional dependency on women.

Many females float through the consciousness of Charles

---

5. Duncan, *Los cuatro espejos*, 10. All subsequent quotations will be cited parenthetically; all translations are my own.

McForbes in his journey toward self-discovery. Among them are
Dora París, a girl he jilts before marrying Lorena Sam; Ruth Viales,
Lorena's childhood friend; Victoria George, who gives birth to
Charles's only son, Tomás, but who later weds another minister,
Alfred George; and Engracia Peña, an older married woman whom
McForbes woos, impregnates, and abandons—she later dies of com-
plications from a botched abortion. His two wives constitute the
Eve/Hagar metaphor, for not only are they joined to Charles, but
they also represent the mutually exclusive cultures he attempts to
reconcile. Ruth and Engracia—one black, the other white—are
shadowy figures who are alter egos of the two female cotagonists,
whereas the brown-skinned Victoria represents Charles's unfulfilled
promise to his child. In terms of the incidents of the narrative, the
story is primarily about McForbes. However, his crisis of identity
is related to his choice of spouses from conflicting cultural, racial,
and social backgrounds. Essentially, the ironic humor of *The Four
Mirrors* enables one to follow the confused antics of a crazed character who goes on a wild-goose chase after himself under the skirts
of his womenfolk.

Structurally, the novel is divided into two main parts of six and
five chapters, respectively. However, neither the primary nor the
secondary narrative threads develops in a linear fashion. Chapters
1, 4, 6, 7, and 11 constitute the external structure of the work,
which portrays Charles and Esther in the upper-class society of San
José, while the inner story, composed of chapters 2, 3, 5, 8, 9, and
10, depicts Charles and Lorena in rural Estrada. Regarding concepts
of time and space in *The Four Mirrors,* Salas Zamora observes:

> The distribution of events in time introduces three moments:
> a) a remote past, which encompasses the facts of Charles's life,
> from his childhood to his definitive departure from town; it
> also includes details about the character's ancestors: parents,
> grandparents; b) a closer past that embraces the time when
> Charles begins his relationship with Esther until he suffers the
> crisis of identity; and c) an immediate past, which encloses the
> length of time the protagonist's crisis lasts. The first and sec-
> ond periods are subordinate to the third, with which the novel
> begins; during the third period of time, the other two are pre-
> sented through introspection.[6]

6. Salas Zamora, "Identidad cultural," 382. My translation.

The creative tension that results from inserting a triple-layered past into the present, like a series of Chinese boxes, provides the impetus for McForbes's double consciousness, which is manifested in the Eve/Hagar paradigm operative in his wives.

Esther Centeno Vidaurre is the classic magnet in the colonized psyche of the protagonist, attracting him from a dissonant, marginalized self toward an alien center.[7] She has been socialized according to the traditional mores and values of the *criollo* class so that certain Eve-like aspects are dominant—beauty, innocence, naïveté, vulnerability, and curiosity. Moreover, she has been protected and dependent all her life, which has led her to be submissive. Esther is the least likely person to marry a black/mulatto ex-farmer like Charles McForbes, even though he is highly educated. Therefore, their marriage evokes the well-known fairy tale "Beauty and the Beast," because all her life the young woman has been taught to hate black people. The typical training of children in an upper-class or bourgeois setting is evident in a scene in which Esther remembers being constantly threatened by her older cousin Magdalena and the family maid with the specter of the "bogeyman," an aged black gardener by the name of Abrahams:

> Only one shadow sullied the daily routine of her childhood: the horrible figure of a Negro who tended gardens in their neighborhood. Not because he would have done anything to harm her, but because Magdalena and the maid—who sometimes shut herself up in another room with Magdalena and the milkman—constantly intimidated her with the black man. If you don't do this or that, that nigger's gonna carry you off. "Unhuh, Esther, he's coming now. The nigger's coming for you." And they would fall out laughing while panic devoured Esther's heart. "Come on, Mister Fly, come get this bad little girl," and Esther would flee to her room, throw herself on her bed, and weep disconsolately.
>
> (Sólo una sombra empañó su rutinaria niñez: la horrible figura de un negro que arreglaba los jardines del barrio. No porque

---

7. Franco, "The Colonised Imagination." Franco employs the term *colonised imagination* to refer to the tendency of Latin American writers, especially during the early period of canon formation, to imitate European tastes, values, and conventions. In this passage the expression "colonized psyche" is used interchangeably as a synonym for the Eurocentric complex.

él le hubiera causado daño, sino porque Magdalena y la em-
pleada—que de cuando en cuando se encerraba con Magdalena
y el lechero—la intimidaban constantemente con el negro. Si no
hacés esto o aquello, te va a llevar el negro. "Ajá, Ester, ahora
sí: el negro viene por vos." Y se reían alborozadas mientras el
pánico devoraba el corazón de Ester. "Venga, Míster Fly, venga
llévese esta chiquita malcriada"—, y Ester huía para echarse
sobre la cama y llorar desesperadamente.) (102–3)

The voice of an omniscient narrator blends with dialogue to display
the virulent racism of Magdalena and the servant. On the other
hand, Esther's father, Lucas Centeno, instills a paternalistic version
of the same lesson in his daughter: "'Come greet this colored boy,'
he would insist, 'tell him: "How you be, boss?"'"—and then Abrahams, encouraged by the doctor's confidence in him, would pat
Esther on the head, grinning from ear to ear" (—Saludá al moren-
ito—insistía él—, decile: ¿cómo le jauar yu?—, y entonces Abrahams, alentado por la confianza del Doctor, acariciaba la cabeza de
Ester, sonriendo, 103). Whenever such encounters occurred, Magdalena and the servant would quickly strip Esther and wash her
with alcohol, warning her about the unsanitary habits of Negroes:
"'Be careful about that pig. Negroes don't even take a bath or comb
their hair. And besides, they come from a place called Africa, where
people eat up little children'" ("Tené cuidado con ese cochino. Los
negros ni se bañan ni se peinan. Y además vienen de un lugar lla-
mado Africa, donde la gente se come a los chiquitos," 103). The
othering of Abrahams in particular and West Indians in general
leaves Esther unprepared to interact with black people as human
beings, and she grows up viewing differences in color, gender, and
class as negative traits associated with those who are not like she is.

Despite attempts at integration by various post–Civil War admin-
istrations in the 1950s and '60s, Costa Rica's educational system
continued to reinforce ugly stereotypes of African-descended people. In the classroom there was nothing in the textbooks to support
the notion that West Indians had a culture or history. Even so, the
teachers would pretend that everything was fine. "When the student
asks his teacher in class, 'why is Peter white and Samuel black,' the
teacher responds that we are all equal and he changes the subject,
leaving the child's question unanswered" (Cuando el alumno le
pregunta al maestro en clase, "por qué Pedro es blanco y Samuel

negro," el maestro responde que todos somos iguales y cambia el tema, dejando al niño con la pregunta abierta, 140).[8] At the private high school Esther attends, she is the ringleader of a group who constantly finds ways to make life miserable for the few black students in attendance: "'Hey, Blackey, Blackey, don't know nothin'-n-n. He don't understand. All Blackey know 'bout is cocoa and bananas.... Everything's dark to him. Monkey head can't understand what the teacher's saying'" ("Hey, Blaky, Blaky no saber nada. No entiende. Blaky sólo entiende de cacao y banana.... Todo está a oscuras. Cabeza de mono no puede ver lo que el profesor está diciendo," 105). As a young adult Esther meets Charles through her father, a trusted authority figure, and with the same curiosity as Eve, Esther interacts with the young widower as she begins to reexamine her attitude about race. Nevertheless, the 180-degree shift from hatred to love of blackness would test the limits of verisimilitude were it not for the fact that McForbes does not really consider himself black. Like Guabo in "Go-o-o-o-al!" Charles is ensnarled psychoemotionally in the Eurocentric complex.

When Esther discovers that her husband is missing the morning after the lecture, she summons her father for help, and their conversation sheds more light on the race, sex, and class vortex in Costa Rica:

> "Dad, I'm not going to permit you to..."
> "*You're* not going to permit *me*, Esther? A Negro that I found one day at the hospital, distraught and disposed to killing himself because his wife had just died from nothing. Yes, from nothing. But she died anyway. And then he left, he went back to the bush where he was hatched, and abandoned a white woman whom he knocked up and then came back; a married woman twice his age. And then he looks for me, asks me for help and I give it to him, and take him into my home against the will of my daughters, and I adopt him as a son; drat it, and then, he makes one of them his lover and marries the other, and one day he gets tired of her and pretends he is crazy..."
> "Daddy, please, I beg you..."
> "Don't interrupt me, Esther. He plays crazy and goes and leaves her. And then both of them have an attack..."

8. Meléndez Chaverri and Duncan, *El negro en Costa Rica*, 140.

(—Papá, no te permito...
—¿No me permitís, Ester? Un negro que yo encontré un día en
el hospital, destrozado y dispuesto a matarse porque su mujer
se había muerto de nada. Sí, de nada. Pero se murió de todos
modos. Y luego se fue, se fue de nuevo al monte donde lo
parieron, y dejó a una mujer blanca con una panza y se vino;
una mujer casada, mucho mayor que él. Y luego me busca, me
pide ayuda y se la doy, y lo recibo en mi casa contra la voluntad
de mis hijas y lo convierto en hijo adoptivo; carajo, y luego,
hace de una su amante y se casa con la otra, y un día de tantos
se cansa de ella, se hace el loco...
—Papá, te ruego que...
—...no me interrumpás, Ester. Se hace el loco y se va y la
deja. Y entonces a las dos les da un ataque...) (110)

Centeno's liberal facade slowly crumbles during the course of his
conversation with his daughter, and the race/gender/class skeleton
upon which the social corpus rests is bared. In an effort to talk
sense into Esther, the doctor invokes his wife's memory: "If your
mother were alive, she'd be telling me: 'this is what you've brought
us to'" (Y si tu mamá viviera me estaría diciendo: a eso nos has lle-
vado, 110). This is certainly ironic because in an earlier passage
when he reminisces about the Centeno family's prestigious lineage,
the distinguished physician reveals that his spouse was not of such
pure stock after all:

> Yes, his family was illustrious, and Lucas Centeno felt guilty
> about its decadence. Because something evil was happening
> now. His only daughter, who for years detested Negroes as he
> watched her grow up, was now in love with one. Perhaps it was
> the Guanacastecan blood of his wife, Doña Aminga Vidaurre.
> Maybe it was that: the Negro blood that was in her. The blood-
> line of a mulatto Castile.

> (Sí, la familia era gloriosa, y Lucas Centeno se sentía culpable
> de su decadencia. Porque algo malo sucedía ahora. Su única
> hija, que por tantos años vio crecer detestando a los negros,
> estaba de pronto enamorada de un negro. Tal vez fue la sangre
> guanacasteca de su esposa doña Aminga Vidaurre. Tel [sic] vez
> fue eso: la sangre de negro que había en ella. Sangre de una
> Castilla mulata.) (74–75)

Several issues emerge in the above text. First, Dr. Centeno poses the inevitable question, "Why my daughter?"—a natural response to those who subscribe to the white supremacist viewpoint. Moreover, the reference to Guanacaste, the northernmost province of Costa Rica, signifies a higher degree of racial mixture, unlike the Central Valley where Centeno's roots are. In the second place, it is tragic that an intelligent, educated, and good-looking man like Charles prostrates himself at the altar of a woman whose family and class regard him with contempt and pity. That tension is central to McForbes's invisibility, for as will be evident in the character Kingsman Moody (in *For the Sake of Peace*), the black male–white female paradigm is the source of intense conflict and violence in the colonized psyche. A third implication of the above passage is that one of the master symbols of racist ideology—*blanqueamiento* (whitening)—is based on the myth of a *castizo* (pure) Spanish heritage. However, the phrase "the bloodline of a mulatto Castile" subverts the image of the Nordic European conqueror/culture that floods the Latin American imagination. Paradoxically, Charles is attracted to Esther because she represents the challenge of an unattainable somatic ideal the society worships, while he simultaneously debases the magma coursing through his individual veins as well as the national bloodline (including Esther's).

True to the patriarchal model of Gisella in "The Ideal Model of Womanhood," Esther is blonde, blue-eyed, and very fair, corporeal features that Charles adores:

> My wife was of distinguished bearing, of Greek elegance, with large eyes and a light trace of Germanic features. She came from a distinguished family, who was no longer rich, but she was still the descendant of wealthy ancestors from a glorious past... blue eyes, slender fingers, lightly rouged cheeks, and she tied up her golden hair with a pink ribbon.

> (Mi esposa era de porte distinguido, elegancia griega, grandes ojos y un ligero rasgo germánico. De familia distinguida, no rica pero descendiente de ricas familias de fecundos pasados... con sus ojos celestes; dedos delgados, mejillas ligeramente rosadas, y recogiendo sus hermosos cabellos de trigo una cintilla rosada.) (10–11)

Moreover, the protagonist wears his wife on his arm like a king bearing his mantle, and their appearance at the lecture is a staged performance, which of course takes place in a very public setting: "The sense of lethargy had begun the night before when Esther and I entered the National Theater triumphantly to listen to that conference on racial minorities in Costa Rica" (La sensación de languidez había empezado desde la noche anterior, cuando Ester y yo entramos triunfantes al Teatro Nacional para escuchar aquella conference sobre minorías raciales en Costa Rica, 10). The hyperbolic, parodic overtones of both passages reinforce the humorous subversion of canonical texts that foregrounds this particular model of beauty as the national standard to the exclusion of all others. Ironically, McForbes thinks that this is the preemptive moment in his life, even though the lecture is the very prong on which he will snag and unravel his false image of himself.

In the character Esther McForbes the Eve/Hagar paradigm is off balance. As a foil for the Hagar aspect(s) of the principle, Esther evokes the dual image of Eve that informs Western culture—the pristine white goddess and the femme fatale.[9] To her credit, Charles's second wife tries to articulate her feeling that something is not quite right with their relationship, and by extension with the national culture. Thus, the argument with her father is an emotional rather than logical defense of her marriage that plays on the stereotype of the "dumb blonde":

> "Daddy," Esther threw herself on him. "Dad, you don't understand, Dad. Charles is like fire. A person runs because fire burns. But she needs the fire, Daddy. The flames destroy everything, but she needs the warmth they provide."
> "Like fire, huh? I'd say he's more like coal."
> "Dad, try to understand. Charles is a strange person; he's neither black nor white. He's beyond those definitions. Perhaps he *is* satanic: a strange mixture in any case, who makes you go crazy. I'm in love, Daddy..."

> (—¡Papá!—Ester se lanzó sobre él—. Papá, vos no podés entender, papá. Charles es como el fuego. Una huye porque el fuego quema. Pero una necesita el fuego, papá. Las llamas lo arrasan todo, pero una necesita el calor que dan.
> —Como el fuego, ¿eh? Como el carbón diría yo.
> —Papá, trata de entender. Charles es una persona extraña; no es ni negro, ni blanco. Está más allá de esas definiciones. Tal

9. Bell hooks, *Ain't I a Woman? Black Women and Feminism,* 31.

vez sea satánico: una mezcla extraña en todo caso, que la en-
loquece a una. Estoy enamorada, papá...) (111)

Because of her total ignorance about other races and classes in
Costa Rica, and her limited experience with men, Charles's white/
mestizo wife is unable to perceive the dilemma her husband faces,
even though she senses a change in him after the lecture. Thus, she
neutralizes his ethnoracial identity (he is neither black nor white)
since she cannot read correctly the signs around her. From the perspective of the dominant culture, Esther Centeno McForbes represents the patriarchal concept of womanhood—the docile, weak,
mindless creature totally dependent on a man. She is cast as the Protected Lady, and in that sense she is the Sleeping Beauty, the image
projected in the opening bedroom scene of *The Four Mirrors*. Metaphorically, she is Eve before the Fall—curious, naive, and vulnerable. Moreover, her posture is rooted in the everyday reality of a
society that adheres to the feudalistic values illustrated in the previous discussion of the Gisella/Bonifacia paradigm in the national
literature. For one thing, Esther is too dependent on male authority
to define her own personhood. For another, she is too used to the
good life—parties, plays, education, travel, luxury, leisure, and servants—to penetrate the surface of things. Esther is wrapped up in
herself, enjoying the physical benefits of her marriage, but not
achieving true emotional intimacy with her spouse. In short, her
privileged race, gender, and class have anesthetized and surgically
removed her from the pulse of life. Furthermore, she feels her husband's vitality, but does not understand its source, and is even afraid
to find out. This is why Esther sees Charles as satanic/strange, for
he is like the serpent/tempter in the Garden. Thus, she can truly
say of their relationship: "The devil made me do it." Esther Centeno McForbes is the allegorical representation of the tangential
positioning of the white Central Valley (symbolized by San José)
with the black Atlantic Coast (symbolized by Estrada).

It is not surprising, then, that McForbes seeks to escape from a
world where he tries in vain to define himself in terms of an insecure
spouse. As he wanders through the streets of San José, the hero reminisces about his past life in Estrada with his first wife, Lorena, other
black women, and his mother, and this aimless movement shifts
the focus of the novel to the inner story. The attack by the *dopí* (evil
white spirit) is allegedly instigated by the couple's enemies, Christian

and Nabe Bowman. Christian, a former rival for Lorena's hand, is
jealous of Charles because the latter is light-skinned, prosperous,
and educated—in short, everything he is not. Nabe resents Lorena
because she knows that Christian has loved her since childhood.
Duncan uses the traditional beliefs and values of the people who
live in rural towns like Estrada as an organizing principle for the
inner story of *The Four Mirrors*. The neighbors believe that

> Lorena's illness was not physical even though the consequences
> of it were. Because it was necessary to remember things just as
> they happened: she was attacked by a malignant spirit. And
> once she had fallen to the floor, screaming and choking, the
> white specter left her there and, to add insult to injury, had the
> nerve to use the front door to exit the house.
>
> ([L]a dolencia de Lorena no era física, aunque las consecuen-
> cias lo fuesen. Porque era necesario recordar las cosas tal como
> sucedieron: fue atacada por un espíritu maligno. Y caída en el
> suelo, gritando y ahogándose, la dejó el espectro blanco, quien
> además con descaro no común, usó la puerta de adelante para
> irse.) (47–48)

At first, Charles has difficulty accepting this explanation of the incident because his formal education has made him question many
things about his nurturing culture:

> It was hard to accept such a supernatural explanation after so
> many years of studying, although they were not so many after
> all. But he was faced with a concrete reality: Lorena sprawled
> out on the cot in some kind of trance and barely breathing.
> And that was real.
>
> (Era duro aceptar una explicación tan mágica después de tantos
> estudios. Aunque, a la verdad, no eran ni tantos. Pero había
> frente a él una realidad concreta: Lorena tendida en el catre en
> una especie de trance y respirando apenas. Y eso era lo con-
> creto.) (41)

Thus, McForbes is torn between disbelief and awe.

With the words "Because they were two irreconcilable worlds,
each one with its own logic" (Porque eran dos mundos irrecon-
ciliables, cada uno con su propia lógica, 42) surging through his

consciousness, the problematic of the novel is explicitly articulated. According to one critic:

> The plot of *Los cuatro espejos* can be reduced to a match-up between two world views: the magical West Indian Weltanschauung of the folk from Limón as against the so-called scientific approach of the white/mestizo dominant group centered in San José, the capital. Charles McForbes is the most important point of contact between the two worlds, and is thus the centre of the conflict. So poignant is the presentation of this conflict that it argues for the existence in the implied author (and perhaps even in the author himself) of a correspondingly intense inner turmoil: an argument that is strengthened by the fact that... there is no real solution offered.[10]

To reiterate, the protagonist is torn between two conflicting value systems represented by the "civilization" of the Central Valley and the "barbarism" of the Atlantic Coast, which is true in theory, but the praxis is more complex than this dichotomy suggests. In fact, one of the goals of *The Eve/Hagar Paradigm* is to illustrate how the implied and real authors of the short stories and novels of the 1970s progressively work out the creative implications of drawing from two spheres that often interface in some aspects but many times diverge in others, especially where religious beliefs are concerned. This happens during the process of syncretism. For this reason, the duppy incident involving Lorena can be viewed as a kind of black science fiction, or an inventive approach to presenting an African-descended spiritual phenomenon (Afro-realism) *on its own terms,* and not necessarily as a "primitive" antithesis of Eurocentric empiricism. There is no "logical," that is, Western, explanation of the occurrence. It just happens according to its own laws.

Even more startling is the strange, but familiar, vision that appears to Charles three times the evening of Lorena's attack: "He looked up just in time to see a horse crossing the railroad tracks, with two riders astride. One of them was facing backward" (Levantó los ojos a tiempo para ver a un caballo cruzando la línea del tren, con dos jinetes a cuestas. Uno de ellos tenía la cara vuelta hacia la cola del animal, 45). The distraught husband thinks that he has been influenced by the fantasies of neighbors and parishioners who

10. Smart, *Central American Writers,* 57.

hold a vigil for Lorena. However, the second time the apparition appears, he recognizes one of the individuals:

> He raised his head to look again at the two horsemen who were crossing the railroad tracks. The horse galloped without moving from its place. Fear ran through the conduits foreshadowed by Nature, and Charles perceived the weathered face of his father, Pete, with eyes perfumed by the dense sequence of dawn.

> (Alzó la vista para mirar de nuevo a los dos jinetes que aún cruzaban la vía férrea. El caballo se daba prisa sin moverse de su sitio. El miedo corrió por los conductos previstos por la Naturaleza, y Charles recordó la cara maltratada de su padre Pete, sus ojos perfumados por la densa secuencia del amanecer.)
> (45)

He then seeks the help of nurse Clarita de Duke, who is the only other person in town with any higher education, and she administers a shot to Lorena until she can get medical help in the capital city. Meanwhile, McForbes is pressured by Ruth, who is also the daughter of an obeah man, to utilize the counterremedy. A significant aspect of the African religious heritage is its focus on the power of healing by means of herbal art or medicine.[11] As Lorena drifts in and out of consciousness, she whispers periodically to her traumatized husband:

> "Charles. Pete says that there's some white powders under the large vase. Did you hear me? Underneath the large vase."
> "Yes ... under ..."
> "Rub your hands with lemon and throw out the powders right now. You have to do it right now."
> "Yes, I'll do it right now. How do you feel?"

> (—Charles. Dice Pete que hay un polvito blanco debajo del florero grande. ¿Oíste? Debajo del florero grande ...
> —Sí ... debajo ...
> —Untate limón en las manos y sacá el polvito ahora mismo. Tenés que hacerlo ahora mismo.
> Sí, sí, voy enseguida. ¿Cómo te sentís?) (51)

11. Barrett, *Soul Force*, 79.

Thus, the rite of exorcism that Lorena requests of her husband is associated with a strong belief in herbal and other natural remedies of traditional medicine (Afro-realism). Nevertheless, McForbes hesitates until he sees the apocalyptic vision for the third and last time:

> The horsemen kept on crossing the tracks. Charles gave the signal agreed upon, and the dogs started to bark. Seconds later, old Pete appeared, fleeing from the rabid canines. When he reached the front of his son's house, he stopped in order to repeat the solemn password. Then Charles saw next to him old Jakel Duke, grandfather of his neighbor Cliff.
>
> (Los jinetes seguían cruzando la vía. Charles hizo la señal convenida y los perros comenzaron a ladrar. Segundos después, apareció el viejo Pete, huyendo de los furiosos canes. Al llegar frente a las casa de su hijo, se detuvo, para repetir la clave solemnemente. Entonces Charles vio a la par de su viejo a Jakel Duke, el abuelo de Clif su vecino.) (46)

This apocalyptic divination—filled with the two horsemen and barking dogs that pursue the ghosts of his ancestors—evokes in a time-frozen capsule the clash of Europe and Africa and the history of slavery/colonization in the New World. In terms of the novel's action, it brings the protagonist to the stark realization that his wife is going to perish. Nevertheless, he takes her to San José.

During her stay in the hospital, Lorena's imminent death allows her plenty of time to reexamine her life, which has been filled with pain, sorrow, and violence. It is a blues litany that embodies the Hagar principle. In addition, Lorena is constantly besieged with a sense of abandonment, exile, and orphanhood, and though she makes a valiant effort to be strong, she is dependent, fearful, bereft, and bitter. Through the insertion of a third-person omniscient narrator into the character's consciousness (interior monologue), it is revealed that her birth was fraught with darkness and foreboding:

> They conceived her one night down by the whispering riverside, and that was not her fault either. And it was rather late when Mary, filled with dismay, discovered that she did not want to have a child for a black voodoo man. She was slow in discovering this just when her advanced stage of pregnancy made it impossible to get any pleasure. She preferred to get rid of it.

But Mr. Sam prepared a "counterremedy" that saved the fetus. And Lorena was born in spite of her mother's criminal intent, but Mary drowned to death right before the astonished eyes of the daughter she tried to kill.

(La engendraron una noche junto al arroyo, que susurraba, y de eso tampoco tuvo ella la culpa. Y fue muy tardía la hora en que María, consternada, descubrió que no quería tener el hijo de un brujo negro. Fue un descubrimiento torpe, hecho cuando ya los meses de embarazo hacían imposible el placer. Prefirió librarse de ella. Pero Mr. Sam preparó una "contra" que le salvó la vida al feto. Y Lorena nació a pesar de los intentos criminales de su madre, pero María falleció ahogada frente a los ojos dilatados de la hija que quiso asesinar.) (96)

In the above passage, the Madonna image of woman is deconstructed as the reader tries to reconcile traditional notions of motherhood with the reality of a near abortion. Moreover, the knowledge of how she began life is a burden of guilt Lorena carries deep in her psyche, a cosmic pain that is reinforced by her constant repetition of the words "it wasn't her fault, she wasn't to blame." The third-person narrative voice effectively conveys the sense of distancing associated with her alienation and anguish. At first, one gets the impression that Mary dies in childbirth, but later it is revealed that she drowns in a flood when the Matina River sweeps away their humble dwelling from low ground. The ten-year-old girl witnesses her mother's violent death and somehow feels responsible for it. The womb/tongue dialectic is operative in Lorena's psyche in that she has never broken free of the enclosed space suggested by her mother's womb, and she experiences emotional suffocation in that prenatal chamber. Conversely, the young woman's inability to channel her angst in positive ways renders her tongue vitriolic, and she drives away her beloved husband with accusations and complaints.

Besides a sense of rejection and guilt, Charles's wife is also the victim of sexual abuse. During their childhood Lorena Sam, Ruth Viales, Charles McForbes, Christian Bowman, Cliff Duke, and Clovis Lince are part of a tightly knit group like brothers and sisters. As they grow up, however, Charles and Christian become rivals for Lorena's affection. Even after Charles weds Lorena, Christian tries to persuade her to divorce him. However, in a scene fraught with ambiguity, Christian attempts to woo Lorena, but his pleas turn to brute force, and he apparently rapes her. Charles goes to jail for a while because he shoots Christian in retaliation, yet in spite of family feuds Christian continues to love Lorena. On the other hand, Christian's spouse, Nabe, is determined to get rid of her rival once and for all. The most agonizing consequence of the affair is that Lorena gets pregnant by Christian, but Mr. Sam and Charles force her to give up the baby for adoption. As Lorena lies dying in the hospital, she has bitter memories of the man-child whom she brought into the world, but who is interned in an orphanage:

> She was also remembering what happened with Christian. Her past suffering because of Nabe's evil works. And the night she woke up in excruciating pain and they called Miss Ann the Wet Nurse. And the trip to San José with the baby. And the empty return home. And the lie: the baby died, the baby died. But without knowing why, she told the truth to Christian.

> (Recordaba también lo sucedido con Cristian. Los sufrimientos pasados por obra de Nabe. Y la noche en que despertó con un dolor terrible y llamaron a Miss Ann la Partera. Y el viaje a San José con el niño. Y el regreso vacío. Y la mentira: el niño ha muerto. El niño ha muerto. Pero sin saber por qué, le dijo a Cristian la verdad.) (96–97)

Like Hagar, Lorena does not have any control or say over the destiny of her son.

In her weakened state of mind, Lorena recalls the scenes of which she daydreamed right before her attack—the setting sun in Estrada; preparing a meal for Charles; the sudden realization that the meat was burning, amid the chorus of spirits and the unexpected visit of the evil one that beat and choked her; the music of her baby's cry at birth; and the sound of Miss Ann's voice saying, "'Yes, it's a man-child'" ("Sí, un hermoso varón," 97). The old woman tries to encourage Lorena, for she is aware that "women's power to give birth and their role as healers make them awesome figures in a sex-oriented culture."[12] Nevertheless, Lorena agonizes over the "loss" of her beloved son, just as Hagar lamented the impending death of Ishmael. Unlike the latter, Lorena does not have the consolation of direct divine intervention.

Although Lorena and Charles are made for each other, she remembers that their relationship began on a troubled note. Mr. Sam

---

12. Steady, "African Feminism," 7.

is anxious to marry them off respectably, but when Charles comes to ask for Lorena's hand, she refuses him:

> Charles wanted to get married. Mr. Sam, red with rage, demanded the same thing. But Lorena was violently opposed to marriage.
> "Well, Daddy, it's that, it's just that . . . If I get married he's gonna think he owns me and he's gonna do whatever he pleases with me. I don't want to be tied to anybody, and anyway . . ."
> "Anyway, what?"
> "It's like I'm already his wife."

> (Charles quería casarse. Mr. Sam, rojo de ira, les exigía lo mismo. Pero Lorena se opuso violentamente al matrimonio.
> —Es que, es que, papá . . . Si me caso va a creer que es dueño mío y va a hacer lo que le dé la gana conmigo. Yo no quiero sentirme amarrada a nadie y de todos modos . . .
> —¿De todos modos qué?
> —Soy su mujer ya.) (82)

In the above scene, Lorena "talks back," or speaks as an equal to her father. Bell hooks asserts that the act of talking back is crucial for those who are oppressed, especially women of color. Not only does the young woman intend to wed Charles on her own terms, that is, as an equal person in the relationship, but she also spurns the conservative morality of the community. Although Lorena risks another whipping from Mr. Sam, she is empowered by her own words. This is crucial in her reinvention of herself within the Eve/Hagar paradigm, and she embodies the womb/tongue conceit to affirm her assertiveness and independence. Hooks concludes that "moving from silence into speech is for the oppressed, the colonized, the exploited, and those who stand and struggle side by side a gesture of defiance that heals, that makes new life and new growth possible. It is that act of speech, of 'talking back,' that is no mere gesture of empty words, that is the expression of our movement from object to subject—the liberated voice."[13]

Lorena Sam marries Charles McForbes, but, like all couples since Adam and Eve, their relationship goes through numerous challenges. Moreover, her untimely death does not allow the couple to produce a child of their own. Unfortunately, Lorena's innocent

13. Hooks, *Talking Back: Thinking Feminist, Thinking Black,* 56, 9.

baby experiences a social death, for "conceived in sin," the black illegitimate man-child remains invisible and trapped within a caste system. As her son he is erased from public existence, just as Ishmael was cast out or erased from Abraham's household. It would be a misrepresentation of the truth to say that the historical Hagar was the victim of rape, but her "consensual" union with Abraham lay within a structure of power and authority she could not possibly have resisted. In contrast, Lorena is legally free, but she is still a victim of sexual abuse. This underscores the reality that the bodily manipulation of women has been one of the most common mechanisms of control in patriarchal cultures throughout the ages.

The motifs of violation and the loss of children are linked to the theme of African slavery and oppression in the Americas, which Lorena ponders on her sickbed:

> Her child, snatched away. How many grandmothers before her, during these shameful four hundred years of crimes... they stole their children only to sell them on the auction block: "I got a Negress and her two gals." "I'm selling them." "I'll sell them together or separate at the client's pleasure." "The oldest one is two years old." "I'll sell them together or separate." And how many sons like her own had been brought into the world through the exclusive will of a slave master?

> (Su hijo, arrebatado. A cuántas abuelas antes de ella, durante estos ignominiosos cuatrocientos años de crímenes... le arrebataron a sus hijos para venderlos en la plaza: "Vendo negra y a sus dos hijas." "Las vendo." "Las vendo juntas o separadamente a gusto del cliente." "La mayor tiene dos años." Las vendo juntas o separadamente. Y ¿cuántos hijos como el hijo de ella, habían venido al mundo por la exclusiva voluntad del esclavista?) (88)

On the one hand, there is a tendency to fall into the victimization mode as the triple themes of race, gender, and class cross and re-cross Lorena's feverish imagination during her prolonged nightmare of death. On the other hand, the young woman feels somewhat empowered as she angrily remembers that females are subject to physical and sexual abuse no matter what the race and class of the perpetrator:

> Only this child was not for a slaveholder but a beast as black as she was. An animal. That's it. But was he really black? Or

perhaps he had acquired with time the characteristics of those who sired one of her ancestors and, at any rate, miseducated little black children in his Sunday school for four hundred years.

(Sólo que este hijo suyo no era de ningún esclavista sino de una bestia tan negra como ella. Una bestia. Eso es. Pero ¿era negro? O acaso había adquirido andando el tiempo las características de quienes engendraron a alguno de sus abuelos y en todo caso, educó a los niños negros en su escuela-iglesia durante cuatrocientos años.) (88)

Essentially, the dilemma of the African-descended female becomes one of resisting not only racial oppression but also sexual and class exploitation. Although *The Four Mirrors* clearly depicts the quest of a male protagonist for a place, identity, and language that make him feel at home in Costa Rica, that search is inevitably linked to the issue of male-female relationships that is also a function of race and class. In this allegory of mutually exclusive colors and cities/cultures, Esther and San José represent the white legend on which the national self-concept is founded, while Lorena and Estrada signify the black West Indian revitalization of the country that remains unacknowledged in the hegemonic discourse. Thus, Alan Persico discusses the ambivalence Charles McForbes has about his marriage to Esther Centeno:

> Part of his motivation to return must have been the feeling of guilt he was experiencing following the words of the speaker at the talk at the Teatro Nacional. He was motivated to find out whether his decision to abandon Limón and seek a new life in San José was anything to feel guilty about. Prior to his return visit to Limón he was of the impression and belief that somehow he was not Black, although, indeed he was fair skinned. Consequently he had acquired new values.[14]

McForbes criticizes the acquisition of material things at the expense of spiritual values, but he is hypocritical since he accrues wealth through his marriage to Esther. Thus, his recognition of the fundamental contradiction of his life confronts him when he is on a slow train bound for Limón:

14. Persico, "Quince Duncan's *Los cuatro espejos:* Time, History, and a New Novel," 17.

> At what precise moment did I lose my own identity? What
> pile of dreams put me in conflict with the culture I had suckled
> from the blackish breasts of my mother, and sipped drop by
> drop on Pete McForbes's pale knee? Look at my skin: shucks,
> it's not black. That is, if it were not for my hair and my fea-
> tures, I could pass for Latino anywhere.
>
> (¿En qué momento preciso perdí mi propia identidad? ¿Qué
> cúmulo de sueños me pusieron en conflicto con la cultura ma-
> mada en los negruzcos pechos de mi madre, y sorbida gota a
> gota desde la pálida rodilla de Pete McForbes? Ustedes pueden
> ver mi piel: pucha, no es negra. Es decir, si no fuera por mi
> pelo y mis facciones yo podría pasar en cualquier parte como
> latino.) (128)

Like Humpty Dumpty, Charles McForbes must strive to put the
pieces back together again to reconstruct the fragments of African
cultures in the New World.

The protagonist's ambivalence about his identity is represented
by the antithesis between his mother's "blackish breasts" and his
father's "pale knee." Nevertheless, Charles recognizes that society
views him as black no matter how light-skinned he is. His two marriages to white (Esther) and dark-skinned/black (Lorena) women,
not to mention the ones he courts in between, externalize his identity crisis. Because of the pendular movement of time in the novel,
it is not clear exactly when Charles has relationships with Victoria,
Engracia, and Ruth, but they appear to take place in between his
two marriages. The pregnant Engracia is given an abortion by Lucas
Centeno (for whom she works and with whom she also has an affair), and dies when the bus she is driving for a group of senior citizens plunges into the Pacuare River. It is suggested that the accident
is the result of a stroke triggered by the wrong medicine Centeno
prescribes. Even though Victoria is in love with Charles and bears
his son, the protagonist abandons her, so she subsequently marries
Alfred George to give her child, Tomás, legitimacy. Faithful Ruth
becomes a surrogate wife to Charles after her friend's death, but he
abandons her, too, along with his house and furnishings, as he seeks
to reenter the comfortable world of San José. In essence, McForbes's
escape from Estrada constitutes his effort to kill the blackness
within. Moreover, his immersion in the Central Valley culture blinds
him temporarily, but it is ironically through the blindness and in-

visibility motifs that the protagonist embarks on a voyage of self-discovery in the very place from which he seeks to run. The tale of two wives/cities alternately places Charles on one side or the other of the Eve/Hagar seesaw.

Through McForbes's consciousness run the complex strains of individual and collective history. On a superficial level is the white legend, the celebration of traditional Euro-Hispanic values played out within the Centeno family album in *The Four Mirrors* (66–74); on a deeper level, and ironically reinforcing the Eurocentric perspective, is the litany of whitening, handed down through generations of McForbeses (129–33). Even more ludicrous is Charles's assertion that "my family didn't put on airs like the Centenos" ([m]i familia no tuvo los aires de la familia Centeno, 129). In fact, that is exactly what they do, for Charles's paternal grandfather, old man Saltiman McForbes, had married Doña Milady Brubanck. Although Saltiman owns the prosperous McForbes Lumber and Service Ltd., and manages to formally educate all eight of his children, he segregates his family from the very black people of the community and constantly nags them to improve themselves through marriage to white or very light-skinned types: "You have to whiten us up, that's the solution, you have to whiten us up" (Hay que ir blanqueando, esa es la solución: hay que ir blanqueando, 130). Charles's father, Pete McForbes, resists this "final solution," and makes his way first to Panama then to Costa Rica to seek his fortune when the family business dissolves from mismanagement and sibling rivalry after Saltiman dies. Pete's supreme act of rebellion comes when he marries the blackest woman he can find and settles down to live among the people of Limón Province. Of course, the McForbes clan writes him off as "a shiftless nigger" (un negro fracasado, 131) in spite of the hard work Pete does to educate Charles and acquire land for him. His most important legacy to his son is the pride in and knowledge of his black roots, which Pete and his unmixed African friend Jakel Duke pass down through oral tradition.

As the protagonist grows up, he is constantly admonished by his father: "Charles: you are black. Papa Saltiman was a poor fool" (Charles: usted es negro. Papá Saltiman era un pobre tonto, 132). This explains McForbes's reference to sipping black culture on his father's pale knee. However, Charles's discomfort with the African component of his identity is illustrated by his use of the pejorative adjective *negruzcos* (blackish) to refer to his mother's breasts, by his lack of acceptance of his features, which one can assume are "negroid" (full lips, wide nose, kinky/curly hair), and by his strong desire to "pass" for Hispanic/white in Costa Rica. Nevertheless, the master symbols of *mestizaje, négritude,* and *blanqueamiento* that are recurrent motifs in *The Four Mirrors* are not mutually exclusive categories, as explained in the following observation:

> From the beginning of the African Diaspora in Europe and the Americas, "whitening" and "darkening" have been dual symbolic processes of classification and identity. Though dominant in nationalist rhetoric, *mestizaje* is not viewed positively in black communities and regions, where, nevertheless, lightness is often considered superior to darkness. "Mulatto" often signifies "free black" as well as "lightened black." In some areas, however, it may mean "darkened white," or just plain "darkened." With the abolishment of slavery between the mid- and late nineteenth century, the terminology became "mulatto/black" in black regions, and "white/mulatto" in regions dominated by peoples of lighter skin color. Extended occupation by U.S. troops in several areas (among them Nicaragua, Haiti, and Puerto Rico) facilitated this process. In many black regions and communities, the word *mestizo* may refer to "black blood" (meaning "darkening"—*negreando*) with no connotation of "lightening."[15]

The alienation, ambivalence, and confusion that result from these conflicting symbols affect not only individuals but also entire communities and nations. Consequently, people become obsessed with race/color, gender/sex, and class/caste as they attempt to map their identities on a spurious social scale. This mania is incarnated in Charles McForbes, Lucas Centeno, and Euclides Herrera (in *Dead-End Street*), but most important in the Eve/Hagar contrapositioning of Charles's two wives, Lorena and Esther.

The figure of the tragicomic mulatto and the theme of passing are related to class and gender issues in *The Four Mirrors*. To wit, Charles's remembered conversations with his lowly female progenitor constitute a powerful presence, or forceful "voice of mother," that is buried in his consciousness and emerges during critical moments of his life. This voice is but another manifestation of the womb/tongue metaphor of the Eve/Hagar paradigm. In a compelling

15. *Report on the Americas,* 18–19.

and provocative essay, Hortense Spillers points out the deep psychoemotional influence of the African American female on her progeny,
especially her male children:

> The African-American male has been touched... by the *mother*,
> handled by her in ways that he cannot escape, and in ways
> that the white American male is allowed to temporize by a fa-
> therly reprieve. This human and historic development—the text
> that has been inscribed on the benighted heart of the conti-
> nent—takes us to the center of an inexorable difference in the
> depths of American women's community: the African-American
> woman, the mother, the daughter, becomes historically the pow-
> erful and shadowy evocation of a cultural synthesis long evap-
> orated—the law of the Mother—only and precisely because
> legal enslavement removed the African-American male not so
> much from sight as from mimetic view as a partner in the pre-
> vailing social fiction of the Father's name, the Father's law.[16]

Thus, Spillers contends that in order to recover an integral part
of his personhood, the African-descended male must acknowledge
and effectively deal with the "female" within himself. Henry Louis
Gates Jr. responds to Spillers's call by clothing her theory in a non-
essentialized garb. He comments: "How curious a figure—men, and
especially black men, gaining their voices through the black mother.
Precisely when some committed feminists or some committed black
nationalists would 'essentialize all others' out of their critical endeavor, Hortense Spillers rejects that glib and easy solution, calling
for a revoicing of the master's discourse in the cadences and tim-
bres of the Black Mother's voice."[17] *The Four Mirrors* features the
cadences and nuances of the black female voice in Charles's mother,
with whom he is connected by birth, and his first wife, Lorena, to
whom he is joined through marriage. During this four-day odyssey
in search of himself, McForbes evokes at a given moment his
mother's image to comfort himself as he wanders through the up-
scale Lomas de Ocloro district, where he is stopped by two "white"
policemen:

> "Hey, boy, where you going at this time of night?" Another
> guy who looked Hispanic went by without their saying any-

16. Spillers, "Mama's Baby, Papa's Maybe: An American Grammar Book," 80.
17. Gates, "The Master's Pieces: On Canon Formation and the Afro-American
Tradition," 36.

thing to him, which I called to their attention. "Look, boy," the one who seemed to be in charge said, "this ain't Limón: watch out now."

(—Moreno, ¿adónde vas a estas horas?—Otro señor, latino, pasó sin que le preguntasen nada, hecho que señalé. —Mira, moreno—me dijo el que parecía ser el official—, aquí no estás en Limón: cuídate.) (120)

Debating over whether he should go back to Esther, Charles muses in another instance about his mother:

> Without knowing why, I began to think about my mother. Raphael, the one with the keen features. Oh, okay. I thought he was the other one. No, go on: he's too ugly. Too ugly? His white teeth highlight the blackness of his skin in the brisk coldness of the store. Yes, he's very black. He looks like an African. Thank goodness! Raphael came out looking like his father; he has good hair. Spanish hair. You know? That's it, hardly what you could call a spade and with good hair.

> (Sin saber por qué, empecé a pensar en mi madre. Rafael el de las facciones finas. Ah, ya. Creí que era el otro. No, que va: es demasiado feo. ¿Demasiado feo? Sus dientes blancos subraya-ban la negrura de su piel en el frío rejuvenecido del aposento. Sí, es negrísimo. Parece un africano. ¡Jesús! Rafael salió al papá; tiene el pelo muy lindo. Pelo español. ¿Sabés? Es así, apenas morenito y con el pelo español.) (121–22)

It is not clear whether Raphael is a brother, who has Pete's "good hair" and the mother's black skin, or a relative or friend of mixed parentage the mother is discussing with someone. The allusion is vague and enigmatic in this passage.

The third time Charles evokes his mother's picture is after return-ing to San José only to find out that Esther and Magdalena have been kidnapped by the Puma, an old gang member. McForbes thinks back to his adolescence when he had been initiated through gang rape by four individuals, and he still feels the emotional pain over the remembered spasm/paroxysm of bleeding and vomiting that made him cry out for his mother's consolation. He thinks:

> As a child, sitting on my mama's lap, I once dared to ask her: "Mommy, how did Jesus sweat blood?" She looked at me, with

that intense look of fighting cocks when they have been beaten by their opponents: "Sonny," she said, with tear-filled eyes, "you'll know in time."

(De niño, sentado en las rodillas de mi madre, osé preguntarle:
—Mami, ¿cómo pudo el Señor sudar sangre?
Ella me miró, con esa mirada intensa de los gallos de pelea cuando han sido vencidos por su contrincante:
—Hijo—dijo, sus ojos nublados—, con el tiempo lo sabrás.)
(157)

Although Charles's fleeting memories of his mother occupy very little space in the novel, they are nonetheless significant because they have been chiseled into his psyche. In short, the mother is the one woman to whose voice he is attuned, for even though he dearly loved Lorena, she was bitter and conflictive. Yet it is ironic that Charles does not name his mother, which might be an attempt to stifle the blackness inside. Be that as it may, the voice of mother never leaves him, which is why he feels guilty about his marriage to Esther. Duncan articulates this sense of shame and betrayal in his commentary on West Indian beliefs: "On matters of sex, the idea was that we blacks are a strong race, and to mix with others is to weaken our race. Marrying a white person was tantamount to treachery for black people in Limón."[18] Charles is haunted by that guilt, and his erratic movement from one pole (woman/city) to the other is symbolic of an intense internal struggle—the two warring forces in the one dark body.

The two wives and the cities/cultures they represent exemplify the Gisella/Bonifacia rift, which is a master trope of female representation in Costa Rican and Latin American (Occidental) literature. Although Esther Centeno McForbes is the second spouse of Charles, she is upstaged in the protagonist's mind as the most important element of his efforts to integrate into national life. As such, she embodies the Eve, or founding-mother, aspect of the Eve/Hagar paradigm, in spite of the fact that she does not bear any children. In terms of female portraiture, Esther is the classic model, for it is this image to which Gisella and, by extension, all female characters must conform. On the other hand, Lorena Sam McForbes, Charles's

18. Meléndez Chaverri and Duncan, *El negro en Costa Rica*, 138.

first wife, encapsulates the Hagar (Bonifacia) portion, for in her life are crystallized all the beleaguered women who "deviate" from the norm, despite the fact that she is much loved by her husband. Ironically, Lorena is also "barren," for even though she gives birth to a child, he is the product of rape and illegitimacy, the bitter fruit of a forced relationship. Thus, the baby is put to death socially, so she does not enjoy the blessings of motherhood. Before examining his life, it is impossible for Charles to achieve balance through the Eve/Hagar paradigm, and that is the reason for his blindness, which is manifest in his inclination to womanize. The hero's imbalanced state of mind and body is expressed in the heart of the novel when, at the moment of Lorena's attack and impending death, he thinks: "They were two irreconcilable worlds." Structurally, this lack of equilibrium is reflected in the work through the initial scenes from Charles's "new" life with Esther in San José, which constitutes the present. However, the layers of pretense under which his identity is submerged begin to peel the night of the lecture at the National Theater. As the action moves toward the immediate and remote pasts, back to his birthplace in Estrada, it becomes evident that the latter is a part of a way of life he has tried to suppress (West Indian culture). It is only when Charles strips himself bare in his blindness and replays the voice of his mother that he begins to ask himself the kinds of probing questions that will lead to his search for an authentic self: "At what precise moment did I lose my own identity? What pile of dreams put me in conflict with the culture I had suckled from the blackish breasts of my mother, and sipped drop by drop on Pete McForbes's pale knee?" Undoubtedly, both paternal and maternal influences are embedded in his psyche, but the voice of the mother is the one that has determined his affective make-up. Paradoxically, Charles identifies with his light-skinned father, the rebel who rejects the white mania and instills black consciousness in his son, but tries to eschew his dark-skinned mother, who lovingly teaches him invaluable lessons about suffering, resilience, and triumph in Estrada (like his mother's breasts, the soil of his hometown is also described as blackish, "el negruzco suelo" [33]). Ultimately, this aversion adversely affects the protagonist's ability to sustain a relationship with any woman. By the end of the novel, McForbes is beginning to appreciate those aspects of his West Indian–Atlantic Coast heritage that can be transferred and transformed into the Hispanic–central highlands environment, but he is still of two minds. To his credit, Charles sees his smiling brown face in the fourth mirror, the one installed in his household, and he accepts the self that must adapt to life with Esther in San José (if he stays with her). Nevertheless, the hero's recovery of his sight is only the genesis of an Afro–Costa Rican consciousness since the novel's outcome remains open.

The Four Mirrors is also a dialectic of ambivalence concerning Duncan's place, language, and identity as a writer. On the one side is the West Indian oral tradition of Anancy tales, musical forms (such as calypso), attitudes, religious beliefs, healing practices, customs, and values in all their richly performative aspects that he inherited during his upbringing in Limón Province. On the other is the weight and attraction of a chirographic (written) Western tradition made dominant by conquest and imposition. The challenge lies in reconciling these mutually exclusive spheres or having them come to terms with each other tangentially. As a step in that direction, Duncan deconstructs the Gisella/Bonifacia rupture by embodying the womb/tongue metaphor in the two wives of Charles McForbes. That is, Esther has the appearance of the ideal model of womanhood, but it is undermined by her ludicrously shallow personality. Moreover, she cannot truly articulate her longings and needs except in a stereotypically gendered fashion, which comes across quite pointedly in the scene when she tries to defend her marriage. Conversely, Lorena is an emotionally scarred woman who "deviates" from the ideal, but in talking back she learns to speak her true-true name before dying. Yet her assertiveness perhaps costs her her life.

The awkwardness of channeling an oral propensity (women are prone to tell their stories instead of writing them) into a written vehicle of communication is a difficulty that surfaces and resurfaces in African Hispanophone literature. For example, Juan Francisco Manzano's *Autobiography of a Slave* (1840), the only extant slave narrative in Spanish discourse, is a powerful testimony of an early writer's awkward attempts to revoice the master narrative in the mode of the black mother, even though the work follows a European model. No matter how much that author desires to write in the romantic vein or adapt other alien forms, the name/figure and voice that he constantly invokes are those of his mother, María del Pilar Manzano, in spite of the fact that the bulk of the narrative documents his turbulent relationship with his master's family.[19] In addition, from what Manzano states in his autobiography, he was not at all attuned to the African-descended oral traditions of the slaves in Cuba, although he undoubtedly heard some stories from his mother, godmother, and other members of the community of free people of color. Nevertheless, Manzano's work, like Duncan's novel, illustrates a historic ambivalence and confliction that have characterized black writing in the New World diaspora. Consequently, through the womb/tongue paradigm embodied in the Eve/Hagar figures, Esther and Lorena (and in Charles's unnamed mother), *The Four Mirrors* speaks to a text like the autobiography, within a counterdiscourse of murmuring, resistance, and dissent that contests the silencing and omission of the black female subject in Latin American literature.[20] Duncan will move closer to resolving that dilemma in *For the Sake of Peace.*

19. Manzano, *The Autobiography of a Slave/Autobiografía de un esclavo: A Bilingual Edition,* introduction and modernized Spanish version by Ivan Schulman, 44–45. This thesis might not be so farfetched when one considers the promise Manzano made in one of his letters to Domingo Del Monte that he would write a true Cuban novel someday. Of course, his premature death obliterated that dream, but the idea of achieving the goal of a true national consciousness reemerges in the Afro-Cuban movement of the twentieth century. There is an underlying connection that belies Manzano's peculiar circumstances and apparent disjuncture with the African-derived oral tradition. See, for example, Rosemary Geisdorfer Feal, "Feminist Interventions in the Race for Theory: Neither Black nor White," 17. Feal presents a compelling argument for assuming an invisible female support system in the works of male writers in her approach to teaching Manzano's autobiography. As her students read the slave narrative, along with Moreno Fraginals's essay "Cultural Contributions and Deculturation" and bell hooks's "Sexism and the Black Female Experience" (in *Ain't I a Woman?*), they were posed a series of questions designed to elicit responses about networking: Was Manzano a typical slave? What was his relationship to writing, and how was he able to gain literacy? Were there any female slaves who did likewise? How was Manzano connected to his mistresses, and how was their interaction with him determined by race and gender? The class wanted to fill in the gaps of Manzano's narrative with invisible black females.

20. Beatriz Pastor, "Silence and Writing: The History of the Conquest," 124.

# 4

## THE HOUSE OF MOODY IN
### *For the Sake of Peace*

*For the Sake of Peace* (1978) is an intriguing historical novel and murder mystery of a young woman who is raped, savagely beaten, and cast into the Pacuare River in Limón Province, Costa Rica. Moreover, the central conflict of the work involves the competition of two young men—the rebel protagonist, Pedro Dull, and the conservative antagonist, Cató Brown—for the affection of the victim, Sitaira Kenton. Although the evidence strongly implicates Cató, Pedro is accused of Sitaira's murder, as well as organizing a strike of banana workers, and he is arrested by the local authorities. He turns himself in and at the end of the novel is awaiting trial. *For the Sake of Peace* is structured around an incident in a small town whose tranquillity is interrupted by the impact of the labor movements of the depression era, in particular the one led by Marcus Garvey. Moreover, the plot reflects a series of historical events that caused the United Fruit Company to lose millions of dollars.[1] On a broader and deeper level, however, the narrative fictionalizes the conflictive forces of Caribbean history over a period of one hundred years from the abolition of Jamaican slavery in 1833 to Jamaican emigration to Costa Rica in the 1930s. Furthermore, *For the Sake of Peace* illustrates many techniques of the new novel, especially with regard to its treatment of time and space. The juggling of past and present, as well as the pendular movement from Jamaica to tropical Costa Rica, allows for the unfolding of a concurrent view of history.[2]

---

1. Royal and Perry, "Costa Rica," 221.
2. Salas Zamora, "Identidad cultural," 378–80. All translated quotations from this essay are my own.

One of the features of the work that commands our attention is the role of its women, who reenact the century-old drama of slavery, oppression, and neocolonialism. Beginning with the youngest and moving back in time, there are five female characters whose stories are interwoven with that of Pedro Dull. The first is Sitaira Kenton, a carefree, elusive figure whose ghost becomes the focus of unresolved conflicts in the community. Second is Sitaira's mother, Mariot Prince Kenton, a social pariah because of her obscure origins and reputation for practicing witchcraft. In addition, both mother and daughter are considered "loose" by other women in the town. Third is Elizabeth Moody Prince, Mariot's mother and Sitaira's grandmother, who during her lifetime is forced to give up her plantation inheritance after consorting with the Haitian freedman Joshua Prince (Mariot's father and Sitaira's grandfather). Fourth is Margaret Moody Dull, Elizabeth's twin sister, who gains custody of her niece, Mariot, after her sibling's premature death. Last and certainly least is Mammy, the ex-slave concubine of Kingsman Moody and surrogate mother to his twin daughters. Yet it is the oral narrative of Mariot Kenton that gives order and meaning to the lives of the dead women as the particularities of Caribbean history play out in the novel. Because she gives voice to her female ancestors and progeny, Mariot is not a secondary character, but emerges as a "cotagonist" with Pedro. Through the tragic story of one female survivor, multiple views of women emerge in the novel, although tradition depicts them primarily as wives/mothers, or conduits of reproduction (the womb). In these roles they are expected not to enter "male space" but instead to remain silent (control the tongue). The preeminence of body suggests *cosificación,* or the objectifying of females in the male imagination. Hence the issues of race/color, gender/sex, and class/caste influence the manner in which the characters of the novel attempt to find a voice through which they will become speaking subjects. Their struggle is concretized in the womb/tongue dialectic, which is an interactive part of the Eve/Hagar paradigm.

In their efforts to inscribe their own identities in history, the women of *For the Sake of Peace* display numerous aspects of the Eve/Hagar paradigm. Because they represent the human condition, they are automatically connected to Eve, but in their capacity for dealing with pain, dislocation, and trauma they evoke Hagar. Moreover, their stories achieve coherence through the first- and third-person narrative voices of Mariot Kenton, but the latter is interwoven with the voice of an omniscient (presumably male) narrator who presents what approximates an official (written) version of history. Paulette Ramsay discusses the use of an omniscient narrator for "communicating the mental images which the Euro–Costa Rican characters hold of Afro–Costa Ricans, since the narrator has privileged access to their thoughts, feelings and motives. For the most part, the author employs this omniscient or third person narrator in an intrusive manner and indicates either by the tone or through the language the narrator commands, the judgments that are to be made by the reader."[3] A more complex version of this dialectic in certain passages of the novel is the placement of a double-voiced omniscient narrator in opposition to a womanist text. Therefore, the dialectic between written and oral accounts is one of the mainstays of the work, which can be restated by considering the parallels among the Eve/Hagar, womb/tongue, and head/hand metaphors. That is, within the context of the encoded discourse that has conventionally been the domain of male writers, the "text" of women's speech defiantly asserts itself from within the veil.

The concept of the maroon narrative is also an excellent approach for analyzing the Eve/Hagar paradigm in the female characters of *For the Sake of Peace*. According to Josaphat Kubayanda, "maroon narrative or poetry deals with marooning and with an underground discursive scheme unfamiliar to dominant discourse." The term *maroon* evokes the slave rebellions and other black resistance movements of the seventeenth through nineteenth centuries in Brazil, Cuba, Ecuador, Jamaica, Haiti, Mexico, and Suriname (as well as the United States). In addition, "marooning enabled the runaway slaves both to challenge and to escape the plantation or post-plantation order. But it was also intended to articulate as independently as possible and within the colonial structure, the socio-cultural and spiritual modes of being of the minority activists. It made it impossible for the dominant order to assume complete control of the discursive world."[4] The radical protagonist, Pedro Dull, is obviously modeled after heroes like Macandal, Cudjoe, Baron and Araby, José Antonio Aponte, and Yanga, to name a few. Less evident in *For the Sake of Peace* is the resistance of the women, who do not

3. Ramsay, "Quince Duncan's Literary Representation of the Ethno-racial Dynamics between Latinos and Afro–Costa Ricans of West Indian Descent," 52.
4. Kubayanda, "Minority Discourse and the African Collective: Some Examples from Latin American and Caribbean Literature," 124.

necessarily engage in open revolt, but through whom a counterdiscourse emerges.

Sitaira is the first figure that embodies the Eve/Hagar paradigm, for it is her funeral in chapters 1, 7, and 8 that frames the incidents. Moreover, her ghost is projected in Pedro's flashbacks, memories, and visions, as well as her mother's dreams, memories, and tales. These parts make up the present, or external narrative, of the novel. Sitaira's romance with Pedro Dull and her rape and murder by Cató in chapters 3, 4, and 5 constitute an inner story of the immediate past. Chapters 2 and 6 form the central core of the remote past. Sitaira is a *prieta,* a dark brown–skinned beauty who is intelligent and independent. In addition, her name (from Latin *cithara* or Greek *kithara*) is derived from the term for "a 30-to-40 stringed lute or musical instrument similar to the modern guitar."[5] This appellation identifies the young character as a person filled with laughter, music, and vitality.

Like Eve and Hagar, Sitaira inhabits domestic space, cooking and housecleaning, but she also intrudes on male territory, performing the heavy labor on the family's farm because her aging and disabled parents cannot do so. Her only sibling, Leonard, is dead. In spite of household responsibilities, the young woman refuses to be domesticated, which in her town means getting married. Thus, Sitaira's fierce assertion of independence is evident in a conversation recalled by her mother, Mariot:

> "Anybody can see that boy love you..."
> "Aw, Mama, tha's what you say. How he gon' love me? He been everywhere, done had too many women to end up fallin' for a country girl like me..."
> "That ain't got nothin' to do with it, child. Yo grandmama..."
> "What about my grandmama?"
> "She was a rich lady and she left everything fo' love..."
> "She was a woman and everybody already know how stupid we women is. But men don' leave nothin' fo' nobody."
> "Where you git such crazy notions from? Who say us women stupid? And I'll tell you somethin' else. I done seen some men leave everything fo' a woman who ain't worth it."

5. *Webster's New World Dictionary of the American Language,* s.v. "sitar."

(—De lejos se ve que ese muchacho te quiere...
—Son cosas tuyas, mamá: ¿qué me va a querer? El ha estado
en tantas partes, ha conocido a tantas mujeres como para ter-
minar enamorado de una campesina como yo...
—Eso no tiene nada que ver, hija: tu abuela...
—¿Mi abuela qué?
—Era una mujer muy rica y lo dejó todo por el amor...
—Era mujer y ya se sabe que las mujeres somos tontas. Pero
los hombres no dejan nada por uno.
—¿De dónde me salís con esas ideas? ¿Quién dice que las mu-
jeres somos tontas? Y te voy a decir que yo he visto cada hom-
bre dejar todo por una mujer que a veces ni vale la pena.)[6]

In spite of the "crazy notions" Sitaira expresses about women, she
has a lot of self-confidence, which the men of the community take
for arrogance, and she plots the course of her life oblivious to what
other people think. Moreover, she is literate and articulate, but she
"code switches," or changes easily from formal to vernacular forms
of language, when communicating with her mother:

"Well, I guess he *is* a womanizer, but now that he in love
with you, he gon' settle down."
"Stop dreamin', Mama."
"It's time fo' a change in yo' life. Work on this here farm's
too hard fo' you, and you know Cornelius ain't gon' get no
better."
"I ain't fo' sale, Mama. Neither am I gon' support no gigolo."
"But Pedro is hardworkin'..."
"Mama, you woke up a lil' dense this mornin'."

(—Es un trotamundos, pero ahora que está enamorado de vos
a lo mejor asienta cabeza.
—Mamá, dejá de soñar.
—Es hora de que busqués un cambio de vida: el trabajo de la
finca es demasiado duro para vos y lo que es Cornelio, no da
señal de componerse.
—No estoy en venta, mamá. Ni voy a mantener a ningún
tarado...
—Pedro es trabajador...
—Hoy amaneciste necia.) (21)

---

6. Duncan, *La paz del pueblo*, 16. All subsequent quotations will be cited
parenthetically; all translations are my own.

Like Eve, Sitaira is assertive, and she deals with her mother as an equal, which is evident in her bold remarks about waking up a "lil' dense." This is not so unusual in view of the social ostracism to which mother and daughter are subjected. Thus, friendship is the only true relationship they enjoy. Nevertheless, the trait known as "talking back" is considered dangerous in females—girl children *and* women—because it means that they are inclined to question authority.[7] Perhaps that is why the town gossips depict Sitaira as brazen and promiscuous, for the young woman does not adhere to the standards of behavior the community feels are appropriate for her color, gender, and class. Instead, she incarnates the womb/tongue metaphor, positioning herself against communal expectations of female conduct and verbalizing such without qualms.

Conversely, Sitaira exhibits the conflictive behavior that seems to characterize many women in Antillean societies. Pat Ellis observes:

> Within society attitudes to male-female relationships and to marriage are ambivalent and contradictory. On the one hand girls are taught from an early age strategies to ensure their survival and that of their families whether a male is present or not. This creates a sense of independence—hence the image of the strong Caribbean women who can cope with anything. At the same time they are also taught that it is not only desirable, but important, to have a male partner; that in the male-female relationship the man is dominant and that the woman is not free to do as she wishes but must defer to her mate.[8]

The reader gradually learns to question the "whore image" of Sitaira as it becomes obvious that both she and her mother are targets of the envious hatred of other mothers and daughters who wish to get Pedro's attention. Although *For the Sake of Peace* presents female voices in a male-authored text, Duncan's characterization of Sitaira militates against the "feminine mode" of portrayal, or the use of the language, images, rhetoric, and literary conventions that reflect the patriarchal view of the female experience. The "feminine mode" is utilized "to characterize a form of literary expression, which reinforces, through appeal to sentiment rather than to intellect, conventional images of women as nurturers who inhabit

---

7. Hooks, *Talking Back,* 9.
8. Ellis, "Introduction: An Overview of Women in Caribbean Society," 8.

domestic spaces; which underscores the sexual and reproductive roles of females; and which dichotomizes women, idealizing them as virgins and goddesses or denigrating them as whores and witches."[9] Sitaira's "femininity" is deconstructed in that she is a devoted caretaker of her parents *and* a sturdy laborer on the farmstead, which can be gender-neutral roles depending on one's circumstances. Yet Duncan does romanticize the initial encounter between Sitaira and Pedro in a scene the latter recalls as he muses on the banks of the Pacuare River: "He looked at the river again and saw her. She was coming toward him, naked, incredibly beautiful, ancestral, and pristine, bubbling with life" (Volvió a mirar el río y la vio: venía hacia él, desnuda, increíblemente hermosa, ancestral y primitiva espesando la sangre, 9). Sitaira seems to Pedro like Eve must have appeared to Adam the first time he saw her, and it is an image the protagonist evokes repeatedly as he mourns his beloved. Although captivated by Sitaira's physical beauty, Pedro is also attracted to her personality—her liveliness, spunk, and rebellious spirit. For example, he also remembers her playful bantering and speculates on the type of conversation they might be having in the present: "'What a cursed life,' he would have told her; and she would have answered, 'Don't be insolent, you blockhead. But crude as you are, I still love you, you bandit'" ("Qué maldita vida le habría dicho y ella; no seás insolente, malcriado. Pero mal hablado y todo te quiero bandido," 9). The interplay of mind and body reduces the saccharin propensity of the love scene in which female and male function complementarily and interdependently.

Conversely, the breathtaking natural beauty of their Eden is converted into a garden of evil, where the jealous Cató Brown gains voyeuristic pleasure from watching the couple. After Cató rapes and murders Sitaira, the place becomes a mud hole replete with decay, destruction, and death—symbolized by the suffocating jungle, killer ants, and circling vultures.[10] This is the concrete reality of Limón Province for those who work its land, and the nightmarish qualities of that torrid setting are illustrated in a scene in which the two grave diggers await Sitaira's funeral cortege:

> "Me, I say this: life ain't worth crap here. This heat . . . Ed, this dam' heat that make ya' drink jarsful of water, that slowly dry

9. DeCosta-Willis, "Afra-Hispanic Writers," 251.
10. Mosby, *Place, Language, and Identity*, 151–53.

you out, that suck yo' bones; this cursed jungle, where a soul
can die all by hisself of anything, and they still work ya' to
death. That's what I mean."

(—Yo lo que digo es esto: que la vida no vale ni mierda aquí.
Este calor... Ed, este maldito calor que lo obliga a uno a beber
agua en tarros de avena, que le va secando a uno de todos
modos, hasta los huesos; esta selva maldita, donde uno con
cualquier cosa se muere, solito, y todavía lo matan a uno. Eso
es lo que yo digo.) (15)

The word *they* refers to the neocolonial systems that have continued
to subjugate the people after the legal abolition of slavery, specifically the North American and English recruiters who baited Antillean workers with El Dorado promises. The love-nest and cemetery
scenes bring together the religious themes of the Adamic/Evenian
exile from paradise, the Hagarian expulsion from Abraham's home,
and the West Indian subject's exile from Jamaica.[11] Thus, images
of dispersal, confinement, and death evoke colonial history as the
present segues back into the remote past through the consciousness
of Sitaira's mother.

In chapters 2 and 6 of *For the Sake of Peace,* the reader is trans-
ported to the postemancipation epoch in Jamaica, the history of
which is essential for piecing together the life of Mariot Prince Kenton, the second Eve-Hagar figure but the most important female
voice in the story. In effect, "The novel's two 'Jamaica chapters'...
display a circularity in the development of events that are repeated
by other characters in Costa Rica. Additionally, these chapters dis-
close the racial dynamic and structure of postcolonial Jamaican society, which leads to the expulsion or exile in Costa Rica. The second 'Jamaica chapter' provides background on the parentage of
Mariot."[12] Into written (men's) history—symbolized by the conflict
between management and labor—Duncan folds oral (women's) narrative, which starts with Sitaira's female ancestors and is brought
up to the time of her demise. When Mariot's white mother, Elizabeth
Moody Prince, dies and her black father, Joshua Prince, is no longer
able to care for her, she is ostensibly rescued by her maternal aunt,
Margaret Moody Dull, who tells her family: "'I need somebody to

11. Ibid., 149.
12. Ibid.

take care of my son, and Mariot can do it. That's all I'm trying to do: employ her so that our blood might not wander about destitute'" (—Necesito [a] alguien que se ocupe de mi hijo y Mariot lo puede hacer. Eso es todo lo que pretendo: emplearla para que nuestra sangre no ande rodando, 126). However, the aunt's "altruism" is a form of exploitation since her son is almost as big and old as his prospective nursemaid. In this manner Margaret avenges the dishonor brought upon her family by her sister's inappropriate relationship with their former slave.

At first Mariot is too young to choose options since she has to depend on the goodwill of people who are relatives and strangers at the same time. Besides getting severe whippings, Mariot is constantly reminded of her parents' "sins." The young girl's torment is even greater as she remembers her mother's tender, loving care, except during those final days when the ravages of tuberculosis did not allow for much physical contact. Mariot's dependent status has thrust her into the age-old conflict between mistress/adult and servant/child in spite of their blood relationship. Margaret Dull, a frustrated, enraged, and neglected wife, uses her body as a weapon against another defenseless female, playing the double role of executioner and victim in the body-trap game. In short, Margaret is "top dog" in the proverbial pecking order, which is an unequal battle with severely limited choices for the victim. The young girl might opt for suicide, flight, or defiance, all of which bring the risk of further abuse or death or both.

Mariot's leap of consciousness occurs when her aunt flogs her during a spell of premenstrual syndrome while they are on board a luxury cruiser in the Caribbean. As the child coughs, she begins to suspect the worst, remembering how her mother had gasped for breath on her deathbed. For that reason, the girl makes a conscious decision:

> She was counseled by who knows what hidden force of the *samamfo,* which made her capable of this supreme act of rebellion.
>
> No one saw her leave, but when Miss Margaret checked the dressing room, neither she nor her Sunday dress was there.
>
> The money her mother had left under the pillow (fifty pounds sterling that someone had exchanged for a coin she did not recognize) only got her detained and delivered to a Mr. Miguelino Sánchez Bonilla, a white man who could hardly speak English.

That seemed strange to her because English was the language of white people.

(Aconsejada por quién sabe qué oculta fuerza del samamfo, que la hizo capaz del supremo acto de la rebelión.

Nadie la vio partir, pero cuando la señora Margaret revisó el camerino, no estaba ni siquiera su ropa de domingo.

El dinero que su madre había dejado debajo de la almohada (cincuenta libras esterlinas que alguien cambió por una moneda que ella no entendía bien), le sirvió para que fuera detenida y presentada a don Miguelino Sánchez Bonilla, un blanco que apenas sabía hablar inglés. Eso le parecía curioso porque el inglés es el idioma de los blancos.) (132–33)

Thirteen-year-old Mariot opts for *cimarronaje* (marronage), or rebellion and flight, but that alternative makes her vulnerable to further exploitation. Although she finds respite from her aunt's authority, she falls into another form of servitude as a domestic in the household of the pedophile Miguelino Sánchez Bonilla, who whisks her away to Costa Rica. In essence, the girl's escape from a ship of fools evokes Hagar's flight into the wilderness as well as numerous suicides of her female descendants during the Middle Passage, who "jumped ship" into shark-infested waters rather than face unspeakable horrors. Implicit in Duncan's stories "Two Roads" and "The Pocomía Rebellion," but explicit in "Ancestral Myths," the *samamfo* is a full-blown symbol of rebellion in *For the Sake of Peace*. Furthermore, it is part of four cardinal tropes in the novel: the *samamfo,* the *cimarrón,* laughter, and the river.[13]

The preceding excerpt also signals a turning point in the narrative perspective with the appearance of a double-voiced omniscient narrator. The first half of the passage (up to the reference to Mariot's Sunday dress) suggests a voice that is attuned to an Afrocentric oral tradition and, thus, one that emits the call of the *samamfo* to which Mariot responds. The second part (from the allusion to the money to the end) represents an intrusive presence, but one that is more reportorial than judgmental. Mariot's mistaken notion about English as the language of white people signifies the color and ethnicity of wealth, power, and privilege in the Caribbean, where "real white people," that is, Anglo-Saxons, are perceived as superior to

13. Smart, *Amazing Connections,* 145.

pretenders like her Spanish-speaking Costa Rican "benefactor." Essentially, the girl's revolt particularizes the Eve/Hagar paradigm in that through the womb/tongue metaphor, Sánchez Bonilla sexually abuses Mariot while she silently ridicules his use of English.

In *For the Sake of Peace,* mutiny begins with Mariot's mother, Elizabeth Moody Prince, who reminds the North American reader of Scarlett O'Hara. Arrogant, pampered, and unruly, Elizabeth rejects the concept of ladyhood defined by Victorian society, which is extolled in a poem by one of her beaux/suitors and set to music by the dark people who still work on the place in the postemancipation period:

> "Oh, little lady, little lady:
> your eyes sparkle like flowers
> your delicate hands like an exquisite palm tree . . ."
>
> ("Oh, pequeña mujer, pequeña mujer:
> tus ojos brillan como las flores
> tus manos finas; palma mayor . . .")
> (40)

Instead, Elizabeth imagines herself as "sugar cane, sweet and strong, delicious and aggressive at the same time" (era como la caña, dulce y fuerte, deliciosa y agresiva a la vez, 40). The author reverses imagery in this scene, contrapositioning the idea of the dainty, fragile, and virtuous creature of Western invention with a flesh-and-blood person with real physical needs and desires. The sweet, strong, and supple sugar cane is something to be savored (alliteration intended), here implying Elizabeth's budding consciousness of her sexuality. Like her granddaughter, Sitaira, would do in her own time, thirteen-year-old Elizabeth Moody loves to wander about the estate in "natural fashion," perfectly in tune with the birds and bees, but causing much consternation in the Big House as well as the quarters. Thus, one is not at all surprised when, after failing to intimidate the fiercely proud ex-slave Joshua with "the voice of authority," Elizabeth relentlessly pursues him with her body, enticing him into her bedroom where his fall is inevitable:

> "Who is it?"
> "Joshua"—uttered in a firm voice, and Little Missy's heart exploded with joy.

"Oh, just a minute."

But she did not put on any clothes. Wrapping herself in a sheet, she told him to come in. The youth entered the room in his Sunday best, his black skin sparkling from a recent bath. He was carrying a bouquet of jasmine in one hand, and in the other a felt hat with an elegant feather.

"I was goin' to church and saw these flowers and brought 'em to you."

Timid Joshua. Tame Joshua now. His boldness was gone with the wind. Then she did not need to blush at all. He was hers now. She had won. Conquered Joshua. Joshua?

"Thank you," she sings, as she takes the flowers and lets go of the sheet, revealing her bold nakedness in all its glory. "Oh, dear," she pretends to be perturbed, and he leaps toward her, trying to cover her up, "I'm so sorry, Missy," as if *he* were to blame for the incident in the orchard, and his original sin made him retreat a discreet distance from her.

(—¿Quién es?

—Josué—firme su voz y en el pecho de la señorita saltó la alegría.

—¡Oh! Espérame un poco.

Pero no se puso la ropa. Envolviéndose en una sábana le dijo que pasara. El muchacho entró luciendo ropas de domingo, su piel opaca señalando el baño recién tomado. Portaba una ramita de jazmines en una mano y en la otra, un sombrero de felpa con una elegante pluma.

—Iba para la Iglesia y vi estas flores y se las traje.

Josué tímido. Josué tímido ahora. Su intrepidez se fugó con el viento.

Entonces ya ella no sintió rubor alguno. Había triunfado. Josué vencido. Josué.

—Gracias...—tomándolas soltó la sábana que entonces dejó al descubierto la mayor parte de su cuerpo y ella dijo "Oh" fingiendo desconcierto y él, precipitándose hacia ella la cubría murmurando "Lo siento señorita" como si hubiera sido culpable de la escena del huerto, y su culpa original lo hizo retirarse a prudente distancia.) (50–51)

The impulsive behavior of Elizabeth, a female of some intelligence although not much formal education, allows her to fall victim to the body trap, thus tipping the scales toward the physical end of the

Eve/Hagar paradigm. Ironically, it is amazing that she is attracted
to a type she has been taught to despise, a question that her family
violently raises just before they kick the two of them off the plantation. As we see from the passage, the tremendous shock waves
that the black male–white female liaison sends throughout Western
society engulf colonial and postcolonial history.[14] From the perspective of the hegemonic classes, such a union represents the unravel-
ing of the social fabric, as articulated in Kingsman Moody's lament
for his "lost daughter":

> "Daddy...I think that we ought to forgive Elizabeth."
> "Never," said the old man, and he turned pale again. "I'll
> never forgive her...That woman trampled on my honor. And
> she had no shame, no sense of decency when she did it, Mar-
> garet; she was not considerate in the least. I, who am some-
> body like Kingsman Moody, a personal friend of the present
> governor and friend to all who have owned this cursed island
> since my father's era. I...I had to walk with my head down,
> without knowing how to face Jamaican society. What she did
> does not have a name."
>
> (—Papá...yo creo que debemos perdonar a Elizabeth.
> —Perdonarla jamás—dijo el viejo, y de nuevo la piel de su
> cuerpo se mudó de color. Eso nunca: esa mujer pisoteó mi
> honor. No tuvo empacho en hacerlo, Margaret, no tuvo con-
> sideraciones. Yo, nada menos que Kingsman Moody, amigo
> personal del gobernador actual y amigo de todos los que ha[n]
> tenido esta condenada isla desde los días de mi padre, yo...yo
> tuve que andar con la cabeza inclinada, sin saber cómo en-
> frentarme a la sociedad jamaicana...Lo que hizo...no tiene
> nombre.) (124–25)

Elizabeth Moody Prince is calibanesque in her rebellion against her
assigned social role, but she succeeds in creating only a different,
not necessarily better, life for herself. In addition, Duncan's play on
the name Prince, and the concept of royalty it suggests, ironically
underscores the reversal of images and roles in this portion of the
novel. When Elizabeth and Joshua (whose name evokes the great
warrior of the Battle of Jericho) are discovered, they are thrown

14. Mosby, *Place, Language, and Identity*, 150–51.

into a pigsty by Kingsman Moody and his overseer/foreman, but it is she who picks up the young man, brushes him off, and leads him away to seek their fortune elsewhere. Whatever happiness Elizabeth has with Joshua is blighted by the fact that they live in poverty, and when she succumbs prematurely to tuberculosis, their beloved daughter, Mariot, is first neglected by her alcoholic father, Joshua, then abused by Elizabeth's vindictive twin sister, Margaret. Consequently, the images of the gallant warrior and prince charming collide with reality.

Like Eve, Elizabeth's independence and backbone cost her paradise, at least from the point of view of a patriarchal society, for she loses wealth, privilege, position, and protection. Similar to Hagar, the young woman is banished from the only family she has, and she must fend for herself in a brave new (cold) world. Thus, the Little Mistress soon learns that the armor of her shining Black Prince will not shield her or her daughter from the hostility and rejection occasioned by her downfall, because Jamaican society will never allow her to forget her part in bringing down the House of Moody. In short, Elizabeth's choice of Joshua as a mate is a travesty of an institutionalized way of life based on an ideology of racial, gendered, and class-conscious hierarchization. For that reason, Duncan "blackens" Elizabeth, or portrays her as one who suffers because of guilt by association with Joshua, thus connecting her to a long tradition of historical and literary outcasts like Hagar. Elizabeth has a direct encounter with Afro-realism.

Margaret Moody Dull, twin sister of the Prodigal Daughter who never goes home again, inherits the family fortune and marries the n'er-do-well Mr. Dull, who wastes her inheritance on wine, women, and song. In contrast to Elizabeth, she becomes the epitome of ladyhood, a concept that was mythified during the nineteenth century. Bell hooks provides a provocative slant on that subject, indicating that the growing economic prosperity of the United States led white Americans to move away from the Puritan religious teachings that had shaped their value system. Accompanying the rejection of fundamentalist Christian doctrine was a change in male perceptions of women. By the nineteenth century white women were no longer regarded as sexual temptresses, which was a legacy of Eve in much misogynist literature. Instead, they were extolled as the "nobler half of humanity." Thus, "ladies" became responsible for directing men's sentiments toward higher impulses. Hooks further comments:

The new image of white womanhood was diametrically opposed to the old image. She was depicted as goddess rather
than sinner; she was virtuous, pure, innocent, not sexual and
wor[l]dly. By raising the white female to a goddess-like status,
white men effectively removed the stigma Christianity had
placed on them. White male idealization of white women as innocent and virtuous served as an act of exorcism, which had
as its purpose transforming her image and ridding her of the
curse of sexuality. The message of the idealization was this: as
long as white women possessed sexual feeling they would be
seen as degraded immoral creatures; remove those sexual feelings and they become beings worthy of love, consideration,
and respect. Once the white female was mythologized as pure
and virtuous, a symbolic virgin Mary, white men could see her
as exempt from negative sexist stereotypes of the female. The
price she had to pay was the suppression of natural impulses.[15]

Like Eve, Margaret Moody Dull must undergo a radical transformation of her will to adjust to an attitude of submission, which a
proper lady must display at all times. Yet she defies her father somewhat by conspiring with Mammy to bring Mariot home after Elizabeth's death. Unfortunately, Margaret unleashes on the child all
the frustration and jealous rage she cannot direct toward her phi-
landering husband and dead sister. She is ambivalent toward her
niece, wanting to shelter the girl but resenting her as a reminder of
the family's shame. This conflictive stance drives Margaret to replicate the biblical Sarah's and her dead mother's pattern of intolerant
behavior toward her servants; therefore, she is the only one of the
five female characters in *For the Sake of Peace* who does not share
any aspect of the Hagar mode. Instead, Margaret embodies the idea
that the transformation of white female iconology from sexual/
sinful woman to asexual/virtuous lady accompanied the mass sexual exploitation of the black female slave or ex-slave, "just as the
rigid sexual morality of Victorian England created a society in which
the extolling of woman as mother and helpmeet occurred at the
same time as the formation of a mass underworld of prostitution."[16]
To reiterate, Elizabeth Moody Prince and Margaret Moody Dull
are socialized according to Victorian morality, which the former

15. Hooks, *Ain't I a Woman?* 31.
16. Ibid., 32.

rejects and the latter embraces. Ironically, the response of the "obe-
dient" twin to their father's lampoon reminds him of his own crucial
role in the scheme of things: " 'Daddy, the only difference between
you and Elizabeth is that what she did was public' " (—Papá ... la
única diferencia entre usted y Elizabeth es que lo de ella se hizo
público, 125). In spite of choosing different paths both sisters ex-
hibit calibanesque tendencies that differ in degree, not kind.

Within the vortex of race, sex, and class is the European/white
man, represented by Kingsman Moody and the generations of slave
masters before him. Also caught up in the whirlwind is Mammy,
slave/concubine to Kingsman Moody and surrogate mother to his
daughters before and after the death of his wife, Elizabeth Margaret
Moody. "Raised" by Moody's father, freed shortly thereafter, and
"treated with deference" by the Moody men, Mammy lives under
the illusion that she is "queen" of the household, even though socially she must play second fiddle to Moody's spouse, when the latter is alive. In fact, Mammy views her new status as a vindication
of her past enslavement, for it is a question of survival and security,
although the latter is more imagined than real. However, as Mammy
bitterly reminisces through interior monologue and dialogue about
her life in the House of Moody, she reveals that she is more a victim
than she realizes. She, too, is caught in the body trap, as apparent
in her conversation with an unidentified interlocutor:

> "I was loyal to both of them for certain: to one because he
> had the decency to separate me from my girlhood ..."
> "Separate you from what?"
> "From the other slaves, because I was too pretty to be mixed
> up with so many brutes."
> "Oh, now I understand!"

> (—Les fui fiel a los dos por cierto; a uno porque desde niña
> tuvo la fineza de apartarme ...
> —¿Te apartó de qué?
> —De los otros esclavos, porque yo era demasiado linda para
> andar así entre tantos brutos.
> —Ah ... ¡eso!) (138)

As Mammy continues to reminisce about her past ordeal, she still
vacillates between fantasy and reality concerning her relationship
with the slave master and his son:

"It's not that I thought about marrying him or anything like
that. After all, a person knows her place. What pained me is
that he didn't even think about me until he got tired of that
skinny little twerp. . . . And now this one's let me down, too,
especially him because with his father it was just a matter of
gratitude.

"But I loved Kingsman . . . I curse that white man . . . I curse
all white people!"

(—No es que yo pensaba casarme con él ni nada. Uno sabe
cuál es su lugar. Lo que me duele es que no se acordara de mí
hasta que empezó a cansarse de la flaca esa . . .

Y ahora, este; él sobre todas las cosas, porque con el padre
fue simple gratitud.

—A Kingsman lo amé . . . maldito blanco . . . ¡malditos todos
los blancos!) (139)

Mammy's dilemma is that of the African-descended woman caught
in a web of circumstances that has entrapped her even in the contemporary era. In addition, her statement of affection for Kingsman
Moody Jr. suggests that she is a "willing" party to her degradation.
Whether Mammy actually "loves her master" is debatable, and it
might very well be the voice of a male author speaking through and
for his character—in other words, gazing on the female as object.
The historical fact is that many enslaved African-descended females
resigned themselves to sexual abuse, retrieving whatever question-
able benefits they could from exploitative relationships. The line of
demarcation between love (eros) and rape is often blurred, and the
application of the terms to specific situations usually depends on a
female's race and class in a society that devalues difference, which
is perceived as a negative otherness.[17]

The incidents in chapters 2 and 6 of *For the Sake of Peace* occur
in Jamaica, an outpost of the British Empire in the Americas. However, in Spanish American countries, African-descended women are
in a similar position of marginality. Lorna V. Williams examines
the condition of female characters of color in *Francisco, El negro
Francisco,* and *Cecilia Valdés,* three Cuban antislavery novels of
the nineteenth century:

It was generally assumed throughout the Americas that blacks
were creatures of nature rather than of culture. Since blacks

17. Ibid., 53.

were primarily engaged in agricultural tasks, the essence of their being was readily equated with the field of their economic activities. In the case of the black woman, the tendency to perceive her as an elemental creature was even more pronounced because she shared the social environment of the black male and consequently was displaced from the moral domain assigned to the members of her sex. In a slave society like nineteenth-century Cuba, where social contact between blacks and whites was regulated by custom and law, the black woman came to be regarded as an exotic presence, at once a productive member of the society, yet outside the prevailing norms of accepted feminine behavior.[18]

Cecilia Valdés is the hot-blooded *mulata,* who is attractive to white men because she is light-skinned. Nevertheless, her position is not too far removed from that of Mammy. Like women of all races, African-descended females have historically been valued mostly for their sexual/reproductive capacities (wombs). However, in contrast to white females, black women have been less likely to elicit admiration, respect, and affection from males of any race. For example, this double standard creates a tremendous conflict within Kingsman Moody Jr. as he reminisces about the pleasures of a massage from Mammy: "Freed by Queen Victoria . . . but still black. Taken by his father, educated, even considered almost like one of the family, but she wore that eternal curse on her skin. She was black" (Liberada por la Reina Victoria . . . pero negra. Recogida por su padre, educada, considerada casi casi de su familia, pero tenía en su piel la eterna condenación: era negra, 46–47). The social construct of race and the physical reality of blackness combine to undermine the biological necessity of gender/sex, and they relegate Mammy to a caste from which she cannot escape.

Duncan's use of the name Mammy to identify this character is pregnant with ambiguity. On the one hand, it suggests an Aunt Jemima figure, one of the favorite stereotypes entrenched in the North American psyche—an asexual, usually fat, long-suffering but, above all, submissive character. Hooks observes:

> The mammy image was portrayed with affection by whites because it epitomized the ultimate sexist-racist vision of ideal

18. Williams, "From Dusky Venus to *Mater Dolorosa:* The Female Protagonist in the Cuban Antislavery Novel," 121.

black womanhood—complete submission to the will of whites. In a sense whites created in the mammy figure a black woman who embodied solely those characteristics they as colonizers wished to exploit. They saw her as the embodiment of woman as passive nurturer, a mother figure who gave all without expectation of return, who not only acknowledged her inferiority to whites but who loved them. The mammy as portrayed by whites poses no threat to the existing white patriarchal social order for she totally submits to the white racist regime.[19]

Mammy's devotion to the Moody twins seems to substantiate that image. On the other hand, Duncan utilizes the name Mammy as a signifier for an inner reality that subverts the stereotype, just as minstrelsy, as it was originally conceived by anonymous slaves/artists, ridiculed the antics of southern whites, who, in turn, imitated what they thought was black reality. In essence, Mammy's testimony is the story of a broken-spirited woman torn between her need to survive and her dream of emerging unscathed from the experience. Contrary to the stereotype, this character is physically beautiful, literate, and energetic even though advanced in years. She is also grateful for having been spared the lash, although she has been scarred emotionally. Mammy is poignantly aware that her "elevated station" in the Big House allows her to occupy only a devalued place/space in the hierarchy, which makes her status a caricature of the womb/tongue metaphor.

According to the tradition of Hagar, the tragedy of Mammy is that of all oppressed females, but especially women who have experienced slavery in the African diaspora. In her provocative study *Just a Sister Away,* Renita J. Weems contextualizes Hagar within the relationship between privileged women of the Bible and their slaves/servants:

> For black women, the story of Hagar in the Old Testament Book of Genesis is a haunting one. It is a story of exploitation and persecution suffered by an Egyptian slave woman at the hands of her Hebrew mistress. Even if it is not our individual story, it is a story we have read in our mothers' eyes those afternoons when we greeted them at the front door after a hard day of work as a domestic. And if not our mothers' story, then it is

19. Hooks, *Ain't I a Woman?* 84–85.

certainly most of our grandmothers' story. For black women, Hagar's story is peculiarly familiar. It is as if we know it by heart.[20]

Mammy attempts to gain a measure of freedom by acquiescence and subterfuge, mistakenly believing that she has the upper hand in the power struggle between herself and Elizabeth Margaret Moody. In this sense, the literary concubine imitates the behavior of the historical Hagar, who became arrogant toward Sarai after her sexual relationship with Abram. "And when she [Hagar] saw that she had conceived, her mistress was despised in her eyes" (Gen. 16:4). It is not certain whether Mammy's only son has been sired by Kingsman Moody, but we do know that she nurses his twin daughters because their own mother refuses to do so. That is why Mammy shows contempt for the "weakling mistress" and casts herself as the "queen" of the household. However, the black woman's blindness to her powerless condition and her denial of the sordid fact that she is nothing more than a sexual object for Kingsman Moody leave her defenseless in the face of his rejection. Weems's womanist interpretation of the biblical ménage à trois analyzes Hagar's situation in this manner: "[T]he story of Hagar and Sarai is about the economic stratification of women as much as it is about the ethnic discrimination of one woman against another. Translated into today's language, Hagar was a domestic; Sarai was her employer."[21] This interpretation of their relationship emphasizes *ethnic*, not racial, discrimination, although a racialized reading is done in the wake of the evolutionary/pseudoscientific theories of Western history.

An exploitative liaison creates a psychoemotional dilemma since the slave/servant has little or no control over her life. Recognizing that reality, Weems observes that "Hagar's body was free, but her mind remained in bonds. What Sarai thought of Hagar had become what Hagar thought of herself; she was property."[22] Although legally free, Mammy's attitude is that of a slave because she loves the Moody men out of a misguided sense of gratitude. In short, unlike Sitaira, the ancient black beauty is portrayed as a willing victim of the body trap, not because she has a physical relationship with a

20. Weems, *Just a Sister Away: A Womanist Vision of Women's Relationships in the Bible*, 1.
21. Ibid., 9.
22. Ibid., 13.

member of the House of Moody but because she seems unable to accept the reality of his true motives—raw lust for her ebony physique.

A comparison and contrast between Duncan's portrayal of Mammy and Nancy Morejón's treatment of the anonymous female persona in one of her signature poems illustrate the nuances among female, feminine, and feminist/womanist characterizations of literary figures. Miriam DeCosta-Willis remarks:

> Nancy Morejón, for example, examines rape, the female body, and the sexualization of racism in her poem "Amo a mi amo" ("I Love My Master"). In an ingenious subversion of the *negrista* texts (with its description of the black woman's eroticized body: hips, thighs, breasts), Morejón creates a black female subject who gazes upon the white male body (eyes, hands, feet, and mouth), an act that clarifies the distance between physical submission and psychological resistance.[23]

The recasting of Mammy lies somewhere between the female and feminine modes because this particular character lacks the "oppositional gaze" that suggests the psychoemotional resistance of Morejón's anonymous caliban.[24] However, Duncan approximates a feminist/womanist posture in the characterization of Sitaira, Mariot, and Elizabeth.

The precarious status of black women in colonial and neocolonial societies has contributed to ambivalent attitudes and contradictory behavior in the complex web of race, gender, and class in the Americas. For example, Verena Martínez-Alier points out that in nineteenth-century Cuba, the road to domestic bliss depended very much on strong family ties. In order to secure the most advantageous liaisons, parents often bartered their daughters for suitable marriage partners. Under such circumstances, white women were better off than black females with respect to the economic benefits of their new social status. In contrast, Lorna V. Williams's analysis of the fictional characters Camila, Dorotea, and Cecilia Valdés reveals that "black women are all members of a disintegrated kinship system. Separated from their parents for one reason or another, the female protagonists are without effective mediators for giving them in marriage. Thus, their basic desire for domesticity stands in

---

23. DeCosta-Willis, "Afra-Hispanic Writers," 249.
24. Hooks, *Black Looks*, 115–31.

marked contrast to their inability to achieve it." Consequently, many mulatto women, and some black ones, settled for a situation that was described as *casa grande* (Big House) and *casa chica* (Little House), or setting up a household as the concubine, not the wife, of a wealthy white man.[25]

Paradoxically, the gender dilemma is just as problematic for the slave mistress as the slave/ex-slave in that Elizabeth Margaret Moody and Mammy are rivals for the attention of a man who exploits them both—the former for childbearing and the consolidation of his legacy, the latter for pleasure. Regarding this irony, hooks observes:

> By flaunting their sexual lust for the bodies of black women and their preference for them as sexual partners, white men successfully pitted white women and enslaved black women against one another. In most instances, the white mistress did not envy the black female her role as sexual object; she feared only that her newly acquired social status might be threatened by white male sexual interaction with black women. His sexual involvement with black women (even if that involvement was rape) in effect reminded the white female of her subordinate position in relationship to him. For he could exercise his power as racial imperialist and sexual imperialist to rape or seduce black women, while white women were not free to rape or seduce black men without fear of punishment. Though the white female might condemn the actions of the white male who chose to interact sexually with black female slaves, she was unable to dictate to him proper behavior.[26]

This statement explains the popularity of Hagar as a literary figure in the works of white women novelists of the nineteenth century. Through this genre they sought to empower themselves to deal with an intolerable situation. This twinning propensity, or the inclination to appropriate the black body as a symbol of freedom for the white, is an illusion, for as long as the black and white females occupy different sides of the socioeconomic fence, cooperation is highly unlikely, if not impossible altogether.[27] One understands, then, why

25. Martínez-Alier, *Marriage, Class, and Colour in Nineteenth-Century Cuba: A Study of Racial Attitudes and Sexual Values in a Slave Society*, 1–21; Williams, "Dusky Venus," 122; Gilberto Freyre, *The Masters and the Slaves: A Study in the Development of Brazilian Civilization*, xvi.

26. Hooks, *Ain't I a Woman?* 153–54.

27. Gabler-Hover, *Dreaming Black/Writing White*, 7, 123.

Mammy is more indignant and broken up than Kingsman Moody over Elizabeth's rebellion, for to the father it is mainly a question of protecting his reputation among his peers; to the black concubine, the girl's failure is her own since she has sacrificed her life and the care of her own child for the twins. Only in the nurturing sense does Mammy approach the Eve half of the paradigm, so one is not surprised that she seeks out the dying Elizabeth and tries to rescue Mariot in spite of Kingsman's opposition. Nevertheless, loyal Mammy is betrayed when Moody abandons her and returns to Scotland to drown his sorrows with brandy in some nameless little village pub. Meanwhile, the House of Moody falls under the management of an ambitious mulatto overseer named M. Brown, who also exploits Mammy sexually. When Brown no longer has any use for the elderly woman, he replaces her with a young girl. Faithful Mammy is left to fend for herself in an unkind world, and she disappears without a trace. The irony of her final destiny is brilliantly underscored as chapter 2 ends with a few lines from a well-known Sankey hymn: "Faith of our fathers living still / We will be true until the end" (Fe de nuestros padres viviente aún / hasta la muerte te seremos fiel, 140).[28] Nevertheless, in this fairy tale gone sour, Mammy's efforts to preserve the seed of Elizabeth and Joshua Prince are not in vain, for Mariot continues the Moody family bloodline, if not its name.

With Mariot Kenton's tale of woe, we are brought back to the present time in For the Sake of Peace (chapters 1, 7, and 8), and one perceives that her life acquires meaning only in retrospect. Because she is the only known survivor of the Moody/Prince family tree, Mariot articulates the individual silences, murmurs, and whispers of all the women who embody the Eve/Hagar paradigm. Through Elizabeth's daughter and Sitaira's mother, oral history emerges at its finest. Mary Chamberlain treats the question of memory and culture in her assessment of the cultural biases in Western philosophy and psychology that view memory as a function of the individual imagination. Chamberlain considers the focus on an individual process to be an unreliable source of history. Specifically, she challenges Eurocentric cultural assumptions by asserting that "the language,

---

28. According to Núñez, a "Sankey hymn, among Jamaican blacks, [is] a hymn accompanied by the beat of a drum; it is sung at wakes on the night of a death" (Dictionary of Civilization, 479).

images, priorities and expectations which shape memory and give it structure and meaning derive from shared, that is social, languages, images, priorities and expectations. In this sense, although the voice may be individual, and differs from one to another, the form memory assumes, the ways in which it is collated and expressed, is collective. It is culturally and socially determined." The communal, functional, and social nature of ethnic memory is a given in many civilizations, including African and African-diaspora cultures, whose oral traditions have been employed to preserve and pass on their legacies in spite of slavery and colonialism. The spirit of Africanity is captured in Duncan's unique symbol of the *samamfo*, which is a spiritual manifestation of Afro-realism. Paulette Ramsay reminds us that "the *Samamfo* is the collective memory of the race which passes from generation to generation and which is active in the religious rites of the people in their struggles and in their experiences."[29] Moreover, the ancestors, the living, and the unborn are all integral parts of that lifeline, and such has significant implications for childbearing.

Janheinz Jahn confirms the strong belief in African philosophy that one's progenitors return through their descendants, observing that "to leave no living heirs behind him is the worst evil that can befall a man, and there is no curse more terrible to put on a man than to wish him to die childless."[30] One might add that the tragedy/curse is even greater for a woman, whose self-definition has traditionally been linked to the reproduction and nurture of the young— the womb/tongue metaphor. Of course, in light of contemporary feminist theory, this aspect of femaleness is often portrayed as subordinate or unnecessary to other considerations. Nevertheless, a balanced view of womanhood and women characters in fiction is more healthy for social relationships, just as it should be for manhood and male figures. Complementarity was the original position of the Adam and Eve relationship, but it was corrupted, resulting in the development of patriarchal models. The compendium of faces and voices of the Eve/Hagar paradigm continues the struggle to restore a balance between mind and body, womb and tongue. African

29. Chamberlain, "Gender and Memory: Oral History and Women's History," 95–96; Ramsay, "African Religious Heritage," 35.
30. Jahn, *Muntu: An Outline of the New African Culture*, 109.

womanism as delineated by Filomina Chioma Steady comes closer to achieving an equilibrium than Alice Walker's womanism, but the latter is still a more holistic perspective than feminism.

Since her own children are dead, Mariot Kenton must find a surrogate descendant, so she chooses Pedro Dull. Inspired by the *samamfo,* the older woman passes on to her cotagonist the knowledge of her family's history:

> Her personal grief. A child's grief. Her mother's prolonged agony, her father's gradual decline from a bottle that made him forget his own name, the glorious tales of the *samamfo,* legends about sacred stools and spiders; and then eternal, cold night fell on their home and, with that darkness, the nocturnal silence of the tomb.
>
> (Su propio dolor. El de la niña. La lenta agonía materna, la decadencia de su padre que a fuer de tomar olvidaba su propio nombre, las gloriosos historias del samamfo, las leyendas sobre banquillos sagrados y arañas; la noche eterna y fría cayó sobre la casa y junto a la noche, también noctámbulo, el silencio del barro.) (105)

The voice of an omniscient narrator segues into a third-person interior monologue as Mariot strives to paint for Pedro word pictures that link past and present in their shared history of suffering and triumph:

> How can this boy possibly know anything 'bout pain or rebellion if he don't know nothin' 'bout work slowdowns on the plantations, or 'bout the burnin' of harvests, or 'bout the destruction of tools; or 'bout those sorrow songs, where solidarity meant a dream of freedom. Centuries-old pain. Bone-deep pain. Includin' betrayal by her Aunt Margaret, who took her after her mama died and made her a servant, mo' like a slave. You better believe she knew what pain was!
>
> (Qué va a ser dolor y rebeldía lo del muchacho que no sabe de trabajos lentos en las fincas, ni de la quema de cosechas, ni la avería de herramientas; ni de las canciones en clave, donde la solidaridad era el sueño de la liberación. Todo eso, todo eso sí que era dolor. Dolor de siglos. Dolor de vena. Inclusive la grosería de su tía Margaret que la recogió después de la muerte de su madre y la hizo sirvienta. Dolor, sí, ¡eso sí era dolor!) (105)

As in other passages, Duncan uses the technique of starting with a sympathetic omniscient narrator, but just at the point when the "nocturnal silence of the tomb" conveys a sense of finality, a third-person interior-monologue voice, representing Mariot's gut-level remembrance of her life, takes over, and she embraces her pain through the telling of *her* story. This is a magnificent renditon of the womb/tongue metaphor, for it gives voice to the collective pain and suffering of the women *and* the men in Mariot's bloodline: her ancestors (grandparents and parents), her dead children (Sitaira and Leonard), and her unborn (hope for another child even in middle age). Tragically, she is an outcast in a nameless swamp community of neocolonial people, and she sees herself as a defeated woman with no successors. Within the African diaspora Mariot is exiled from her homeland, Jamaica, but she has little hope of establishing a place and home in Costa Rica, especially now that her bloodline has dried up.[31]

In the months following Sitaira's death, Mariot and Pedro draw closer to one another in order to assuage their mutual grief. At one point Mariot's anguish drives her to think about seducing Pedro, but it is not clear whether this "act" occurs in her imagination/ dreams or in fact/reality. For his part, Pedro is not aware of his connection to the Moody clan, but it is implied during the course of the narrative that the young man is the illegitimate offspring *(hijo natural)* of Margaret Dull's roving husband, whose first name is never given, and Pedro's nameless black mother. As the cotagonists remember Sitaira, Mariot tells Pedro additional stories about her life with Cornelius Kenton, a former member of a train crew who has suffered severe head injuries in a derailment. Moreover, it is revealed that shortly before the accident, an anonymous prattler had told Cornelius a tale of cuckoldry, "Brother Anancy and Tucuma," to hint at his wife's infidelity. Whether or not there is truth in this anonymous accusation, the violent "expulsion" of Pedro and Sitaira from paradise nullifies the African concept of blood and lineage, and the Kentons are left without heirs. With Sitaira and her brother, Leonard, out of the way, Mr. Brown, father of the implied murderer, Cató, and owner of the banana plantation where Pedro Dull and other exploited laborers are preparing to strike, sees an opportunity to suppress the labor movement. Coincidentally, Brown

31. Mosby, *Place, Language, and Identity,* 165–66.

is the illegitimate son of the mulatto administrator M. Brown, who
had tried to pass for a Scotsman after Margaret Dull sent him to
Puerto Limón in search of the runaway Mariot. This pretender is
the same M. Brown who abused Mammy. However, unlike his
father, Brown is very black. No one in the village knows the whole
truth, not even all the members of the Brown and Kenton families.
Believing that Cató is responsible for her daughter's murder, Mariot plots secret revenge on the Browns by hiring Pedro as an assassin
because she feels it is futile to appeal to the law for justice. However,
Pedro does not have the heart to kill the mentally deranged Cató.
Later, the protagonist is arrested for his affiliation with the Garvey
movement. For this reason, the authorities accuse him of inciting
the workers and then try to blame him for killing Sitaira. In desperation Mariot mobilizes the workers to join her in Pedro's defense.
In short, "this complex novel, composed of flashbacks, multiple
perspectives, and interpolated poems, songs, and biblical sermons,
reveals tensions within the West Indian community in Limón over
the past and the future. The death of Sitaira, a young Afro–West
Indian peasant, exposes the open wounds of class, caste, and color
in the province."[32] The color and class consciousness among the
Antilleans elicits a radical response from the work's cotagonists,
who strive to unite the community in the face of oppression.

Mariot Prince Kenton embodies the Eve/Hagar figure par excellence because she is active and passive, assertive and submissive, independent and dependent. Although victimized by men like Miguelino Sánchez Bonilla and women like her Aunt Margaret, she also
enjoyed a happy marriage and family life before her husband's accident and the death of her children. Since Cornelius is present in
body only, Mariot must capture the spirit of both within her own.
Out of her ancient pain, dislocation, and exile she begins to reinvent
herself symbolically with Pedro. Except for the Brown family, most
of the town's inhabitants—curiosity seekers, tale bearers, would-
have-been suitors, and female ex-rivals—attend Sitaira's funeral,
even though few do so out of real sympathy for her parents. The
truly compassionate ones are Sebastián, the Bribrí Indian; the
Sánchez family; Mr. López, who appears to be a surrogate father to
Pedro; and the Chinese couple who owns the local tavern. Sitaira's
death is metaphorically transferred to Pedro through guilt by former

32. Ibid., 153, 145.

association, and the two characters are symbolically linked by their rebellion (marronage). It is not surprising that Pedro becomes the object of persecution, for his real crime is organizing the laborers against the blaxploitation of Brown. However, his arrest and pending trial, along with Sitaira's demise, render them both Christlike figures as they are made sacrificial offerings by pharisees like Brown and the local preacher, who condemn all labor-protest activities for the sake of peace *(por la paz del pueblo)*. Sitaira's ghost celebrates the coming together of the citizens to protest, and her mirth at the end of the novel confirms this spirit of survival and jubilance: "But they all heard in the distance the resounding laughter of a woman who was coming from the river" (Pero todos oyeron a lo lejos una carcajada de mujer que venía del río, 187). Her defiant laughter is symbolic of the community's resilience and strength, and the river represents the continuing flow of life.

In every society women are significant tradition bearers, for they have constituted an oral infrastructure that undergirds accounts written mostly by men. Hence, expressions like "old wives' tales" and "women's talk," usually employed disparagingly, take on new meaning when one considers the tremendous part females play in transmitting culture.[33] The individual stories of female characters in *For the Sake of Peace* are muted by distances of time and place, even though their collective saga emerges from clashing and complementary perspectives. However, the voice of Mariot Prince Kenton, that tremendous "voice refound" of African-descended women figures in diaspora literature, helps Pedro Dull fill in the lacunae of his own past, especially those parts that have not been related by his mother and grandfather.[34] Furthermore, the hegemonic discourse is verbalized by an omniscient narrator/historian, while the resisting discourse is channeled through Mariot's voice of ethnic memory. Together, these discourses form a dialectic that constitutes a tale of greed, violence, and prejudice in the Caribbean and the Americas, but also one of survival, healing, and triumph. They are the fragments of memory captured in the reconstructed word—Afro-realism.

As previously stated, *For the Sake of Peace* can be read as a maroon narrative because it addresses the issues of race, gender, and

33. P. Ellis, "Introduction," 109.
34. Abena P. A. Busia, "This Gift of Metaphor: Symbolic Strategies and the Triumph of Survival in Simone Schwartz-Bart's *The Bridge of Beyond*," 289.

class in a postcolonial context and in a contestatory fashion, unlike
any other work of prose fiction in Costa Rican literature. Moreover,
the novel demythologizes the image of paradise invented by Colum-
bus and perpetuated for centuries by writers with an exclusively
Eurocentric worldview. Thus, some critics see the novel as part of the
new-historicist or revisionist tendency in twentieth-century canonical literature, while others view it as a "postmodern" work that
challenges the feudalistic, patriarchal institutions on which Costa
Rican and other Latin American societies are established. Although
it deconstructs those structures, *For the Sake of Peace* also reveals a
sensibility that militates against "the indeterminacy of meaning
and the decenteredness of existence" associated with postmodernism.[35] If anything, Duncan seeks to extract meaning out of the splin-
tered, disjunct pieces of Caribbean history and recenter them in
the African-derived concept of the *samamfo* as a literary construct
of Afro-realism.

Concerning black spirituality, Ian Smart perceives the relationship between Mariot Kenton and Pedro Dull as a re-creation of the
Kemetian myth of Horus/Osiris, who is the son/brother-consort of
his mother, Isis. He comments:

> The primal connectedness between Señora Mariot and Pedro,
> her daughter Sitaira's lover, is established through the agency of
> the *samamfo,* clearly manifested in the narrative itself prior to
> the older woman's offer of herself to the young Pedro. The pro-
> found mythical significance of the event is highlighted through
> the use of the future tense to narrate a past action, a recollec-
> tion. The great moments of mythical action are always beyond
> the limits of ordinary time, manifested in the sequential pas-
> sage from past to present to future. The mythical moment is
> the eternal now.[36]

Whether this is a conscious choice or not, the Isis/Horus/Osiris allegory parallels the Hagar/Ishmael story and approximates the Mariot/
Pedro relationship in that role reversal is evident in these relationships. Duncan's use of myth situates the action of the novel within
the postcolonial specificity of a banana plantation of the 1930s. At

35. Joseph Childers and Gary Hentzi, eds., *The Columbia Dictionary of Modern Literary Criticism,* 233.
36. Smart, "Quince Duncan," 103.

the same time, it centers the "strategies of resistance" within the discourse of the oppressed group while "othering" what bell hooks refers to as "a pervasive politics of white supremacy which seeks to prevent the formation of a radical black subjectivity" in canonical literature.[37] In short, the unfolding of the Eve/Hagar paradigm within the liberation movement of the West Indian population in *For the Sake of Peace* represents a "blackening," or radical transformation, of perspective in the Latin American imagination. Although not immediately apparent, the transformative nature of Duncan's fiction will have a significant impact on Costa Rican literature through the prizewinning novel *Dead-End Street*.[38]

37. Hooks, *Yearning: Race, Gender, and Cultural Politics*, 26.
38. Richard Jackon refers to the transformative nature of contemporary African Hispanophone writing as a new humanism in Western literature. See *Black Literature and Humanism in Latin America*.

# 5

# A Voice from Down Under in
## *Dead-End Street*

The concept of identity manifests itself on various levels. One speaks of an individual identity, or unique personality; a collective identity, or shared disposition; and a national identity, or body politic. Like the other six nations of Central America, and like the continental entity that composes Latin America, Costa Rica has forged its identity on a vision of history that flies in the face of empirical truth. The myth of Euro-Hispanic settlerhood, or the white legend, permeates every level of society.[1] As Dorothy Mosby observes:

> This national myth of whiteness or "Europeanness" in Costa Rica has been perpetuated historically to give the country its sense of difference and identity amid the majority mestizo, indigenous, and Afro-Creole or Afro–West Indian cultures of its Central American neighbors by emphasizing its genetic and cultural proximity to the European conquerors. Black writers defy the notion that Costa Rica is a "white," Latin, Hispanic country absent of ethnic diversity.[2]

The basis of the mythologizing tendency is the continental Eurocentric complex discussed in chapter 2 of the present study. Therefore, as in other nations of South America, in Costa Rica "[t]he national myths that assert the dominance of the traditional Hispanic culture over that of the descendants of West Indians are tied to a need to consolidate a sense of nationhood and belonging, even if it means the exclusion and marginalization of immigrant identities.

---

1. Kyle Longley, "Resistance and Accommodation: The United States and the Nationalism of José Figueres, 1953–1957," 3.
2. Mosby, *Place, Language, and Identity,* 24.

The origins of these myths have their foundation in the patterns of colonial rule and neocolonial ventures in investment capitalism." *Dead-End Street* (1979) explores the implications of Costa Rica's one-sided perspective of history and articulates some unresolved sociopolitical issues that resurfaced in the aftermath of the 1948 Civil War. Because that event was a watershed in the country's history, Duncan utilizes it to scrutinize and challenge traditional notions of self, community, and polity. In doing so the author demythologizes the white legend by juxtaposing various oral/unofficial and written/ official perspectives of history and by subtly recasting Costa Rica's national identity in terms of its racially and ethnically diverse population. Ironically, this "raceless" novel won Costa Rica's prestigious Aquileo Echeverría literary prize for 1979.[3]

*Dead-End Street* is a circular work that begins and ends with the dilemma of Carlos López, who is a member of the Social Democrat Party that represents a fragile coalition between the urban working and middle classes. When his son Daniel and other student demonstrators are beaten and arrested by plainclothes detectives for protesting against government corruption, Carlos experiences a severe emotional crisis and begins to question the value of his own military service in the Civil War. He abruptly finds out about Daniel's detention and hospitalization from a news bulletin on his car radio the afternoon of April 11, 196_, which is Private John's holiday.[4] Not only do the police attack the students, they also attempt to

3. Ibid.; Smart, "Quince Duncan," 105.
4. Richard Biesanz, Karen Zubris Biesanz, and Mavis Hiltunen Biesanz, *The Costa Ricans*, 20. Private Juan Santa María was a young soldier in the Costa Rican army who helped the Nicaraguan troops overthrow William Walker, a *filibustero*, or soldier of fortune, from the southern United States. The *World Book Encyclopedia* informs us that Walker first tried to conquer lower California and Sonora, Mexico (1853), then invaded Nicaragua (1855) and set himself up as president (1856–1857) in an effort to recolonize the "darker peoples" of Central America (s.v. "Walker, William"). Ronald N. Harpelle observes in *The West Indians of Costa Rica: Race, Class, and the Integration of an Ethnic Minority* that shortly thereafter, these latter-day conquistadores decided to capture Costa Rica as well, but President Juan Rafael Mora declared war on them after witnessing Nicaragua's humiliation. Walker and his military adventurers were routed and chased back into Nicaragua. "The success of Juan Rafael Mora's forces in the struggle against the invaders played an important role in the development of Costa Rican nationalism. With the triumph of the National Campaign, Costa Rica finally had a number of heroic national figures. The most significant to emerge was Juan Santa María, a young man who sacrificed his life in the battle of Santa Rosa. The youth's sacrifice was credited with the defeat of the mercenaries and the salvation of Costa

cover up their misdeeds by labeling the protestors "Communist agitators" and "pot smokers." At first, Carlos does not want to seek help from his father because of their long-standing differences from the era of the Civil War. The elder López had fought with the troops of President Rafael Ángel Calderón Guardia *(los calderonistas)*, and the younger with those of the victorious revolutionaries under José Figueres *(los figueristas)*. However, Carlos feels betrayed when Salchicha Gutiérrez (alias *el Comandante*), his former comrade in arms and minister of defense in the second Figueres administration, is not held accountable for the beating. Instead, Gutiérrez is transferred to another post. Furthermore, the government blocks Carlos's efforts to sue *el Comandante,* so he goes to his father, Don Caliche López, for moral support.

Although the men of the López family are the primary characters in the work, it is the secondary personage Doña Carmen López whose voice creates a counterhegemonic discourse. In fact, this female character is potent as a counterpoint to the dominant discourse represented by Don Euclides Herrera, an illustrious descendant of the Spanish conquistadores, because the men of her family are either dreamers or in denial of reality. Similar to other Eve/Hagar figures in Duncan's narrative, Doña Carmen is an unlettered person of humble origin, but this does not prevent her from rebelling against her designated place in society, which she does in an unobtrusive manner. Consequently, it is easy to overlook her importance in the novel. In effect, Doña Carmen is the embodiment of the Eve/Hagar paradigm, but this is displayed in a uniquely challenging manner. Specifically, this female character operates like Anancy the Spider, a trickster figure from the corpus of Afro–Costa Rican oral traditions who resorts to astuteness and dissimulation to survive or

---

Rica. Juan Santa María's death became the country's leading symbol of patriotism, and the National Campaign marked the most important political event of the nineteenth century" (5–6). The irony of Juan Santa María's status as national hero stands out in that historically there have been "efforts to deny his *non-European* appearance" (192n13; emphasis added). Harpelle's source on the National Campaign and its aftermath is Carlos Monge Alfaro, *Historia de Costa Rica* (San José: Librería Trejos, 1978); his reference on the controversy over Juan Santa María is Stephen Paul Palmer, "A Liberal Discipline: Inventing Nations in Guatemala and Costa Rica, 1870–1900" (Ph.D. diss., Columbia University, 1990). Consequently, it is not a coincidence that Duncan chose this particular hero (Juan Santa María) and holiday (Private John's Day) to dismantle the white legend, and this choice reinforces the use of Doña Carmen as Anancy the Signifying Spider.

triumph or both.[5] Furthermore, signifyin(g) is the process through which Doña Carmen reverses and undermines the white legend in *Dead-End Street*. It is necessary to comprehend the novel's structure and relationships among its characters before discussing this trope.

In the opening scenes of the novel, the López father and son have not spoken to each other since that fateful day twenty years earlier when Carlos had joined the opposition party. Nevertheless, Don Caliche adores his grandson Daniel and has already appealed to his former *patrón,* Don Euclides Herrera, to intervene on the youngster's behalf. During the course of the story both Don Caliche and Carlos go through identity crises that reveal serious doubts about their respective roles in the conflict. It is Doña Carmen, Don Caliche's third wife and Carlos's second stepmother, who first sees that the Civil War was futile no matter what faction they supported because none of the parties established a government that was truly committed to the people.

*Dead-End Street* comprises nine chapters that are constructed around a series of flashbacks, memories, and dreams presented in a conversational mode through five characters: Carlos, Daniel, Don Caliche, Doña Carmen, and Don Euclides. The framework of the novel, which consists of chapters 1, 2, 3, and 9, shows the interaction between Carlos and various officials. Moreover, these chapters are structured around the incidents of police brutality. In these sections the narrative voice, which is predominantly first-person singular, alternates between participatory (past) and interpretative (present) modes. That is, Carlos reevaluates his own participation in the Civil War at the time of Daniel's troubles. In chapters 4, 6, and 8—the inner core of the novel—Don Caliche recounts his role in the struggle to Doña Carmen. Through an ongoing dialogue with his wife, the elder López begins to reexamine the significance of the Civil War to himself, his community, and nation. Chapters 5 and 7 feature the story of the Herrera dynasty, which interweaves with the external framework and inner core of the work. Through the memories related by Don Euclides to his son Frenillo, the story of the

5. Mosby, *Place, Language, and Identity,* 35. We are reminded of the character Ruby in "A Gift for Grandma." Ileana Villalobes Ellis articulates the political and social consequences of the Costa Rican Cival War of 1948 in "Entre los cerros y el muro: Análisis e interpretación de *Final de calle.*"

Olympians, or the mythical version of Costa Rican history, unfolds. Yet the voice of Doña Carmen emerges from down under as the most powerful one, informing the work with an engaging orality.

Essentially, the internal drama of Carlos López constitutes the central conflict of *Dead-End Street*:

> I'm crossing the mountains again just like that morning when I left behind a father weighed down by grief and indignation and joined Fermín Solano and Salchicha Gutiérrez, while Don Gustavo stayed behind because he had a cold. I'm crossing the mountains in the coldness of Ochomongo, with a mixture of unmistakable pleasure and pain on my palate, because the notion of conspiracy, the supreme moment of illumination, drew me toward rebellion, like a son of light, because rebels alone define history.
>
> (Volver a cruzar los cerros como aquella mañana en que, dejando atrás a un padre agobiado por el dolor y la indignación, me reuní con Fermín Solano y Salchicha Gutiérrez, mientras don Gustavo se quedaba atrás porque estaba resfriado. Cruzar los cerros, en medio del frío de Ochomogo, con una mezcla de placer inenarrable y dolor en el paladar, porque la conspiración, el supremo momento de lucidez me lanzaba a la rebelión, como un hijo de la luz, porque sólo los rebeldes definen la historia.)[6]

Carlos's allusion to the "son of light" simile continues the revolutionary stance of Duncan's earlier novels and stories, where the rebel/*cimarrón* who defines history is often a martyr figure such as Pedro Dull and Sitaira Kenton, or Jean Paul and Mama Bull. However, the intergenerational conflict between the male members of the López family represents the country's inability to redefine itself at the crossroads of change. The enterprise fails because the society still adheres to patriarchal models and structures.

Doña Carmen, the lone *cimarrona* (female rebel) and incarnation of the Eve/Hagar model, symbolizes the conscience of the nation. In addition, she is a humanized version of Anancy the Spider, a close cousin to the Signifying Monkey. Rather than incorporate an Anancy story into the narrative text of *Dead-End Street* (as he does in *For the Sake of Peace*), Duncan subtly inserts the animal protagonist

---

6. Duncan, *Final de calle*, 19–20. All subsequent quotations will be cited parenthetically; all translations are my own.

through the voice of the secondary character Doña Carmen, who repeats and revises, repeats and reverses, repeats and contests the national mythology in myriad ways. As a metaphorical trickster, Anancy's role is multivalent, for signifyin(g) is a deeply embedded performance that transcends cultures. In fact, its origin can be traced back to African rhetorical forms, many of which emphasize linguistic virtuosity, an oral performance of "art for art's sake." Thus, while the Signifying Monkey is peculiar to the black oral tradition in the United States, signification (in oral and scribal terms) exists in other American settings where there are African-descended people.[7] Roger Abrahams provides a user-friendly definition of this fluid process:

> Signifying . . . can mean any of a number of things; in the case of the toast about the signifying monkey, it certainly refers to the trickster's ability to talk with great innuendo, to carp, cajole, needle, and lie. It can mean in other instances the propensity to talk around a subject, never quite coming to the point. It can mean making fun of a person or situation. Also it can denote speaking with the hands and eyes, and in this respect encompasses a whole complex of expressions and gestures. Thus, it is signifying to stir up a fight between neighbors by telling stories; it is signifying to make fun of a policeman by parodying his motions behind his back; it is signifying to ask for a piece of cake by saying "My brother needs a piece of cake."[8]

Signifyin(g) manifests itself in numerous ways, but its essence involves parody, or repetition and reversal, indirect argument or persuasion, implication, and oblique verbal or gestural acts or both. Moreover, the signifier can utilize any number of rhetorical devices, or "master tropes," like metaphor, metonymy, synecdoche, irony, or hyperbole. In addition, "the black rhetorical tropes subsumed under signifying would include 'marking,' 'loud-talking,' 'specifying,' 'testifying,' 'calling out' (of one's name), 'sounding,' 'rapping' and 'playing the dozens.'"[9] Indigenous (self-generative) genres like signifyin(g) constitute the transformed roots, branches, and seeds of African modes of seeing and being in the world, and they are

7. Gates, "Blackness of Blackness," 286.
8. Abrahams, *Deep Down,* 51–52.
9. Gates, "Blackness of Blackness," 286.

present in myriad forms throughout the diaspora. This aspect of Duncan's Afro-realism parallels Henry Louis Gates Jr.'s theory of African American literature.

As Doña Carmen and Don Caliche reminisce about the Civil War, she recalls her loving relationship with her first husband, Salomón González, who often described her as *chocolate* (dark brown) in contrast to himself, who was *cremita* (cream colored or vanilla). These gustatory images may well symbolize mutual terms of endearment for the spouses since Doña Carmen constantly reminisces about their sexual relations in terms of fruit: "As usual the savor of mangoes in Carmen's mouth..." (Como siempre un sabor a mango en la boca de Carmen..., 38). Thus, chocolate and vanilla are not necessarily racial markers. On the other hand, this ambiguity points toward resolution when the terms are placed in the context of offhand references to Salomón's other body parts: "black, almost curly or crispy hair" *(pelo negro, casi crespo)*, "firm buttocks" *(nalgas plomizas)*, and "bony legs" *(piernas huesudas)* (38). By *specifying/naming* the somatic and corporeal features associated with blackness, Doña Carmen reverses the tendency of the national myth to privilege white (light) skin, "good (blond) hair," thin features, fleshy legs, and flat buttocks. Salomón is fair-skinned, but his physical features are "blackened," which is the case with a lot of mixed populations in the Caribbean and Central and South Americas. The national hero Juan Santa María is a case in point. In terms of the Eve component of the paradigm, the "white" and "black" bodies of husband and wife are complementary and interdependent, and their essential/sexual union is symbolically rendered in the mango, a tropical fruit, which is the ideal representation of an authentic Costa Rican identity. However, the Hagar (dark) element is perceived as a threat to the mythological body politic, so it must deconstruct white supremacy through signifyin(g).

Carmen's memory of Salomón's father is a second catalyst for signification: "[T]he old man was white as a ghost, with white skin, white clothes, the only spot of color bein' his feets splattered with brown mud" ([B]lanco como un fantasma el viejo, blanca la piel y la ropa y sólo los pies manchados por el barro trigueño, 39). The negative polarities established between white ghost/skin/clothes and brown muddy feet are pulled toward the center in the blended relationship between Carmen and Salomón, which is evidence of a lengthy historical process of which she is only vaguely aware. However, contemporary studies have documented that "in the pre-industrial period there were several *pueblas* (non-white reservations, both urban and rural) in central and northwestern Costa Rica where indigenous and black people lived. It was also common for upper-class Hispanic men, including clergy, to take young slave women as concubines, producing mixed-race 'godchildren' who would carry their father's surname."[10] Moreover, this amalgamation is but the tip of the iceberg in the question of national identity, as historian Michael Cutler Stone observes:

> Racial mixing was apparently more socially acceptable in rural than in urban Costa Rica. The 19th century rise of coffee brought the evolution of a predominantly male, racially mixed working class emigration to rural areas, while *pardo* women stayed in the cities as domestics. This brought men and women of color in contact with those of European blood, fostering interracial unions, whether legitimate or otherwise. Poverty meant late and limited access to matrimony for both *pardo* men and women (suggesting lower rates of reproduction), and higher rates of infant mortality. Additionally, the salience of the terms *pardo* (colored) *trigueño* (wheat colored), and *rubio quemado* (burnished red) suggests that the color line in 19th century Costa Rica was sufficiently fluid and negotiable to ease the colonial black population's assimilation.[11]

The allusion Doña Carmen makes to "reddish brown or wheat colored mud" *(barro trigueño)* is her way of "testifying," that is, of "coloring" her father-in-law, the symbol of the Costa Rican white peasant/settler. This testimony does not deny the presence of Euro-Spanish ethnicity, but it does affirm the reality of others that have been embedded in the national psyche. This "disappearance" or erasure of the black element from the Costa Rican cultural, racial, and social corpus is the subject of several provocative studies.[12] It

10. Royal and Perry, "Costa Rica," 220.
11. Stone, "The Afro-Caribbean Presence in Central America," 11. Stone provides charts and tables to substantiate his findings.
12. See the following works by contemporary Costa Rican historians and other scholars: Oscar Aguilar Bulgarelli and Irene Alfaro Aguilar, *La esclavitud negra en Costa Rica: Orígenes de la oligarquía económica y política nacional*; Tatiana Lobo Wiehoff and Mauricio Meléndez Obando, *Negros y blancos: Todo mezclado*; and María Teresa Ruiz, *Racismo: Algo más allá que la discriminación*. They build on Meléndez Chaverri and Duncan's trailblazing study, *El negro en Costa Rica*.

is interesting that Doña Carmen does not refer to herself as *negra* because that term is not socially acceptable when it stands for black skin in Latin America. However, *negra* can be used as a term of endearment for women of all colors. As illustrated by the situation of Aracely Brown in "Go-o-o-o-al!" women of dark complexion are considered social hindrances or objects of pleasure or both. They are considered less desirable as mates because it is not likely that they will function as instruments for lightening/whitening up the race *(blanquear la raza)* and thus as "agents of improvement" for a family's status. People often use all kinds of euphemisms—*mestizo, moreno, mulato, pardo, trigueño,* ad infinitum—to keep from naming blackness. Consequently, racial ambiguity in these passages is a trope to signify on the white legend, for it suggests the ambivalence of the nation toward its own identity formation and identification in view of its mixed heritage.[13] As an Eve/Hagar figure, Doña Carmen stands outside the Eurocentric matrix and is, thus, endowed with a double vision and a double voice, which she renders in the vernacular. Consequently, the oblique verbal and gestural acts of signifyin(g) enable her to engage the leadership of the nation through her richly nuanced private conversation with her second husband.

The macho Don Caliche remembers with pride his good fortune with women. After the death of his first wife (Carlos's mother) in childbirth, he marries Doña Tomasa, who helps raise the boy. In fact, Carlos loves his first stepmother dearly, and she is the one who prevails on Don Caliche not to kill his only son if they meet on the battlefield. Doña Tomasa and Doña Carmen are friends and neighbors, but the former dies during the war, and Don Caliche eventually marries the widowed Doña Carmen. It seems unlikely that this yucca farmer and baker-turned-soldier would marry a dark woman, for he represents the European-settler mentality on which the national myth is founded. However, such are the contradictions of race, gender, and class relations in Latin America, as elsewhere. Like the average peasant and worker of his era, Don Caliche feels threatened by the influx of foreigners, in this case the West Indians who were imported by international business interests as cheap labor.[14] This fear and insecurity are evident in Don

13. Jackson, *Black Image,* 1–9; *Report on the Americas,* 18.
14. Meléndez Chaverri and Duncan, *El negro en Costa Rica,* 91–93. See also Royal and Perry, "Costa Rica," 218; and Purcell, *Banana Fallout,* chaps. 2 and 3.

Caliche's memory of a discussion with young Carlos over the black presence in Costa Rica:

> "Daddy," the boy interrupted, "that affair about Don León's ordering them to get even with the *ricardistas*..."
> "Don Ricardo was always one to exaggerate...You can't pay no 'tention to him."
> "What about the Negroes?"
> "What about the *nigras,* son?"
> "Don Ricardo and Don León signed a decree that prohibits black people from going to work on the Pacific Coast. The minister was Don León. And then Don León, you saw for yourself, fired all the blacks who were already working in the Pacific region. All of them except one, who's his brother's friend."
> "I don't know where you git all that nonsense from, boy; that's all lies made up by cheap politicians."
> "They're not lies, Daddy, they're injustices."
> "Well, whaddaya want? Ya want them *nigras* to take bread outta our mouths, huh?"
>
> (—Papá,—interrumpió el muchacho—y eso de que don León mandó darle chincha a los ricardistas...
> —Don Ricardo fue siempre un hombre exagerado...no hay que hacerle mucho caso.
> —Y...lo de los negros...
> —¿Qué es lo de los negros?
> —Don Ricardo y don León firmaron el decreto que prohíbe a los negros ir a trabajar al Pacífico. El ministro era don León. Y luego don León, usted ha visto, despidió a todos los negros que trabajaban en el Pacífico. Todos menos uno que es amigo de su hermano.
> —No sé de dónde toma[s] estas cosas...son inventos de los politiqueros.
> —No son inventos, papá: son injusticias.
> —Bueno, ¿y qué quieren? ¿Que los negros nos vengan a quitar el pan?) (28)

Don Caliche's hostility is based on his resentment of the *blackness, maleness,* and *foreignness* of the West Indians, who look strange, speak English, and practice different customs from the white/*mestizo* population, and who consider themselves superior to the *pañas* (Spanish-descended nationals). On the other hand, just as the Span-

ish conquerors took African and Amerindian females as concubines, many peasant settlers cohabited with or married *criollas de
color*—the Spanish-speaking African-descended women born and
acculturated in the Americas. Thus, the union between Don Caliche
and Doña Carmen reflects a well-established pattern of miscegenation in Costa Rica and throughout Latin America. It is one of the
many contradictions peculiar to the race-gender-class construct. In
this setting Doña Carmen, the metaphorical Anancy, is by necessity
a trickster figure who belies the racist myths Don Caliche has begun to question but to which he still clings at gut level.

Doña Carmen models the Eve/Hagar archetypes in that she is
assertive, courageous, and enterprising in spite of her lowly origins
and illiteracy. For example, that she cannot read and write is obvious in her recall of taking a letter to Doña Tomasa to read to her.
Thus, Carmen constantly berates herself, repeatedly peppering her
remarks with expressions like "medio bruta" (uncouth), "tonta"
(stupid), and "testaruda" (thick-skulled) (41–42). However, there
is a subtle process in play such that Anancy the Spider undermines
her own opinion of herself as dumb. That is, "the use of repetition
and reversal (chiasmus) constitutes an implicit parody of a subject's
own complicity in illusion."[15] Doña Carmen is well aware that she
has other qualities that compensate for her lack of a formal education. For one thing, she is a shrewd, intelligent person, possessing
"mother wit," or the ability to comprehend things through one's
common sense, experience, and traditional wisdom. Therefore, this
unlettered woman clearly understands that poor people should unite
in spite of their political affiliations:

> Salomón González—that's what my first husband name was—
> well I knowed Salomón and Don Caliche was good friends,
> even though the baker wan't a Communist, both him and my
> husband was on the same side and was defendin' the same
> thing.
>
> (Salomón González—así se llamaba mi marido—yo sabía pues
> que Salomón y don Caliche eran buenos amigos, y aunque el
> panadero no era comunista, tanto él como mi marido estaban
> del mismo lado y defendiendo lo mismo.) (35)

15. Gates, "Blackness of Blackness," 289.

For another, unlike Esther in *The Four Mirrors,* Carmen is not intimidated by a man when defending her own point of view. Essentially, she is one of the first people in their community to sense that the war is between the haves and have-nots, although she claims that she did not have any idea of the meaning of those events at the time they happened:

> But the truth is these days, it's more clearer and clearer that the worl' divided between those who has somethin' to kill hunger with and those who is dirt po'. But, you know, truth is, now I see it but I didn't have the foggies' notion when I was talkin' wit' Salomón that mornin'.
>
> (Pero la verdad es que ahora en estos momentos, va quedando claro que el mundo está dividido en los que tienen con qué matar el hambre y los que están pelados. Pero la verdad es que eso lo pienso ahora, pero no se me ocurría cuando hablaba con Salomón esa mañana.) (56)

Such Eve/Hagar-like qualities of humility and submissiveness clash with Carmen's firm belief in her instincts, even though she assumes that posture. Because Doña Carmen is unlettered, she does not set much store by any political ideology, but instead relies on the black concept of signifyin(g), which is essentially a "folk" notion that defies the interpretation of meaning in language through book-learned sources.[16] Thus, her understanding of world affairs is based on such knowledge. For example, she challenges Salomón to open his eyes to the ugly realities behind the *caldero-comunista* (conservative) coalition he so blindly supports. No matter what rhetoric and tactics the politicians use, they all betray the people:

> Salomón got so worked up and I knowed it, and almos' always whenever I seen 'im half crazy like that, I shut my mouth. But that mornin' I ain't gave 'im no slack. No indeed, I ain't gave 'im no slack 'cause it seemed to me real strange that Somoza's "Nicas" was helpin' our government, since Somoza was a shameless dictator and traitor.
>
> (Salomón se estaba enojando y yo lo sabía, y casi siempre cuando yo lo veía medio arrancado me quedaba callada. Pero

16. Ibid.

esa mañana no le aflojé. No le aflojé nada porque es que a mí
me parecía raro eso de que los nicas de Somoza estuvieran
ayudando al gobierno, siendo Somoza un dictador sinvergüenza
y traidor.) (58)

In spite of her submissive pose, Doña Carmen tries to convince her
spouse of the obvious—that the conservatives and rebels are one
and the same: "Somoza's 'Nicas' help the government troops, and
his enemy 'Nicas' help y'all. But they's all buyin' from the same
sto'... And I know I'm stupid and all that, but I don't understand
it" (los nicas de Somoza apoyan al gobierno y los nicas enemigos
de Somoza los apoyan a ustedes. Unos y otros pelean en las mismas
tiendas... Y es que una es bruta y todo, pero yo no entiendo eso,
59). Again, through metaphor ("they's all buyin' from the same
sto'") and chiasmus/repetition and reversal ("And I know I'm stupid and all that"), words that appear to inform her husband are
really intended to persuade him not to take part in a vain struggle
from which he as a poor person will gain no benefits. When indirec-
tion fails, Doña Carmen boldly confronts Salomón by assuming an
independent, assertive (Eve-like) stance:

> "You wanna know the real truth? I ain't never knowed how to
> be submissive. No matter how much I used to tell myself how
> I oughta listen to my husband, I ain't let up offa Salomón 'til I
> seen him git *real* mad, and then I got scared. But I wan't fright-
> ened of 'im, just had respect for 'im."
>
> (—Y la pura verdad es que yo nunca supe ser así resignada.
> Nunca, por más que hable y diga que una debe atenerse a lo
> que dice el hombre, no me le he aflojado a Salomón, hasta que
> lo vía todo bravo, y a veces con eso me entraba un miedo. Y
> no tenía que tenerle miedo, pero es una especie de respeto.)
> (59)

All of the preceding passages illustrate the vitality of the womb/
tongue metaphor in the delineation of this womanist character, for
Doña Carmen's ease and skill in using language are her forte. Moreover, it is a performance culled from a tradition of people who
value verbal exchanges and face-to-face encounters *in and of themselves*. Signifyin(g) is the masterful use of language in oral contexts,
but when it is transferred into written discourse it can be employed

to create "'speakerly texts' or those that privilege the representation of the speaking black voice."[17] One can virtually hear Doña
Carmen's richly toned, penetrating voice "loud-talking," "marking,"
and "sounding off" at Don Caliche about her memories of the war
and her first husband, Salomón. The reader can also imagine the
ironic inclination of Carmen's head, the sly grin on her face, the
quizzical expression in her eyes, the index finger punctuating the
air, and, most important of all, the hands placed deftly on the hips
(arms akimbo) from time to time as she cajoles, challenges, and
persuades Don Caliche while making fun of the politicians and the
gullible masses who believe in their lies. The womb/tongue metaphor is the core of the Eve/Hagar paradigm in *Dead-End Street,*
for the "minor" figure Doña Carmen becomes a talking book—the
vital link between the opposing forces of orality and writing. As an
Eve figure, she is a helpmate and confidante for the elder López,
who is forced to reexamine certain inconsistencies of the Civil War
that are still unresolved in his mind, and she is the nurturer and
counselor to Carlos, thus preparing the way for their reconciliation.
As a Hagar model, she represents the lowest rung of society, and
therefore the most ignored, least respected, and, certainly, most invisible. In short, Doña Carmen is the last person anyone would
consult about national or world affairs.

When Carlos comes to look for his father, Doña Carmen greets
him warmly, although at first their chitchat is somewhat awkward.
However, since Don Caliche has gone to Don Euclides to plead his
grandson Daniel's case, Carlos promises to return later. The reader
learns through the sifted memory of Doña Carmen's interior monologue that father and son finally do reconcile: "Thank God he
spared me to see the day the two of 'em could talk. Po' Tomasa" (De
modo que Dios me hizo la gracia de vivir para verlos hablando.
Lástima Tomasa, 33). In spite of the family feud, Doña Carmen remembers her stepson with fondness and is even proud of him:
"And many times I would tell Doña Tomasa: that boy don't
walk like no baker's son, but like a congressman or bishop. But,
you know, maybe she expected too much from him, maybe she did"
(Y muchas veces se lo había dicho a doña Tomasa: ese muchacho no
camina como hijo de panadero, sino como un diputado o un obispo.
Pero ella esperó quizás demasiado de él, quizás, 34). In short, as

17. Ibid., 296.

Anancy the Spider, Doña Carmen not only helps Don Caliche and Carlos López to reconcile with one another, but also gets them to connect to a diverse national history/reality that the formal/hegemonic discourse disguises as the white legend.

Doña Carmen is a rebel at heart, a trait that links her to other females of the Eve/Hagar paradigm in the fiction of Duncan. Moreover, her spirit of resistance surfaces when the situation demands, which is what surprisingly attracts the conservative Don Caliche López to her:

> He watched Carmen get up, take the tin plate in her hands weathered by time, get up, take the enameled tin plate into her hands worn by endless hours of water and dishrags, grease and sweat from a million painful days and nights, watching her children die or barely survive, with an empty heart due to her husband's absence, the one she loved so much; he saw her move away, enter the kitchen, and he was thinking about her, *about the rebellion that they shared and that united them,* about the hopes and dreams they had in common that they tried to transfer into the future without knowing how, because nobody had bothered to tell them.

> (Miró a Carmen levantarse, tomar entre sus manos golpeadas por el tiempo el plato de lata esmaltada, levantarse, tomar entre sus manos golpeadas por las horas de agua y trapos, grasas y sudor en un millar de días y noches dolororsas, mirando a los hijos morirse o sobrevivir apenas, vacío su pecho por la ausencia de su marido que ella quiso tanto, la miró alejarse, entrar en la cocina, y estaba pensando en ella, *en la rebelión que compartieron y los unía,* en los sueños y esperanzas comunes que intentaban trasladar al futuro sin saber cómo, porque nunca nadie se tomó la molestia de decir cómo.) (45–46; emphasis added)

Through these conversations with his spouse, Don Caliche begins to concede that he has betrayed himself and his own people by supporting the oligarchy out of gratitude for significant gains—social security, health care, and an eight-hour workday—but at the expense of fundamental privileges like the rights to vote, to exercise free speech, and, above all, to protest peacefully: "And he knowed it, yeah, he knowed it like a person know the sky's above his head, that the struggle wan't 'bout mistakes. It was a war between the haves and have-nots. But how could he make peoples understand that?" (Y sabía, sabía como quien conoce que el cielo está sobre su cabeza, que la lucha no era contra los errores. Que la lucha devenía entre los adinerados y los pobres. Pero, ¿cómo hacérselo entender a la gente? 50–51).[18] The goading, needling, cajoling remarks uttered by his wife in the name of tough love have brought him to the point of despair, the exact opposite of the hope with which Don Caliche had enthusiastically gone to war:

> How could he get peoples to understand when he hisself and, just like him, many other supporters of Calderón had been involved in arrestin' members of the opposition party? Yeah, him too. In the name of the Doctor and wit' all the authority 'vested in him, he had also done these things in good faith and with the conviction that he was doin' the right thing.

> (¿Cómo hacérselo entender a la gente, si además él mismo, y como él muchos otros calderonistas habían participado en la detención de oposicionistas?
> Sí, él mismo.
> En nombre del Doctor y con toda la autoridad del caso, él también con toda su buena fe, con la convicción de que hacía lo mejor.) (51)

---

18. Biesanz, Biesanz, and Biesanz, *The Costa Ricans,* 23–32. The 1940s was a decade filled with turmoil in Costa Rica. Various factions clustered around two prominent political figures: Dr. Rafael Ángel Calderón Guardiá, an arch-conservative who saw himself as a benevolent dictator, and Otilio Ulate, publisher of the newspaper *Diario de Costa Rica.* Ironically, Calderón was supported by the Communist-led faction under Juan Rafael Mora, and Ulate was backed by a tenuous coalition of oligarchic elites, idealistic reformers, and opportunistic activists. *Dead-End Street* portrays this conflict by casting Salomón González and Don Caliche López, Doña Carmen's first and second husbands, respectively, as *calderonistas,* or supporters of Calderón, while suggesting that people like Carlos López and his cohorts are *oposicionistas* or *ulatistas,* supporters of Ulate who also opposed Calderón. To complicate matters, a third figure came on the scene around 1942. José "Pepe" Figueres had been exiled, but he continued his opposition to both groups from abroad. Thus, he became a charismatic symbol of resistance and was a key player in the Partido de Acción Democrática (Social Democratic Party), an organization that provided him with a solid political base as well as potential soldiers in 1945. By February 1947 the country was plagued by sabotage, assassinations, armed conflict between the police and youth groups, strikes, closed banks and other businesses, as well as general chaos. Thus, on March 10, 1948, Figueres's "revolutionary forces," called *figueristas,* began their "War of National Liberation" from their base of operation in La Lucha. However, the battle lasted only about a month, for a cease-fire was declared on April 13, and peace negotiations were begun on April 18.

Through a third-person interior-monologue voice, Don Caliche pain-fully raises questions he has not allowed himself to even think about for years:

> Why was a family of peasants with the rich peoples? And why was he, the son of a peasant, grandson of a peasant, a baker—no mo', no less—a descendant of peasant settlers, sent to ar-rest one of his own? No, no, he couldn't make 'em understan' that the government was a good one in spite of its mistakes; he couldn't do it 'cause he wan't clear 'bout the whole matter hisself.

> (¿Por qué una familia campesina estaba con la causa de los ri-cos? ¿Y por qué él, hijo de campesino, nieto de campesino, panadero no más, descendiente de colonos campesinos, era en-viado a detener a uno de los suyos? No, no podia recurrir a la gente. No podía hacerles comprender que el gobierno, por en-cima de sus errores era un gobierno bueno; no podía, porque él mismo no tenía claro todo el cuadro.) (52)

Don Caliche does not have the answers to these questions. His wife might not either, but she sets him to thinking.

Doña Carmen's oral testimony, the source of unrecorded histor-ical information about the Civil War of 1948, is intrahistory, or the unwritten story. First, her anecdotes are relevant because they re-veal the perspective of everyday people who were victimized by both sides in the conflict. For example, there are constant references to a water tank that was dynamited in San Joaquín, leaving the vil-lage without a water supply. The *calderonistas* and *figueristas* blame each other for the atrocity, but the people suffer. Second, through Carmen's understanding of her first husband's involvement with the Communist Party, it becomes clear that the foot soldiers were used as pawns by the conservative and liberal factions. Thus, Car-men reveals that she constantly worried about the survival of her-self and their eleven children, but when she finally gets the news of Salomón's death, she shows the same courage and strength as Hagar by taking matters into her own hands. She joins the ranks of the local revolutionary party. Doña Carmen's memory of that day sums up her bittersweet, tragicomic life and that of the nation:

> And now that I think about it, I'm gonna do it. I'm gonna join the Committee of Mercy 'cause somethin' like that have to be

important enough for a man as intelligent as you is, with a wife and 'leven kids, to go fight 'til they kill 'im dead like some dog. And anyway, I don't even wanna be on the same side as Don Gustavo. I wanna follow in yo' footsteps, Salomón.

"Is the dead man your relative, lady?"

And you know, I was thinkin' 'bout the Court of Immediate Sanctions and 'bout my kids and my parents, and I said, naw, I ain't never had no husband and I lef' there with the taste of sweet mangoes in my mouth, rememberin' his hairy chest, and short, half-kinky hair, his butt covered with smallpox pimples, and, goodness, his weight on top of me, and how the bugger used to say silly stuff like his skin vanilla and mine chocolate.

(Y ahora que lo pienso lo voy a hacer. Voy a entrar al Comité de la Mercé porque tiene que ser importante la causa para que un hombre tan inteligente como vos, con once hijos y mujer, se haya ido a pelear hasta que lo maten como a un perro. Y de todos modos, no quiero estar del mismo lado de don Gustavo. Quiero seguir del lado tuyo, Salomón...

—¿Es pariente suyo el muerto, señora?

Y es que yo estaba pensando en los Tribunales de Sanciones Inmediatas y en mis hijos y en mis padres y dije que no que yo nunca tuve marío y salí a la calle con una gana del olor a mango dulce, su pecho velludo, su pelo corto medio chuzo, sus nalgas salpicadas por manchas de viruela, sus piernas gruesas, pesado el condenado, diciendo cosas que yo nunca tuve tiempo de oír, como cremita la piel de él, como chocolate el mío.) (108)

The cynical stance of this Anancy figure is sweetened by her allusion to the taste of mangoes, as the womb/tongue metaphor triggers memories of love for Salomón and for Costa Rica. Furthermore, this posture inspires the heroine to coax the men of the López family into mending fences, which is symbolic of the need for the nation's healing and restoration.

In terms of verisimilitude, it is necessary for Doña Carmen's story to be implanted within the text (story) of the male protagonist in *Dead-End Street* because her perspective is not to be found in any written accounts. Because history is written primarily by the conquerors, it had been difficult to perceive alternative points of view until the recovery and rescue of dissenting texts in the late twentieth century. Because of the ironclad acceptance of the white legend, black characters in *Dead-End Street* are conspicuous by their absence or invisibility, which is a deliberate technique to underscore the irony of Costa Rica's identity crisis. For example, as Carlos tries to interrogate other victims who were beaten and arrested along with Daniel, he appeals in vain to "Black Tony," another minor character in the novel, to join him in a lawsuit against the government:

> Black Tony, Daniel's bosom buddy, was his last hope. But Tony remembered his father's warning that before 1948 Negroes couldn't even travel beyond Turrialba. So even if the police had beaten him up and his back carried battle scars, like welts of cat-o'-nine-tails, he did not dare sign a statement against them that would ultimately damage the party.

> (El negro Tony, compañero inseparable de Daniel, era el último que quedaba. Pero Tony tenía presente que le dijo su padre que antes del 48 los negros no podían pasar de Turrialba y por ese motivo aunque había sido golpeado y tenía la espalda magullada no se atrevía a firmar una demanda que podía perjudicar al Partido.) (110–11)

Carlos the revolutionary reveals his academic understanding of the situation when he admonishes Tony for not cooperating with him in seeking justice for the incidents of police brutality:

> "Good grief, son. I took to the hills to fight for that same party. I'm one of the founders of that party. This whole thing cost me some blood."
> "Me, too," shot back Tony, almost yelling. "The *mariachis* [the cops] even killed my older brother in Paradise Valley."

> (—Pero por Dios muchacho...yo fui a pelear: yo soy fundador de ese partido. A mí me costó sangre esta cuestión...
> —A mí también—dijo Tony casi gritando—a mi hermano mayor lo mataron los mariachis en Paraíso.) (111)

Historians corroborate the presence of racial and class tensions in Costa Rica, citing the series of immigration laws, government decrees, economic sabotage, and numerous Jim Crow practices that made life almost unbearable for aliens and citizens of Antillean origin during the twentieth century.[19] Nevertheless, many West Indians and middle-class whites like Carlos were idealistic enough to believe

19. Harpelle, *West Indians of Costa Rica*, 97–109.

in the deferred dream of constitutional changes that would bring equality and justice. However, a concrete incident in Black Tony's life (police brutality against black males) blows up that dream, and the phenomenon of Afro-realism functions through the Eve/Hagar paradigm in Doña Carmen's story. Consequently, Black Tony reminds Carlos (and the reader) that reality falls far short of the ideals encoded in the national text, and in doing so he supports Carmen's viewpoint, namely, that the government does not truly represent the people.

In order to illustrate the hegemonic discourse in *Dead-End Street*, Duncan employs excerpts from Costa Rican newspapers and magazines, thus articulating the official history codified in the textbooks. For example, the *Tribuna,* organ of the conservative coalition, reports,

> The Pacific Navigation Company was pleased to announce to its clients that in spite of the difficult conditions occasioned by the war, it would continue offering its regular service in the Central American ports, courtesy of Felipe J. Alvarado and Company, S.A.... "Good men will govern the Nation," he said, "and we will have peace."

> (The Pacific Navegation *[sic]* Company anunciaba a sus clientes con gusto que a pesar de las difíciles condiciones creadas por la guerra, seguiría ofreciendo el servicio regular a los puertos centroamericanos. Felipe J. Alvarado y Cía. Sucs. S.A.... hombres de bien gobernarán la República—dijo—y habrá paz.) (31)

To this end, the white legend, articulated by the aged *patrón* Don Euclides Herrera, is the foundation of the dominant discourse the newspaper supports:

> At what point had his noble lineage lost its strength? Was not his own father, Don Julio Herrera Hamilton, among the architects of the national European culture? What had happened between the time he went into exile and the moment the blue vote of the *echandistas* [Echanda's followers] was cast? There was a sort of empty space in the construction of his version of events that did not permit him to understand things well, but he still had to hold on to the honor he had inherited from the Salvatierra and Sanch families, from the Centenos and Moras....

What had happened to a world where it used to mean something when you mentioned the names Orlich, Urbina, Mora...?

(¿Dónde perdió su fuerza su misma hidalga estirpe? ¿No estuvo
don Julio Herrera Hamilton, su padre, entre los forjadores de
la cultura nacional-europea? ¿Qué había comenzado a suceder
entre el momento en que emprendió su exilio y el vote azul
echandista? Había una suerte de vacío en la construcción de su
versión de los hechos, que no lo dejaba interpretar bien. Pero
tenía que aferrarse aún al honor heredado de los Salvatierra y
los Sanch, de los Centeno y de los Mora....

¿Qué le sucedió al mundo, donde tenía un sentido preciso
decir Orlich, Urbina, Mora...?) (64–65)

Don Euclides's interior monologue represents a concept of self/
nationhood established during the nineteenth century by the first
generation of writers known as the Olympians, or those born in the
1850s and '60s.[20] Moreover, those architects of national culture
were obsessed with European models, especially English and French
ones (and to a lesser extent Spanish); thus, their own social paradigm was circumscribed to the Central Plateau of Costa Rica, where
San José is located.

During the nineteenth century, the Central Valley also became the
heart of the coffee-growing agribusiness that gave the nobility of
Costa Rica a chance at economic solvency, for at the beginning of
the colonial era the province had been an impoverished area on the
margins of prosperous metropolises such as Mexico City, Guatemala
City, and Lima. It is important to note that the Olympian notion of
national culture deliberately excluded those regions of Costa Rica
where Amerindian and African-descended groups were found, as
well as the cattle-raising and mining areas where significant portions of the population were of mixed ancestry. Hence, the myth
that entered the twentieth century projected an image of Costa Rica
as a country with a 98 percent "white" population.[21]

Ronald N. Harpelle summarizes the intimate relationship between the white legend and the national identity in Costa Rica:

20. Álvaro Quesada Soto, "Identidad nacional y literatura nacional en Costa
Rica: La 'generación del Olimpo,'" 102. Among these writers were Manuel de
Jesús Jiménez (1854–1916); Jenaro Cardona (1863–1908); Manuel González
Zeledón, alias "Magón" (1864–1909); and Ricardo Fernández Guardia (1867–
1950).
21. Ibid., 103. See also Smart, "Literary World," 294.

Costa Ricans take pride in a concept of history that sets them apart from neighboring republics. According to popular lore and academic postulations, when the Spaniards arrived in Costa Rica they discovered a very small indigenous population that could provide sufficient labor for the development of the large haciendas that came to characterize other parts of Latin America. Instead the Europeans became poor immigrant farmers who developed a more egalitarian society because of a common heritage. Accordingly, the lack of a sizable indigenous population also meant that miscegenation was uncommon and Costa Ricans remained "racially" pure. Therefore, Costa Rica, unlike its neighbors, developed into a peaceful "white settler" society where the Catholic Church dominated and everyone shared Spanish ancestry.[22]

The counterhegemonic text that deconstructs the preceding model of nationhood emerges from the collective voices of civilians like Doña Carmen, for Don Caliche and Carlos López provide the accounts of the foot soldier and guerrilla, respectively. Through the womb/tongue metaphor, oral history and ethnic memory are utilized to reinterpret the events of the Civil War of 1948 and its aftermath twenty years later. History and myth are sifted through the characters' conflicting visions and multiple discourses, which results in a national identity based on alienation, confusion, and anguish. On the one hand, Carlos López's perspective forms a shaky bridge between Don Euclides's and Don Caliche's points of view, just as the middle class barely holds its own between a recalcitrant but dying oligarchy and the amorphous masses. On the other hand, Doña Carmen's testimony is the most significant in the novel because it inspires the men to search their souls for the good of self, community, and nation. Whether Carmen is actually a black woman is less relevant than her experience of suffering indignities and injustices in a supposedly democratic society. Like the other Eve/Hagar figures we have examined in Duncan's fiction, Doña Carmen is "blackened" by her shared history of fighting oppression along with the López men. Thus, it is appropriate that signifyin(g), a rhetorical device from the African-derived oral tradition, be utilized to make the

22. Harpelle, "Assimilate or Emigrate? West Indian Strategies for Survival in Costa Rica, 1930–1949," 97.

case for the diversity and multiplicity of heritages that constitute the national body. Nevertheless, the anguish expressed by the ex-guerrilla protagonist, Carlos López, echoes that of a nation that refuses to look at the discrepancies between its fantasy and its reality, and such blindness leads inevitably to a *final de calle,* or dead-end street.

Carlos López is considered an existential figure because of the alienation, confusion, and doubt he expresses throughout the novel, as well as the lack of meaning in his postwar efforts to redefine history. Moreover, the protagonist's deep sense of loss is symbolized by the inability to find his house: "And you cannot even find the street that leads you back home" (Y no puedes hallar la calle que da a tu casa, 112). Not only does Carlos feel the absurdity of his individual plight, but he is also anxious about the ridiculous predicament of his country. He wonders if he should regroup and go back to the battlefield without the Fermíns and Salchichas of the world, knowing like Hernán Cortés that the ships have already been burned, or break through the wall of corruption and complacency. That question is left unresolved and the work open-ended. On the surface, Carlos as existential antihero is a way of examining Costa Rica's identity crisis through the specific trope of marginalization:

> In spite of appearances, the novel *Dead-End Street* depicts a rather well-defined schism between the perspective of the principal narrator and the social sector that is the protagonist of the novel and whose point of view must be presented. It is primarily through existentialism that Duncan has been able to accomplish this subtle distancing of the mestizo-bourgeois sector, a distancing that is basically carried out in the confrontation and conflict characteristic of his earlier fiction.[23]

The Eve/Hagar paradigm in the character of Doña Carmen has presented a distinct reading of *Dead-End Street*. Viewed from another angle, the womb/tongue and head/hand metaphors are deconstructing signifiers for Duncan's achievement at inserting the Afro–Costa Rican aesthetic into the national canon. There is a difference between an African-descended author whose culture informs his

---

23. Ian Isidore Smart, "*Final de calle* y la estética negra." All translated quotations from this essay are my own.

works and one who is pigeonholed by the Eurocentric imagination. By winning the highest national prize for literature, Duncan's stature as an artist improved tremendously, but it also showed that his art was not trapped by race, gender, and class. Thus, within the context of a national dialectic, the significance of the author's notes at the beginning of the novel becomes clear: "*Dead-End Street* is above all a novel. It tries to be faithful to the facts, as told to us by the popular sectors who are its protagonists, without ceasing from being an interpretation" (*Final de calle* es ante todo una novela. Intenta ser fiel a los hechos tal como la cuentan los sectores populares protagonistas, sin dejar de ser una interpretación, n.p.). It is one writer's way of looking at his homeland's place, identity, and language in the world of literature.

Not only does Doña Carmen recite an alternative view of Costa Rican history, but she also embodies that revisionist history. She is both a character that signifies and the vehicle of signifyin(g)/signification on the white legend. Through selecting a vernacular construct from the Afro–Costa Rican tradition, Duncan challenges the polarity between orality and literacy that privileges scriptural practice (writing) over nonscriptural performance. In the process the author re-creates a talking book that also plays on the devices of creolization, double vision, and double voicing. The latter two concepts provide an excellent insight into the ways that "'outsider' conventions" intersect with "'insider' knowledge and practice" to offer a more holistic way of interpreting reality:

> These terms help to describe processes of creolization because they take into account the dual or multiple factors that interaction involves, yet they work against either/or, is/isn't polarization. "Doubling" establishes an oscillation between contrasting perspectives but does not reify them into entities. Double voicing refers to the articulation of a dual cultural consciousness, shaped through social and personal conflict and expressed in oral and written mediums. Double vision is itself a double-voiced concept, in that speakers and writers use it to refer to both bicultural existence and to special powers of sight that cross the boundaries between the visible and the invisible, the material and the immaterial dimensions of reality. By extension, double voicing and double vision offer ways to talk about relationships between two (or more) sign systems, modes of inscription, and ways of approaching literature texts and artifacts.

Sometimes they take on a more concrete character when two voices, two scripts, two systems of meaning occur side by side.[24]

If we read the two systems that merge in Duncan's fiction as currents that flow from the Afrocentric and Eurocentric discourses, then the resolution of their conflict can be obtained by the eclectic manipulation of both/and rather than either/or. This is what the author suggests that New World writers can achieve through the theory and practice of Afro-realism, and this is what has been explored in terms of the interactive, interdependent, and complementary aspects of the Eve/Hagar paradigm in the fictional works of the present study. In that manner, the wounds sustained through exile, dispersal, forced migration, and enslavement/colonization are healed through adaptation, renewal, and transformation in the New Jerusalem—the blending of Limón and San José.

24. Grey Gundaker, *Signs of Diaspora/Diaspora of Signs: Literacies, Creolization, and Vernacular Practice in African America*, 4–5, 10–11.

# CONCLUSION

As we have seen throughout *The Eve/Hagar Paradigm in the Fiction of Quince Duncan,* there are certain red flags raised when male authors create female characters, just as there are problems with members of any hegemonic group who portrays figures occupying a marginal status in a given society. Whether the matter involves race/color, gender/sex, or class/caste, there is a general consensus that it is very difficult, if not impossible, for the dominant individual or class to speak for the subordinate ones within a context of inequality and injustice. The perception of difference and the negative ways in which that perception is depicted in literature lie at the heart of postcolonialism and postmodernism, theories that have been entertained in this study but found to be untenable in and of themselves. Instead, Afro-realism as a theory and praxis has been the approach to exploring Duncan's fiction of the 1970s. Moreover, this approach falls within the context of a global theory espoused  by Joyce Ann Joyce:

> An African-centered ideology is an African-American intellectual concept that places all of Africa (not just ancient Egypt) and its history at the center of its research and pedagogical investigations. An African-centered approach is interdisciplinary, with practitioners who are historians, philosophers, sociologists, psychologists, cultural analysts, anthropologists, and literary critics. An African-centered ideology is comprehensive with its goal of influencing both the intellectual and the emotional components of Black lives.[1]

Like that of other contemporary writers, Duncan's fiction is challenging and complex. For example, his novels and short stories do reflect

---

1. Joyce, "African-Centered Womanism: Connecting Africa to the Diaspora," 539. In *Black Writers and Latin America: Cross-cultural Affinities,* Richard L. Jackson traces the history of cultural and literary ties among New World black writers, many of whom do use an African-centered ideology in their works.

some of the traits associated with postmodernism. In the works examined, male protagonists like Guabo Brown ("Go-o-o-o-al!"), the anonymous artist ("Ancestral Myths"), and Charles McForbes *(The Four Mirrors)* experience a strong sense of alienation, absurdity, fragmentation, and meaninglessness—similar to the classic existentialist hero of Western literature. On the other hand, many of the women figures, as well as men like Pedro Dull *(For the Sake of Peace)*, almost invariably seek wholeness, spirituality, and connectedness to their history, and they embrace values that are rooted in precolonial systems, although the latter have been tempered by the American experience. This transformative process is evident in the lives of Mariot Prince Kenton *(For the Sake of Peace)*, Ruby ("A Gift for Grandma"), Sophisticated Lady ("Sophisticated Lady"), the anonymous old woman ("Two Roads"), Mama Drusilda ("Family Ties"), Miss Spence ("A Letter), and Lorena McForbes *(The Four Mirrors)*.

As stated earlier, four major tropes recur in Duncan's fiction: the *cimarrón*, the *samamfo*, the river, and laughter. However, the symbol par excellence for struggle, especially the women's efforts to re-center self and community, is the *samamfo* because it embodies an African-dominant worldview—that there are spiritual and material realities we must respect. To that end, the Eve/Hagar paradigm captures the strong tendency toward spirituality and resistance while provoking the characters to reestablish balanced ties to males and children within the spaces of family, home, and community. Conversely, those women who are out of touch with that potent life force experience a sense of failure, as does the Educator ("The Watchman's Light"); or they are self-destructive, like Aracely Brown ("Go-o-o-o-al!"); or they do not survive, like Mammy *(For the Sake of Peace)*. For this reason, Afro-realism has been proffered as an indigenous alternative to the "post" theories because it is rooted in the matrix of reconstituted African-descended cultures in the New World that form the context of African Hispanophone writing.

The fiction examined in *The Eve/Hagar Paradigm* also treats many of the topics of postcolonial theory from the perspective of a writer who has experienced neocolonialism in Latin America. Considering the lingering oppression of people in developing nations, especially that which is perpetuated by multinational entities, one could easily pose this question: How "post" is postcolonialism? In fact, Duncan raises this very issue through the voices of male and female characters, and the dynamics of that questioning informs every aspect of his fiction, which challenges/engages the canon:

> [T]he hyphenated form of the word "post-colonial" has come to stand for both the material effects of colonialism and the huge diversity of everyday and sometimes hidden responses to it throughout the world. We use the term "post-colonial" to represent the continuing process of imperial suppressions and exchanges throughout this diverse range of societies, in their institutions and their discursive practices. Because the imperial process works through as well as upon individuals and societies "post-colonial" theory rejects the egregious classification of "First" and "Third" World and contests the lingering fallacy that the post-colonial is somehow synonymous with the economically "underdeveloped."[2]

Neither is the postcolonial writer aesthetically "underdeveloped," for the craft of writing is a vehicle deliberately manipulated to present a world of one's own invention. More than any factor, the culture(s) experienced by an artist determine(s) the language, forms, and sensibility of his or her art, while race, gender, and class might shape the outlook or the position from which he or she speaks. Duncan expounds on the notion of *ficciología* (ficciology), a group of theoretical and methodological approaches to the study of literature developed by other colleagues and him:

> As the art of the written word, fiction is a part of a correlated whole. Certainly it has its own relative autonomy in relation to its sources, but at the same time, it is integrated into its milieu in a double sense: as an expression of the ideological system of a social group and as a medium of that same system in order to provide cohesion to collective thought. Therefore, as a system, fiction is not a simple aggregate of elements. It is a new, empowered reality, qualitatively distinct from the one in which it originated. It is produced according to a preexisting aesthetic code in that society (at least partially). Each work of fiction emerges, then, from the community, as a product of the work of an author inserted in that social ambience. And each work of fiction as the product created by social circulation is integrated into a communal reality when it documents and in-

2. Ashcroft, Griffiths, and Tiffin, *Post-colonial Studies Reader,* 3.

terprets collective experiences, thus stimulating reflection on them and the will to transform the real happenings.[3]

The preceding theory of fiction is grounded in Duncan's own premises about literature, as well as studies by Ariel Bignami (*¿Qué es la literatura?* [What is literature?]) and Nestor García Canclini (*La producción simbólica* [Symbolic production]). In addition, the Costa Rican author's "ficciology" is strongly rooted in the African-descended oral traditions, whose collective, functional, and social nature has been well established. Ideally, *afro-realismo* is an eclectic, holistic, and restorative approach to writing similar to the African-centered literary criticism formulated by Joyce: "An African-centered literary criticism embraces a communal doctrine that has its roots in the interconnectedness and well-being of all Blacks in Africa and the diaspora. It is essential to note here that many of the societal values indigenous to traditional African culture have now been weakened seriously by corruption and disruption."[4] Afro-realism does not ignore the syncretistic experiences of Africans living in the New World diaspora. Nevertheless, it does eschew the dehumanizing, unethical, and spiritually vapid cultural tendencies that are based on the commodification of people and celebration of things. More than anything, the signifyin(g) trope calls attention to the black writer's need to meet the challenge of rehumanizing language and literature in the Western world. Consequently, the talking book–speakerly text within *Dead-End Street* is a model worth emulating.

How well does Duncan convey the female voice? In order to address that issue, one must first understand some basic assumptions about feminist theory and practice. As discussed earlier, the feminist mode involves the privileging of the female voice, which conveys the total experience of being female—that is, all the psychological, emotional, intellectual, physical, sexual, and spiritual factors affecting the female gender. In addition, many would argue that the feminist mode can be conveyed only by a female artist, writer, or intellectual. For example, Rosalyn Terborg-Penn reports that "a radical feminist approach to black women's history would view victimization as the major theme, with patriarchy, whether white

3. Duncan, "Visión panorámica," 79.
4. Joyce, "African-Centered Womanism," 541.

or black, as the basis for oppression."[5] An example of the latter is the Combahee River Collective manifesto.[6] On the other hand, African feminism is more inclusive and less inclined to pander to the woman-as-victim motif. She comments:

> First, it begins with the cosmology common to traditional African women who lived during the era of the slave trade. Because the African heritage of most women indigenous to New World societies originated then, this cosmology provides a common source for historical analysis. Second, the theory eliminates the "white filter" in that it looks to black standards for interpreting culture, values, initiatives, activities, and organizations. In doing so, the theory is uniquely a black woman's theory. Third, the theory can be applied cross-culturally through time in order to assess women's roles and activities during and after slavery, as well as women's battle against human oppression. Here the variables in the liberation struggle are more diverse than in any other theory, because they include race, gender, sexuality, class, religion, and culture, all areas of human activity in which black women have achieved in spite of discrimination.[7]

In the fictional world explored in *The Eve/Hagar Paradigm*, there are characters like Mammy and Esther McForbes who are depicted in the feminine mode, while others such as Sophisticated Lady,

5. Terborg-Penn, "African Feminism: A Theoretical Approach to the History of Women in the African Diaspora," in *Women in Africa,* ed. Terborg-Penn and Rushing, 28.
6. Childers and Hentzi provide the following information about the collective: "The Combahee River Collective is a group of feminists of color who began meeting together in Boston in 1974. The collective took its name from a military campaign conceived and led by Harriet Tubman in 1863, which freed more than 750 slaves. Initially the group focused primarily on consciousness-raising rather than political activism, though individual members were involved in a variety of causes ranging from lesbian politics to sterilization abuse. Members also formed a study group and established Kitchen Table: Women of Color Press. The Kitchen Table Press has provided a means of publication for creative writing and social criticism that might not otherwise have made it into print via a mainstream press. In April 1977 the collective issued 'A Black Feminist Statement,' which explains the group's history and outlines an agenda for feminists of color; the statement had a significant influence on subsequent feminist criticism, particularly in its stress on the interconnections among oppressions based upon gender, race, class, and sexual orientation" (*Columbia Dictionary,* 49).
7. Terborg-Penn, "African Feminism," 29.

Sitaira, and Lorena McForbes are speaking subjects whose "oppositional gaze" and propensity to "talk back" situate them close to but not entirely within the feminist/womanist mode. A third group consists of characters like Myra, Ruby, and Miss Spence, who develop self-reliance, independence, and survival strategies in balanced relationships with the men in their lives—their husbands or sons. Although some of the female characters victimize each other or resort to infighting (Margaret and Mariot, Margaret and Elizabeth), one can assume an invisible network of supportive relationships among males and females because those who struggle and triumph cannot do so in isolation. In fact, an awareness of a powerful force like the *samamfo* implies that someone has passed down this knowledge to the individual. In the case of Mariot Prince Kenton, her father, Joshua, was the repository of her oral history, but she was separated from him at such an early age that others (including some unknown women) would have had to reinforce this value system as she grew up. Thus, Mariot is a significant tradition bearer in *For the Sake of Peace,* even though such is neither recognized nor appreciated by the black community, except by Pedro Dull, to whom she attempts to pass on the legacy. However, his ability to do likewise is truncated by his impending death. Despite the problematic of death and destruction, the Eve/Hagar principle embodied in Duncan's female characters allows the reader to experience the life-giving, restorative inclination of his fiction.

Joyce calls for the reexamination of feminist/womanist works of art and theories of literature by African-centered writers and scholars so that they do not mimic the rhetoric and internalize theories that are inconsistent with the value systems of black communities globally. This does not mean that sexism should not be challenged the same as racism or classism. However, it does signify that male and female artists and intellectuals need to find some common ground. She also calls our attention to a very important aspect of contemporary criticism often overlooked by canonical feminists:

> In her book *Africana Womanism: Reclaiming Ourselves,* Clenora Hudson-Weems joins Afrocentric sociologists Delores Aldridge and the late Vivian Gordon in her desire to distinguish Africana womanism from feminism and to emphasize unabashedly the importance of the family to the Africana womanist. While most African-American womanists stress Black male sexism through discussions around differences, the Africana

womanist focuses simultaneously on deconstructing Black male sexism, reconstructing the Black family, and paradoxically achieving female psychical and professional autonomy.[8]

This is what a sensitive black male writer like Duncan achieves in his theory and practice of Afro-realism by means of the concrete signifyin(g) trope from the Afro–Costa Rican oral tradition. Consequently, the African-centered intellectual communities throughout the world would do well to consider this kind of writing and critique as they attempt to reestablish harmonious, equitable relationships between men and women.[9]

To reiterate, the female characters in Duncan's fiction are outstanding contemporary literary representations of the ancestral mother Eve and the Egyptian matriarch Hagar in that their lives reflect in various degrees the conditions experienced by those historical figures. However, Duncan's women figures reinvent the paradigm along contemporary lines. The fact is that these personages are unique in Costa Rican discourse for several reasons. In the first place, they understand the realities of being females in patriarchal societies, but this does not necessarily prevent them from defining themselves according to a culturally unique vision, or from collaborating with the men in their lives. Second, the females come in all ages, classes, colors, occupations, shapes, and sizes—practically from the cradle to the grave—and many of them transcend the limitations or meet the challenges of those specific biological, cultural, and social circumstances. In this respect, they break from the traditional portrayal of young "white/beautiful" female heroines. Third, female characters in the stories and novels of Duncan are neither angels nor whores, but saints *and* sinners in that they represent living, flesh-and-blood beings who miss the mark at times. When that occurs, some seek redemption in spirituality while others opt for worldly, and often not so healthy, alternatives. Even more important, they might also make any choice in between, which is what every human being does.

In the absence of an authentic black female writer in Costa Rican fiction, Duncan successfully inserts the black female subject into the canon. His women figures may not be considered "politically cor-

8. Joyce, "African-Centered Womanism," 546.
9. Ibid., 549.

rect" when measured against radical feminist ideology, nor should they. As an enthusiastic response to Aldridge, Gordon, and Hudson-Weems's call, *The Eve/Hagar Paradigm* posits a return to the reciprocity that defined gender relations before the Fall and even afterward in some cultures in Africa. There is a prevailing belief that Christianity and Islam destroyed the mutual, interactive, and complementary relationship between men and women once these religions influenced significant portions of the world's populations.[10] To a large extent this is true, especially with respect to Islam, but it must be pointed out that Jesus treated women with dignity, equality, and respect, as a perusal of the Gospel reveals. It is just that he recognized and worked within the culture and gender-based division-of-labor patterns of his times because his purpose was ultimately to achieve a spiritual, not social, revolution. No economic, political, or social transformation is everlasting without a fundamental change in human nature—a conversion of the heart. The women who embody the Eve/Hagar principle succeed in demarginalizing and recentering black or oppressed females or both, thus presenting some outstanding examples of "cultural heroism," or heroic women who act, defy, and challenge the dominant system.[11] Furthermore, the act of writing through the reconstructed voice of the black female is an approach that augurs well for the healing and restoration of human identity in contemporary Latin American and Western literature. For that Quince Duncan is to be commended.

10. Ibid., 541.
11. Kubayanda, "Minority Discourse," 113.

# WORKS CITED

## WORKS BY QUINCE DUNCAN

*Una canción en la madrugada.* San José: Editorial Costa Rica, 1970.
*Los cuatro espejos.* San José: Editorial Costa Rica, 1973.
*El negro en la literatura costarricense.* San José: Editorial Costa Rica, 1975.
*La rebelión Pocomía y otros relatos.* San José: Editorial Costa Rica, 1976.
*La paz del pueblo.* San José: Editorial Costa Rica, 1978.
*Final de calle.* San José: Editorial Costa Rica, 1979.
"El modelo ideal de la mujer: Un análisis ficciológico de estereotipos sexistas en la narrativa costarricense." *Káñina* 9 (July–December 1985): 97–101.
*Cultura negra y teología.* San José: DEI, 1986.
"Visión panorámica de la narrativa costarricense." *Revista Iberoamericana* 53:138–39 (January–June 1987): 79–94.
"Black Images and the Eurocentric Complex in Latin America." The Birmingham Talks: Jemison Visiting Professor Lectureship, transcribed by Dellita Martin-Ogunsola. Speech recorded at the Hulsey Center, University of Alabama at Birmingham, March 27, 1995.
*Un señor de chocolate: Treinta relatos de la vida de Quince.* San José: FUNDEXED de la Universidad Nacional, 1996.

## OTHER SOURCES

Abrahams, Roger D. *Deep Down in the Jungle.* Chicago: Aldine, 1970.
Aguilar Bulgarelli, Oscar, and Irene Alfaro Aguilar. *La esclavitud negra en Costa Rica: Orígenes de la oligarquía económica y política nacional.* San José: Progreso Editorial, 1997.

Ashcroft, Bill, Gareth Griffiths, and Helen Tiffin, eds. *The Post-colonial Studies Reader*. London: Routledge, 1995.

Barrett, Leonard. *Soul Force: African Heritage in Afro-American Religion*. Garden City, NY: Doubleday, 1974.

Biesanz, Richard, Karen Zubris Biesanz, and Mavis Hiltunen Biesanz. *The Costa Ricans*. Englewood Cliffs, NJ: Prentice-Hall, 1982.

Brathwaite, Edward Kamau. "The African Presence in Caribbean Literature." *Daedalus* 103 (1974): 73–109.

Busia, Abena P. A. "This Gift of Metaphor: Symbolic Strategies and the Triumph of Survival in Simone Schwartz-Bart's *The Bridge of Beyond*." In *Out of the Kumbla*, ed. Carol Boyce Davies and Elaine Savory Fido, 289–303. Trenton: African World Press, 1990.

Captain, Yvonne. "Writing for the Future: Afro-Hispanism in a Global, Critical Context." *Afro-Hispanic Review* 13:1 (spring 1994): 3–8.

Castellanos, Rosario. *Mujer que sabe latín*. Mexico City: SepSetentas, 1973.

———. "Woman and Her Image." In *A Rosario Castellanos Reader: An Anthology of Her Poetry, Short Stories, Essays, and Drama*, ed. and trans. Maureen Ahern, 236–44. Austin: University of Texas Press, 1988.

Chamberlain, Mary. "Gender and Memory: Oral History and Women's History." In *Engendering History: Caribbean Women in Historical Perspective*, ed. Verene Shepherd, Bridget Brereton, and Barbara Bailey, 94–110. New York: St. Martin's Press, 1995.

Childers, Joseph, and Gary Hentzi, eds. *The Columbia Dictionary of Modern Literary Criticism*. New York: Columbia University Press, 1995.

Clarke, John Henrik. "New Introduction." In *The Cultural Unity of Black Africa*, by Cheikh Anta Diop, i–xv. Chicago: Third World Press, 1978.

Cobb, Martha K. *Harlem, Haiti, and Havana: A Comparative Critical Study of Langston Hughes, Jacques Roumain, and Nicolás Guillén*. Washington, DC: Three Continents Press, 1979.

———. "Images of Black Women in New World Literature: A Comparative Approach." In *Women in Africa and the African Dias-

*pora: A Reader,* ed. Rosalyn Terborg-Penn and Andrea Benton Rushing, 237–45. Washington, DC: Howard University Press, 1996.

Coleman, James. *Black Male Fiction and the Legacy of Caliban.* Lexington: University Press of Kentucky, 2001.

Cypess, Sandra Messinger. *"La Malinche" in Mexican Literature: From History to Myth.* Austin: University of Texas Press, 1991.

Davis, Lisa E. "Alienación e integración del negro caribeño en la obra reciente de Quince Duncan de Costa Rica." *Casa de las Américas* 21:124 (1981): 154–58.

———. "The World of the West Indian Black in Central America: The Recent Works of Quince Duncan." In *Voices from Under: Black Narrative in Latin America and the Caribbean,* ed. William Luis, 149–62. Westport, CT: Greenwood Press, 1984.

DeCosta-Willis, Miriam. "Afra-Hispanic Writers and Feminist Discourse." In *Women in Africa and the African Diaspora: A Reader,* ed. Rosalyn Terborg-Penn and Andrea Benton Rushing, 247–62. Washington, DC: Howard University Press, 1996.

———, ed. *Daughters of the Diaspora: Afra-Hispanic Writers.* Kingston and Miami: Ian Randle Publishers, 2003.

Deen, Edith. *All the Women of the Bible.* New York: Harper and Row, 1988.

Diop, Cheikh Anta. *The African Origin of Civilization: Myth or Reality?* Ed. and trans. Mercer Cook. Chicago: Third World Press, 1974.

———. *The Cultural Unity of Black Africa.* Chicago: Third World Press, 1978.

Ellis, Pat. "Introduction: An Overview of Women in Caribbean Society." In *Women of the Caribbean,* ed. Pat Ellis, 1–24. London: Zed Books.

Feal, Rosemary Geisdorfer. "Feminism and Afro-Hispanism: The Double Bind." *Afro-Hispanic Review* 10:1 (January 1991): 25–29.

———. "Feminist Interventions in the Race for Theory: Neither Black nor White." *Afro-Hispanic Review* 10:3 (September 1991): 11–20.

———. "Reflections on the Obsidian Mirror: The Poetics of Afro-Hispanic Identity and the Gendered Body." *Afro-Hispanic Review* 14 (spring 1995): 26–31.

Fenwick, M. J. "Female Calibans: Contemporary Women Poets of the Caribbean." *Zora Neale Hurston Forum* 4:1 (fall 1989): 1–8.

Fernández Retamar, Roberto. *Caliban and Other Essays.* Trans. Edward Baker. Minneapolis: University of Minnesota Press, 1989.

Franco, Jean. "The Colonised Imagination." In *Spanish American Literature since Independence,* 1–15. New York: Barnes and Noble, 1973.

Freyre, Gilberto. *The Masters and the Slaves: A Study in the Development of Brazilian Civilization.* Trans. Samuel Putnam. New York: Alfred A. Knopf, 1956.

Frymer-Kensky, Tikva. *Reading the Women of the Bible.* New York: Schocken Books, 2002.

Gabler-Hover, Janet. *Dreaming Black/Writing White: The Hagar Myth in American Cultural History.* Lexington: University Press of Kentucky, 2000.

Gates, Henry Louis, Jr. "The Blackness of Blackness: A Critique of the Sign and the Signifying Monkey." In *Black Literature and Literary Theory,* ed. Henry Louis Gates Jr., 238–321. New York: Routledge, 1984.

———. *Loose Canons: Notes on the Culture Wars.* New York and Oxford: Oxford University Press, 1992.

———. "The Master's Pieces: On Canon Formation and the Afro-American Tradition." In *The Bounds of Race: Perspectives on Hegemony and Resistance,* ed. Dominick LaCapra, 17–38. Ithaca: Cornell University Press, 1991.

———. *The Signifying Monkey: A Theory of Afro-American Literary Criticism.* New York: Oxford University Press, 1988.

Giovanni, Nikki. *The Selected Poems of Nikki Giovanni.* 1968. Reprint, New York: William Morrow, 1996.

Gordon, Donald K. "Alderman Johnson Roden: The Tailor-Poet." *Afro-Hispanic Review* 2 (May 1983): 9–12.

———. "Expressions of the Costa Rican Black Experience: The Short Stories of Dolores Joseph and the Poetry of Shirley Campbell." *Afro-Hispanic Review* 10:3 (September 1991): 21–26.

———. *Lo jamaicano y lo universal en la obra del costarricense Quince Duncan.* San José: Editorial Costa Rica, 1989.

———. "The Socio-political Thought and Literary Style of Quince

Duncan." *Afro-Hispanic Review* 7:1–3 (January–September 1988): 27–31.

Greene, J. Lee. *Blacks in Eden: The African American Novel's First Century.* Charlottesville: University Press of Virginia, 1996.

Gundaker, Grey. *Signs of Diaspora/Diaspora of Signs: Literacies, Creolization, and Vernacular Practice in African America.* New York: Oxford University Press, 1998.

Haberly, David T. "The Literature of an Invisible Nation." *Journal of Black Studies* 7:2 (December 1976): 133–50.

Hall, Stuart. "Cultural Identity and Cinematic Representation." *Framework* 36 (1989): 68–81.

Hansberry, William Leo. *Africa and Africans as Seen by Classical Thinkers.* Ed. Joseph E. Harris. Washington, DC: Howard University Press, 1981.

Harpelle, Ronald N. "Assimilate or Emigrate? West Indian Strategies for Survival in Costa Rica, 1930–1949." *Secolas Annals* 23 (1992): 97–109.

———. *The West Indians of Costa Rica: Race, Class, and the Integration of an Ethnic Minority.* Montreal: McGill-Queen's University Press, 2001.

Henderson, Stephen. *Understanding the New Black Poetry.* New York: William Morrow, 1973.

Hodges, Carolyn R. "Introduction: Reflections on the Art of Literary Translation and the Legacy of Langston Hughes." *Langston Hughes Review* 4:2 (fall 1985): vii–xii.

hooks, bell. *Ain't I a Woman? Black Women and Feminism.* Boston: South End Press, 1981.

———. *Black Looks: Race and Representation.* Boston: South End Press, 1992.

———. *Talking Back: Thinking Feminist, Thinking Black.* Boston: South End Press, 1989.

———. *Yearning: Race, Gender, and Cultural Politics.* Boston: South End Press, 1990.

Jackson, Richard L. *The Black Image in Latin American Literature.* Albuquerque: University of New Mexico Press, 1976.

———. *Black Literature and Humanism in Latin America.* Athens: University of Georgia Press, 1988.

———. *Black Writers and Latin America: Cross-cultural Affinities.* Washington, DC: Howard University Press, 1998.

———. *Black Writers and the Hispanic Canon.* New York: Twayne, 1997.

———. "The Shared Vision of Langston Hughes and Black Hispanic Writers." *Black American Literature Forum* 15:3 (fall 1981): 89–92.

Jahn, Janheinz. *Muntu: An Outline of the New African Culture.* New York: Grove Press, 1962.

Joyce, Joyce Ann. "African-Centered Womanism: Connecting Africa to the Diaspora." In *The African Diaspora: African Origins and New World Identities,* ed. Isidore Okpewho, Carole Boyce Davies, and Ali Mazrui, 538–54. Bloomington: Indiana University Press, 1999.

Joyner, Nancy Carol. "Postprandial Postmodernism." Presidential address, South Atlantic Modern Language Association, Atlanta, November 4, 1995.

Kubayanda, Josaphat B. "Afrocentric Hermeneutics and the Rhetoric of *Transculturación* in Black Latin American Literature." In *Latin America and the Caribbean: Geopolitics, Development, and Culture—Conference Proceedings,* ed. Arch R. M. Ritter, 226–40. New York: CALACS/ACELAC and OCPLACS, 1984.

———. "Minority Discourse and the African Collective: Some Examples from Latin American and Caribbean Literature." *Cultural Critique* 6 (spring 1987): 113–30.

LaCapra, Dominick. Introduction to *The Bounds of Race: Perspectives on Hegemony and Resistance,* ed. Dominick LaCapra, 1–16. Ithaca: Cornell University Press, 1991.

Lobo Wiehoff, Tatiana, and Mauricio Meléndez Obando. *Negros y blancos: Todos mezclado.* San José: Editorial de la Universidad de Costa Rica, 1997.

Longley, Kyle. "Resistance and Accommodation: The United States and the Nationalism of José Figueres, 1953–1957." *Diplomatic History* 18:1 (winter 1994): 1–28.

Manzano, Juan Francisco. *The Autobiography of a Slave/Autobiografía de un esclavo: A Bilingual Edition.* Ed. Ivan A. Schulman. Trans. Evelyn Picon Garfield. Detroit: Wayne State University Press, 1996.

Martínez-Alier, Verena. *Marriage, Class, and Colour in Nineteenth-Century Cuba: A Study of Racial Attitudes and Sexual Values in a Slave Society.* Cambridge: Cambridge University Press, 1975.

Martin-Ogunsola, Dellita. "Invisibility, Double Consciousness, and the Crisis of Identity in *Los cuatro espejos.*" *Afro-Hispanic Review* 6:2 (May 1987): 9–15.

———. "Translation as a Poetic Experience/Experiment: The Short Fiction of Quince Duncan." *Afro-Hispanic Review* 10:3 (September 1991): 42–50.

———, ed. and trans. *The Best Short Stories of Quince Duncan/ Las mejores historias de Quince Duncan.* San José: Editorial Costa Rica, 1995.

Mbiti, John S. *African Religions and Philosophy.* Garden City, NY: Doubleday, 1970.

McManners, John, ed. *The Oxford Illustrated History of Christianity.* Oxford: Oxford University Press, 1990.

Meléndez Chaverri, Carlos, and Quince Duncan. *El negro en Costa Rica.* San José: Editorial Costa Rica, 1972.

Meyers, Carol L. *Discovering Eve: Ancient Israelite Women in Context.* New York: Oxford University Press, 1991.

Minority Rights Group, ed. *No Longer Invisible: Afro–Latin Americans Today.* London: Minority Rights Publications, 1995.

Moreno Fraginals, Manuel. "Cultural Contributions and Deculturation." In *Africa in Latin America: Essays on History, Culture, and Socialization,* ed. Manuel Moreno Fraginals, trans. Leonard Blum, 5–22. New York: Holmes and Meier, 1984.

Mosby, Dorothy E. *Place, Language, and Identity in Afro–Costa Rican Literature.* Columbia: University of Missouri Press, 2003.

Neubert, Albrecht, and Gregory M. Shreve. *Translation as Text.* Kent: Kent State University Press, 1992.

Núñez, Benjamín. *Dictionary of Afro–Latin American Civilization.* Westport, CT: Greenwood Press, 1980.

Pastor, Beatriz. "Silence and Writing: The History of the Conquest." In *1492–1992: Re/Discovering Colonial Writing,* ed. Rene Jara and Nicholas Spadaccini, 121–63. Minneapolis: Prisma Institute; Minneapolis: University of Minnesota Press, 1989.

Persico, Alan. "Quince Duncan's *Los cuatro espejos:* Time, History, and a New Novel." *Afro-Hispanic Review* 10:1 (January 1991): 15–20.

Phillips, John A. *Eve: The History of an Idea*. San Francisco: Harper and Row, 1984.

Powell, Lorein, and Quince Duncan. *Teoría y práctica del racismo*. San José: DEI, 1988.

Purcell, Trevor W. *Banana Fallout: Class, Color, and Culture among West Indians in Costa Rica*. Los Angeles: Center for Afro-American Studies Publications, 1993.

Quesada Soto, Alvaro. "Identidad nacional y literatura nacional en Costa Rica: La 'generación del Olimpo.'" *Canadian Journal of Latin American and Caribbean Studies* 17:34 (1992): 97–113.

Ramsay, Paulette. "The African Religious Heritage in Selected Works of Quince Duncan: An Expression of Literary Marronage." *Afro-Hispanic Review* 13:2 (fall 1994): 32–39.

———. "Quince Duncan's Literary Representation of the Ethnoracial Dynamics between Latinos and Afro–Costa Ricans of West Indian Descent." *Afro-Hispanic Review* 17:2 (fall 1998): 52–60.

*Report on the Americas: The Black Americas, 1492–1992*. New York: NACLA, 1992.

Royal, Kathleen Sawyers, and Franklin Perry. "Costa Rica." In *No Longer Invisible: Afro–Latin Americans Today*, ed. Minority Rights Group, 215–24. London: Minority Rights Publications, 1995.

Ruiz, María Teresa. *Racismo: Algo más allá que la discriminación*. San José: DEI, 1988.

Ryken, Leland, James C. Wilhoit, and Tremper Longman III. *Dictionary of Biblical Imagery*. Downer's Grove, IL: InterVarsity Press, 1998.

Salas Zamora, Edwin. "La identidad cultural del negro en las novelas de Quince Duncan: Aspectos temáticos y técnicos." *Revista Iberoamericana* 53:138–39 (1987): 377–90.

Sapir, J. David. "The Anatomy of Metaphor." In *The Social Use of Metaphor*, ed. J. David Sapir and J. Christopher Crocker, 3–32. Philadelphia: University of Pennsylvania Press, 1977.

Sell, Henry T. *Studies of Famous Bible Women*. London: Fleming H. Revell, 1925.

Smart, Ian Isidore. *Amazing Connections: Kemet to Hispanophone Africana Literature*. Washington, DC: Original World Press, 1996.

———. *Central American Writers of West Indian Origin: A New Hispanic Literature.* Washington, DC: Three Continents Press, 1984.

———. *"Final de calle* y la estética negra." *La Nación Internacional* (July 19–25, 1984): 22.

———. "The Literary World of Quince Duncan." *CLA Journal* 28:39 (March 1985): 281–98.

———. "Quince Duncan." In *Dictionary of Literary Biography: Modern Latin American Fiction Writers,* 145: 100–107. Detroit: Sage Publications, 1994.

———. "Religious Elements in the Narrative of Quince Duncan." *Afro-Hispanic Review* 1:1 (May 1982): 27–31.

Spillers, Hortense. "Mama's Baby, Papa's Maybe: An American Grammar Book." *Diacritics* 17:2 (summer 1987): 65–81.

Steady, Filomina Chioma. "African Feminism: A Worldwide Perspective." In *Women in Africa and the African Diaspora: A Reader,* ed. Rosalyn Terborg-Penn and Andrea Benton Rushing, 3–21. Washington, DC: Howard University Press, 1996.

Stone, Michael Cutler. "The Afro-Caribbean Presence in Central America." *Belizean Studies* 2–3 (1990): 6–42.

Terborg-Penn, Rosalyn, and Andrea Benton Rushing, eds. *Women in Africa and the African Diaspora: A Reader.* Washington, DC: Howard University Press, 1996.

Teubal, Savina J. *Hagar the Egyptian: The Lost Tradition of the Matriarchs.* San Francisco: Harper and Row, 1990.

Van Dijk, Teun A. *Elite Discourse and Racism.* Amsterdam: Benjamins, 1987

Van Sertima, Ivan, and Runoko Rashidi, eds. *The African Presence in Early Asia.* 1985. Reprint, New Brunswick, NJ: Transaction Publishers, 1988.

Villalobos Ellis, Ileana. "Entre los cerros y el muro: Análisis e interpretación de *Final de calle.*" Tesis de grado, Costa Rica, Universidad Nacional, 1982.

Walker, Alice. "In Search of Our Mothers' Gardens." In *In Search of Our Mother's Gardens: Womanist Prose,* by Alice Walker, xi–xii. San Diego: Harcourt Brace Jovanovich, 1983.

Weems, Renita J. *Just a Sister Away: A Womanist Vision of Women's Relationships in the Bible.* San Diego: LuraMedia, 1988.

Whitten, Norman E., Jr., and Arlene Torres. "To Forge the Future in the Fires of the Past: An Interpretative Essay on Racism, Domination, Resistance, and Liberation." In *Blackness in Latin America and the Caribbean: Social Dynamics and Cultural Transformation,* comp. and ed. Norman E. Whitten Jr. and Arlene Torres, 3–71. Bloomington: Indiana University Press, 1998.

Wideman, John Edgar. "In Praise of Silence." *Callaloo* 22:3 (1999): 547–49.

Williams, Claudette. *Charcoal and Cinnamon: The Politics of Color in Spanish Caribbean Literature.* Gainesville: University Press of Florida, 2000.

Williams, Delores. *Sisters in the Wilderness: The Challenge of Womanist God Talk.* Maryknoll, NY: Orbis Books, 1993.

Williams, Lorna V. "From Dusky Venus to *Mater Dolorosa:* The Female Protagonist in the Cuban Antislavery Novel." In *Woman as Myth and Metaphor in Latin American Literature,* ed. Carmelo Virgilio and Naomi Lindstrom, 121–35. Columbia: University of Missouri Press, 1985.

Wynter, Sylvia. "The Eye of the Other: Images of the Black in Spanish Literature." In *Black Writers in Hispanic Literature,* ed. Miriam DeCosta-Willis, 8–19. Port Washington, NY: Kennikat Press, 1977.

Zapata Olivella, Manuel. *Las claves mágicas de America (Raza, clase y cultura).* Bogotá: Plaza and Janes, 1989.

# INDEX